Uppies and Downies

The extraordinary football games of Britain

Uppies and Downies
© English Heritage 2008

English Heritage
is the government's statutory
advisor on all aspects of the
historic environment

Kemble Drive
Swindon SN2 2GZ
www.english-heritage.org.uk

Design by Jörn Kröger
Series designer Doug Cheeseman

Production by Jackie Spreckley
Maps by Mark Fenton
For image credits see page 186

Malavan Media is a creative
consultancy responsible
for the Played in Britain series
www.playedinbritain.co.uk

Printed by Zrinski, Croatia
ISBN: 978 190562 4645
Product code: 51322

Uppies and Downies
The extraordinary football games of Britain

Hugh Hornby

Editor Simon Inglis

Shrove Tuesday 2007 – young and old, fathers and sons, daughters too, follow the silver ball through the back streets of St Columb Major in Cornwall, where Town and Country have been vying for Shrove Tuesday honours since at least 1594. In 1846 the antiquarian Richard Edmonds described St Columb as the only place 'where gentlemen now unite with the rest of the inhabitants in this diversion'. A mile and a half separates the goals, but tradition requires that the ball (held in the leading player's right hand) should not leave the town centre before an hour of play has passed.

Page One 'Turning up' the ball in Ashbourne, Derbyshire on Ash Wednesday 2006. Ashbourne is the only location where a special platform has been built for this purpose. The decorations on the ball reflect the interests of the guest of honour, in this instance former player George Handley, who scored for the Up'ards in 1975 and who therefore opted not to face the crowd before turning up the ball, to avoid any hint of bias.

Page Two Old habits die hard at Kirkwall in 1974. A characteristic of most games of *Uppies and Downies* is that anyone can join in at any time, and for as long as they are able and willing.

Contents

Foreword

by Simon Inglis, Played in Britain series editor

It is impossible to become a true fan of any sport without developing at least some sense of history. Knowledge of past results, past events and past players is the common currency of fandom. No match, no single encounter can be viewed in isolation. Rather, each one forms part of a wider and more profound narrative.

But however individuals develop this appreciation, whether by study or by osmosis, invariably their understanding of how the present fits in with the past is shaped by an overarching, orthodox view of how their particular sport has evolved.

In recent years several challenges have been made to the received narrative of football history (by which we mean both Association football and rugby). Revisionist historians have taught us, *inter alia*, that the basic concept of two teams of equal numbers, playing at a designated location to an agreed set of rules, was by no means the brainchild of ex-public schoolboys in Victorian Britain.

Uppies and Downies, it is hoped, will be seen as contributing further to this re-examination of history.

By visiting and closely observing all fifteen of the surviving mass participation games that feature in this book, Hugh Hornby has been able to demonstrate that not only is the world of *Uppies and Downies* still alive and fiercely competitive, but also that it has a culture and even a science of its own, related to, but distinct from developments in soccer and rugby.

In short, that teams of *Uppies and Downies* were not superceded by the Uniteds and Rovers of today, but enjoyed, and continue to enjoy a parallel existence, rooted not in everyday football but in once-a-year, or 'festival football'.

Compared with previous studies in the *Played in Britain* series, there is precious little architecture in this book. Streetscapes and landscapes aplenty for sure, and a good deal of spirited play. A surprising amount of water too.

But to be frank, readers will find very little actual football.

Indeed only in a few of the games does kicking even take place at all.

Moreover, only in Workington are the competing teams actually called 'Uppies' and 'Downies'.

Yet the majority of festival games did start out as football, and have always been contested by players representing different parts of their town or district; the Up part of town against the Down part, the Town versus the Country, or an equivalent.

We therefore trust that players and supporters of the games featured will forgive us for bracketing them all under the one, *Uppies and Downies* flag of convenience.

For most of his travels around Britain, Hugh was accompanied by Peter Holme, whose numerous photographs offer a valuable adjunct to the text.

As a football fan, I find their combined efforts hugely entertaining. As a historian, I shall never think of the game's history in quite the same way again.

I hope readers will be equally enlightened, but more than that, will seek to attend these games in person, whether as players, spectators or, as we shall see, as both...

Welcome to the extraordinary football games of Britain.

Preparing one of the goals before the Shrove Tuesday match at Alnwick, Northumberland. Opposite, festival football's board directors, at St Columb, Cornwall (*far left*), Atherstone, Warwickshire (*centre left and far right*), and Duns, Berwickshire (*centre right*).

Joseph Strutt sums up the *Played in Britain* ethos in his seminal study of 1801, *The Sports and Pastimes of the People of England*.

In order to form a just estimation of the character of any particular people, it is absolutely necessary to investigate the Sports and Pastimes most generally prevalent among them.

1. Uppies and Downies

Ashbourne prepares for its annual Shrove Tuesday match with an exclusive in the local newspaper. The Derbyshire town is one of fifteen towns and villages where mass participation, festival football games still take place, in one form or another. But only in Ashbourne is so much attention paid to the decoration of the ball itself.

If you are new to the subject of festival football, this book may appear to be a study of a dying sub-culture within modern Britain.

Where once there were possibly hundreds of towns and villages hosting games that would fit into the category of *Uppies and Downies* – a catch-all description that, as we shall see, incorporates several diverse strands – now only fifteen locations remain (*see opposite*).

Yet for those readers who have witnessed or participated in any of the games featured in this book, the culture of *Uppies and Downies* is not moribund at all.

Rather, it is a treasured part of local history, and an opportunity for people of all ages to come together in celebration of communal values.

Some observers may dismiss games of *Uppies and Downies* as quaint customs, survivors of a pre-industrial era, akin to morris dancing or well-dressing.

They may consider them just a bit of fun, or as opportunities primarily to imbibe large quantities of alcohol in the name of some vague tradition.

But as we shall see, most of the games are a genuine test of sporting prowess and physical endurance, in conditions that few professional sportsmen or women would countenance.

Indeed for the players on the day, these games, and the rivalries they engender, are as hard fought and as meaningful as any major sporting encounter.

Before delving into the history and evolution of the phenomenon that is *Uppies and Downies* therefore, we must look at the basic elements that these apparently disparate games have in common.

What exactly is it that makes them so extraordinary?

Festival football

First and foremost, games of *Uppies and Downies* are played only at specific times on the calendar.

As detailed in Chapter Three, the majority take place between late December and March or April, concentrated within three periods; first Christmas and New Year, then Shrovetide and finally Easter.

In most locations only one game is played per year, although in Ashbourne, Kirkwall and St Columb Major two games are played, and in Workington three are staged within a nine day period, starting on Good Friday (*see page 188 for the schedule*).

Because these games are rooted in the calendar our preferred term for them is 'festival' rather than either 'traditional' or 'folk'.

After all, before the codification of football and its subjugation to regular fixtures and schedules in the late 19th century, the terms 'traditional' or 'folk' could reasonably be applied to football in all its variant forms, as played casually at any time of the year.

But the games featured in this book are neither routine, and nor are they mere kickabouts.

Instead, they should each be considered as local showpiece games with a special resonance, and to which certain time-honoured rituals and celebrations are attached.

For example, four of the games featured in *Uppies and Downies* (at Hallaton, Haxey, Alnwick and St Ives) are preceded by gatherings and processions, in which »

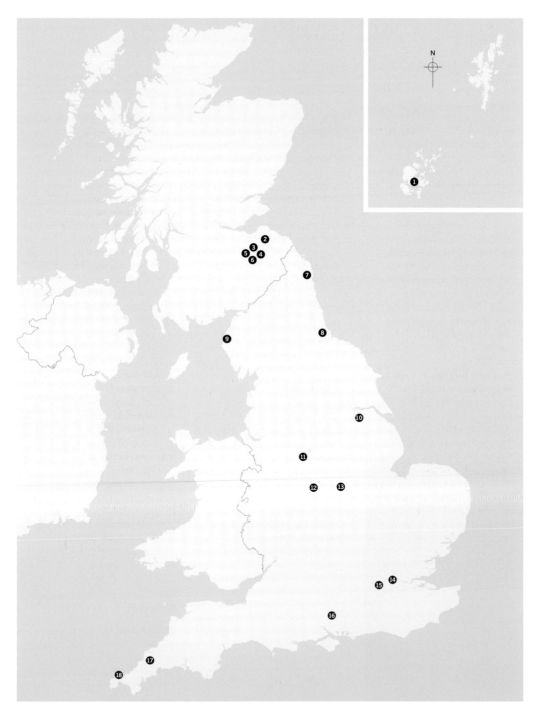

◀ Firm evidence for the existence of games of *Uppies and Downies* has been found in over 80 cities, towns and villages around Britain, although it is safe to say that the actual number is certainly much higher. Mass football played on festivals was undoubtedly a national phenomenon.

This map shows where the 15 surviving games featured in this book currently take place.

Also featured are the three schools where other extraordinary forms of football survive.

As will be noted, none of the locations are within major towns or cities. Indeed, among these places, only Workington has a population above 10,000.

▼ Night games in **Hobkirk**, in the Scottish Borders, with only the fluorescent jackets of some of the players offering any illumination in the gloom of a February evening.

Duns apart, all the games in this book take place during winter or spring, and it is usual for the action to continue well after dark. *Uppies and Downies* thus becomes a multi-sensory experience.

Hunkering down in an unlit field, or chasing an opponent down a narrow country lane requires not only steady nerves but also local knowledge. Hearing and touch become increasingly important as players seek to follow the action and, not least, try to locate the ball. Even one's sense of smell seems heightened as the aromas of mud and sweat drift across the night air.

In the dark, the games are often intensely visceral, yet also curiously magical.

≫ costume, music, food and drink play an important role.

At Hallaton and Haxey the games do not even feature balls.

At the former the contest involves three small wooden barrels (known confusingly as 'bottles'), while at Haxey the rival teams fight over a two foot long leather cylinder containing a length of thick rope, known, for reasons which will become apparent, as the 'hood'.

Extraordinary indeed.

Yet all these games and their pre-match rituals have much in common with sporting events of more recent vintage. Think, for example, of the crowds travelling to London for FA Cup or Rugby League Challenge Cup Finals, decked in fancy hats and rosettes, eating, drinking and singing.

On such occasions, celebrating the event is as important as the event itself.

Mass participation

A second defining feature of *Uppies and Downies* is that they invite mass participation. There are no limits on the number of players, no requirement for each team to be of equal size, and no age restrictions (other than for children's games, which are staged before the main events in Kirkwall, Jedburgh, Ancrum and Hallaton).

Just as importantly, unlike other sports where there exists a clear distinction between players or athletes on one hand and spectators on the other, in most games of *Uppies and Downies* (though not at Duns or Alnwick) no such distinction exists.

Not only are there no physical barriers between spectators and participants, nor are there any rules to prevent a spectator from joining in whenever he or she feels the urge. Equally, it is common to see players drop out of the action to join the crowds, or to nip off to the pub or the shop, or to take up a different position in order to rejoin the action at a later time.

In this sense, *Uppies and Downies* is unique. Everyone can participate for as long or as little as they feel able and willing.

They do not even have to make any special preparations to join in.

There are no team uniforms or colours in festival football, and therefore no easy way of telling who is playing for whom.

That said, the regular players will know, because the vast majority of players, being local, are known to everyone.

Boundaries and goals

Games of *Uppies and Downies* offer participants a freedom of movement that is rare today. For one precious day only, within reason, the town or village in which they live becomes their playground.

This is because, unlike games played on pitches, for the most part festival football knows no boundaries. Rather, it is played in streets, alleyways, parks, commons and fields, across roads, rivers, harbours and any other barrier, natural or otherwise, that might lie between the starting point (usually in the centre of the town) and the two goals.

Certain areas might be deemed by convention to be out of bounds, such as churchyards, gardens or business properties. Railway lines and major roads raise issues of safety but are sometimes overrun.

Traffic must wait, shoppers stand aside, and the police will maintain only a watching brief as players roam as far and as wide as they see fit, in an attempt to shake off opponents and reach the goal.

At Ashbourne, where the goals are three miles apart, play can extend over six square miles. At St Columb Major, Cornwall, it can extend even further, within an area of up to 25 square miles. Yet in other locations all the action might be contained within a few streets.

Whatever the terrain, paved or ploughed, on dry land or in water, the once-a-year licence to run and play in what is normally a busy street, or to dash through a market place, or to wade across a stream or swim across a pond, offers a truly liberating experience.

It is, moreover, one that the vast majority of players exercise with respect. After all, once play ends and the world returns to normality, they must live and perhaps work within the same environs in which they played. With freedom comes responsibility.

Goals and scoring

In most games of *Uppies and Downies* goals are not formed by posts and nets, but are instead functional structures such as buildings, bridges, walls, doors, gates or fences. To score, a player must touch the ball against them.

Or, as is common for those playing 'Down' (meaning down river), to score the ball must enter a body of water, such as the harbours at Kirkwall and Workington.

At Ashbourne there are modern purpose-built goals, formed by stone plinths embedded into the side of a river bank. These are on the sites of two mills that used to constitute the goals. To count, the scorer must be actually in the river before touching the ball against the plinth. The equivalent for the Doonies at Jedburgh, in the Scottish Borders, is to roll the ball across a road that covers the now-culverted Skiprunning Burn, which marked the original goal.

At St Columb Major in Cornwall the two goals are barely visible granite troughs, set into the roadside. But players can also score by carrying the ball over the parish boundary.

At Haxey, Lincolnshire, the hood (the equivalent of the ball) must cross the threshold of certain pubs, while in Denholm, Roxburghshire, one goal is a bridge, while the other is a hedge-line (although not everyone seems sure of the exact point).

At Sedgefield in County Durham the goals are called 'alleys'. In Scotland goals are 'hailed', not scored, and in Hobkirk, until the 20th century, balls were carried not just to certain houses, but were touched against the back of the kitchen hearth.

Similarly in Duns, Berwickshire, the married players had to carry balls into the church and touch them against the pulpit. This was known as 'kirking' the ball.

For their unmarried opponents, balls had to be touched against the hopper of a mill, where the miller would dust the scorer's hat and coat with flour. Hence, for the bachelors, scoring was called 'milling'.

At Atherstone, Warwickshire, and St Ives, Cornwall, there are no goals at all. Instead, the player in possession of the ball at an appointed hour is deemed the winner.

Only at Alnwick are there goals – called 'hales' (*see page 7*) – that resemble those used in football or rugby, probably because the game was relocated from the streets to an open field in 1828.

A contest within a contest

Teamwork plays an integral part in the physical struggle required to convey the ball to the point at which it can be scored, or hailed.

But in some games of *Uppies and Downies*, such as at Ashbourne, that combined effort can ultimately break down into a second contest at the goal, to »

▲ Members of the **Uppie** team arrive from their heartland in Kirkwall, to take part in the Boys' Ba' on New Year's morning, 2006.

As the name suggests, an Uppie represents that part of the town which is 'up' from the harbour.

In towns with a river, playing 'Up' or 'Down' equates to either up or downstream.

The usual factors deciding team membership are birthplace, residence or family ties. But there are other selections, such as Married v. Bachelors, or Town v. Country. At Hallaton teams are named after villages. At Alnwick they are named after parishes.

Below is a list of team names used over the centuries. Note that only in Workington are the teams actually called *Uppies and Downies* (pronounced as *Doonies* in Scotland).

Team names past and present

Uppies and Downies Workington
Uppies and Doonies Kirkwall, Jedburgh, Denholm, Ancrum, Hobkirk and Scotland generally
Up'ards and Down'ards Ashbourne
Upalongs and Downalongs St Ives
Upper and Lower Town Workington
Uppergate and Priestgate Workington
Uppey-gyates and Downey-gyates Workington
Up-Streeters and Down-Streeters Chester-le-Street
Up-the-Gates and Down-the-Gates Kirkwall
Up-Town and Down-Town Workington, Witney

Easties and Westies Lilliesleaf
Eastenders and Westenders Hawick, Dorking
Eassla and Wassla Hawick
Northenders and Southenders Stromness
Toonheiders and Toonfitters Jedburgh
Town and Country St Columb Major, Sedgefield

Atherstone balls are the largest seen in *Uppies and Downies* and are either inflated or filled with water. Kicking is more common than in other games.

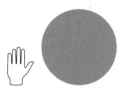

Ashbourne balls (like those at Kirkwall) are filled with cork to be sturdy and buoyant, and, in common with Atherstone balls, are slighter flatter than a sphere when viewed from the side.

Workington balls are stuffed tightly with flock or horsehair and each weighs around 2lbs (910g).

The smallest balls are those used in Scottish Border games of handba' and in Cornish hurling. The former have a leather case, stuffed with either sphagnum moss, flock or hay. Hurling balls are made with an applewood core encased in silver.

» determine which team member will be accorded the ultimate honour of actually scoring.

Equally the leading players might draw lots in the midst of the final heave.

At Kirkwall the scorer may not even be the player finally acclaimed as the game's 'champion'. He may be another prominent player who has performed well over the years.

At Sedgefield 'alleying' the ball is also only part of the game. Once that has occurred the players return to the centre of the town where a secondary struggle begins to see which player can pass the ball three times through a bull ring set into the ground.

Similarly, Atherstone's game is in two phases. The first phase is a general kickabout in which many participants, young and old, are encouraged to have a kick of the ball. This is followed by a second competitive phase, for more vigorous players only.

At Sedgefield, as at Ashbourne and Kirkwall, the prize is not just victory but the ball itself, which the scorer then gets to keep for life.

Own goals

A further crucial difference between *Uppies and Downies* and games such as soccer and rugby is that instead of trying to score in one's opponents' goal, the object is to score what might be termed an 'own goal'. That is, the balls are the spoils of war, to be brought home in triumph.

The games start with the ball being 'thrown up' (or 'turned up' in Ashbourne), often by an invited guest, from a point roughly midway between the two goals.

In most instances this central point is in the heart of the town or village, for example in the market place or outside the chuch.

But the aim then is move the ball back to one's own goal, not to advance into enemy territory.

The number three

The number three bears a significance in all manner of belief systems, customs and folklore, whether it be the Holy Trinity, the three wise men, the Three Graces or the three bears.

It also crops up repeatedly in the rituals of *Uppies and Downies*.

At Ashbourne the ball must be touched three times against the goal in order to score. At Workington it must be thrown up into the air three times at the hailing point.

At Hallaton, each of the three bottles, or barrels are dropped three times before play can start.

Three balls are also contested at Duns, as they were also once at Dorking. At Alnwick the best of three goals wins.

Finally, as mentioned earlier, at Sedgefield the ball is passed three times through the bull ring, both at the start of play and at the conclusion.

Duration

Games of *Uppies and Downies* vary in their length. At St Columb the hours are from 4.30pm to 8.00pm. As Ashbourne they start at 2.00pm and must end by 10.00pm at the latest. At Kirkwall the men's ba' is thrown up at 1.00pm but there is no time limit and games can continue long into the night. The same applies at Workington, where the throw off is not until 6.30pm.

Given that the majority of games take place in winter or spring, this means that most of the play takes place after darkness falls.

The shortest encounter, and also the most compact in terms

of terrain, is at Duns, where some games end within half an hour.

Football or handball?

As conceded in the Foreword, it may be contentious to describe *Uppies and Downies* simply as a variant of football. Certainly there is very little kicking to be seen in some games, and none in others.

In each case (*as illustrated left*) the size and/or weight of the ball used gives a fair indication of what kind of game is played.

In the Scottish Borders, where the balls are small and soft, a more accurate description of the games would be handball (or rather handba'). In Cornish hurling too, where the ball is small and hard (and coated in silver) the ball is almost exclusively handled.

Ashbourne's game is described by its players as 'hug ball', and one would need a stout pair of boots and strong knees to kick a Kirkwall ba'.

But it is true to say that from a historical perspective (as detailed further in Chapter Two), with the exception of Cornish hurling all the games in this book started out at one time or another as a form of football, however ill-defined, with some fully evolving into handball and others retaining only an element of kicking.

But then in Gaelic, American and Australian Rules football, and of course rugby football, handling features prominently, and even in Association football the goalkeeper is allowed to handle. In early versions of soccer, outfield players could stop the ball with their hands.

So 'football' is a broad church, and in the context of *Uppies and Downies* it is essential to take a catholic view.

This is a genus not a species.

▲ The calm before the storm. In **Kirkwall** (*above right*) the ball is rarely thrown and almost never kicked. The threat is therefore more from the weight of the scrum than the ball itself. Sturdy planks are thus placed in front of doors and windows at waist height, but panes of glass are left uncovered.

Every plank has been pre-cut and labelled for the property concerned, and then bolted into place by a team of workmen, who do the rounds twice a year. Theirs is a well-honed operation.

In those locations where the ball does fly around more randomly, such as **Atherstone** (*above left*) and **Jedburgh** (*centre left*) whole shop fronts are covered, by bespoke shutters or by chipboard or chicken wire. But in other locations, such as Workington, where most of the play is on open ground, no boarding up is necessary.

Inevitably, however much protection is in place, windows are occasionally damaged, along with street signs, trees and plants.

Where there is a committee, such as at Kirkwall and **Ashbourne** (*lower left*), joiners and glaziers – who may themselves be keen players – are usually on hand to carry out repairs. But in some situations property owners have been known to fund repairs themselves or claim on their insurance. In other places, players' fundraising will cover costs.

▲ Nowhere in *Uppies and Downies* will you see **team colours** being worn, nor kit that might easily identify a player's team. Some players may occasionally be seen in souvenir shirts, as at **Hallaton** (*above*), but these usually relate to the game as a whole rather than the individual's allegiance.

Rugby shirts appear to be the garment of choice, partly because they are strong enough to cope with the rigours of play, but also because many of the players are themselves members of rugby clubs.

At **Kirkwall** (*top right*), Uppies and Doonies wear their determined 'game faces' before the start outside St. Magnus Cathedral, sizing each other up and preparing to hoist one of their number up into the air to grab the ball from the throw up, as in a rugby line-out.

Footwear is also important, and sometimes even indicative of a player's role. These players at Kirkwall (*right*) have donned tough boots, wrapped with gaffer, or duct tape, for added ankle and leg protection. They will no doubt be concentrating their efforts in the scrum, where a firm foothold is vital on a range of surfaces.

In contrast, younger and more lightweight players wear trainers, so that, if passed the ball, they can sprint away from the mass of bodies for a quick breakaway.

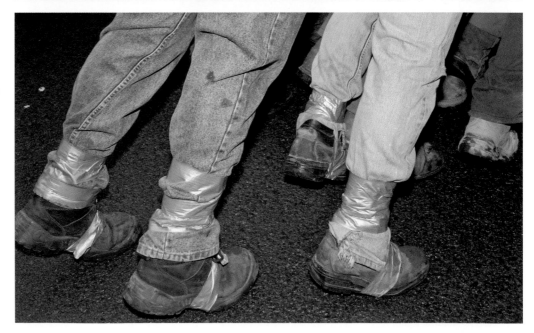

Rules

It is often said, not least by the players, that in *Uppies and Downies* there are no rules. It is an obvious way of underlining their distinctiveness and impressing outsiders.

However, this has never been quite the case. It is true that there are very few *written* rules (other than at Alnwick). But no mass encounter could ever have survived without a verbally agreed set of conventions.

Thus players know when and where games are due to start. They are made aware that play should not stray into certain areas.

They understand the aims of the game, and most of all they are made repeatedly aware, by older and more experienced players, of what actions are permitted within the spirit of the game. When a player goes down, for example, or is injured and cannot get clear unaided, play is generally halted.

Meanwhile, in most Scottish games and in Workington the art of 'smuggling' the ball – that is, hiding it on one's person or in a secret place – and of making decoy runs without the ball, is not only tolerated but admired. Yet not so in Ashbourne.

At Ashbourne and Kirkwall there are game committees, to organise pre-match events and to help raise funds for the balls and for charities. But these committees do not run the games per se. The players do that themselves.

Still, *Uppies and Downies* have had to adapt to the modern world.

So, in most locations it has been agreed that players must not convey the ball in motor vehicles (after numerous incidents in which exactly such a ploy was tried). Time limits have also been tightened. Ashbourne's game used

THROWING OUT THE BALL. SHROVE TUESDAY CHESTER-LE-STREET.

to stop at midnight. Now it ends at 10.00pm, to make it easier for both the players and the local police.

Increasingly, games are influenced by the use of mobile telephones, which allow players to communicate over long distances and even call up reinforcements.

And yet while issues such as this do have to be taken into account, and occasionally collective decisions do have to be made, the overall lack of a controlling authority adds to the special appeal of these games.

Indeed compared with the multiple clauses and amendments that litter the rulebooks of modern codified sports, where increasingly arcane interpretations of the rules confuse even professional players and coaches (let alone the spectators), the simplicity of *Uppies and Downies* remains one of its greatest assets. It takes just minutes to grasp the basics.

▲ Up-Streeters and Down-Streeters gather in **Chester-le-Street, County Durham**, as one of the Dalkin family throws out the ball for the start of the Shrove Tuesday game in 1913. Dalkin's, based on Front Street, were a firm of saddlers and harnessmakers who had been supplying balls for the game for over 60 years. The game was last played in the town in 1932.

The majority of games of *Uppies and Downies* start in this fashion, either from an upper storey window

(as at Atherstone) or from the market cross (Kirkwall), or in the case of St Columb Major, from the top of a stepladder.

Known as the 'throw-up', 'throw-out' or, in Ashbourne, as the 'turning-up', the honour is usually performed by a local dignitary, a former player or sponsor of the game, or by an invited celebrity.

When facing the ball before it is thrown up, players from both sides intermingle. They at least know who is on which side.

▶ Wherever you play or watch mass football, there are three rules for dressing: make sure your clothes are warm, make sure they are waterproof and make doubly sure they are old or dispensable.

At **Hobkirk**, as in other games played in the Scottish Borders, bulky jackets, designed for work in construction or on the roads, are the preferred mode of dress. This is as much for their capacity to hide smuggled balls as for their warmth.

Although males predominate in *Uppies and Downies*, support from women has been a longstanding feature. Female players have been known to score, but more often they are to be seen either urging on their menfolk from the sidelines or, as seen at **Haxey** in Lincolnshire (*below right*), adding their muscle at the rear of the scrum (or 'sway' as it is called in Haxey).

During the 18th century the married and unmarried fishwives of Inveresk, east of Edinburgh, went one further. According to the *Statistical Account of Scotland*, 'As they do the work of men, their manners are masculine, and their strength and activity is equal to their work. Their amusements are of the masculine kind. On holidays they frequently play at golf; and on Shrove Tuesday there is a standing match at football.'

Apparently the married women usually emerged as winners.

Violence

Mass football is undeniably a tough and physical pursuit. But it is far from the 'bloody and murthering practise' described by the Puritan Philip Stubbes in 1583.

In medieval times, as detailed in the following chapter, much of this hostile reporting emanated from those who, like Stubbes, sought to suppress football. But even in more recent years historians have all too easily damned mass football on the evidence of a few, isolated deaths.

For example James Walvin, writing about the Shrove Tuesday games in Derby, in *The People's Game*, published in 1975 (*see Links*), noted that 'in keeping with the unrestrained traditions of popular footballing violence, the Derby game claimed its share of victims.'

In fact, only one death was ever confirmed at Derby, when John Snape drowned in the River Derwent in 1796.

Moreover, between 1800 and 2007 the total death toll at the games featured in this book stands at nine.

Of these, five drowned – as we shall see, water play is an integral part of certain games, such as at Ashbourne and Workington – while two died from heart attacks and one from hypothermia.

A ninth man was killed at Denholm, it is thought in the early 20th century, after being impaled on railings.

This is not to minimise these fatalities. But compared with the number of players' deaths arising from games such as rugby and football, and the considerably higher death tolls recorded in American football – 33 in 1908 alone – *Uppies and Downies* has a remarkably good record.

Injuries are another matter.

No statistics exist to assess whether festival games are any more likely to result in injury than other contact sports, or indeed other mass gatherings such as rock concerts or outdoor screenings of major events.

But clearly it is an issue, for example at the Hallaton bottle kicking game. Larger games such as this do require the presence of ambulances and medical back-up, and the public purse does have to bear the expense (as is also true of street festivals and demonstrations).

Another commonly-expressed view is that mass football offers an opportunity for rivals to settle scores. Again, James Walvin wrote 'sometimes quarrels spilled over into murder after the game,' but offered no real evidence to back this up.

Even recent revisionist works are influenced by the prevailing view. Adrian Harvey's *Football: The First Hundred Years* (*see Links*) claims, for example, that 'some games ventilated the hostility between rival groups...'

But hostility within the game should not be confused with hostility away from it. While there will always be flare-ups in the heat of the moment, as in any contact sport, deliberate wounding arising from a feud is almost non-existent.

As would be expected when a small town or village supplies both sets of players, there is a line of acceptable behaviour which neighbours are unlikely to cross.

Uppies and Downies is therefore much more about fun and fellowship than violence and victimisation. This is not the stigmatised 'mob' of a town bent on destruction. Rather, it is the community at play, revelling in its own backyard.

Post match handshakes between members of the Married and Unmarried teams at Duns in Berwickshire. In games of Uppies and Downies, where neighbours and workmates often oppose each other, there is little scope for grudges or lingering disputes, particularly as the players all tend to meet up in the pub afterwards. One of the strengths of *Uppies and Downies* is that the games are largely self-policing, and anyone contravening the spirit of the game risks becoming a social pariah.

2. History

It is entirely possible that mass participation football arrived in Britain courtesy of the Normans. The French game *soule*, pictured here in an 1835 engraving and especially popular in Brittany, was similar to *Uppies and Downies* in several respects, being played on holidays, in the streets, with goals in ponds or streams. It was finally suppressed in the 19th century.

Association football, invented in Britain and by far the world's most popular sport, is frequently described as 'the people's game'.

But there also exist several other variants of football, each of which has been adopted and moulded by different sectors of society in different parts of the world, and which may equally be said to belong to 'the people'.

Quite clearly *Uppies and Downies* is one of these variants. And yet it is also one whose place in football history is the least understood.

One reason for this is the fact that so much of what we know of football in the pre-modern era derives from texts and sources that focus almost exclusively on violence and lawlessness, or on prohibition.

Yet there is also a body of evidence which points to mass participation, festival football being a longstanding and positive characteristic of national life, if only we read more closely between the lines.

Until recent probings by such revisionist historians as Adrian Harvey and John Goulstone (*see*

Links), the received narrative has generally portrayed football's evolution as a linear path, from the primitive to the civilised.

Along this path, three main trends are generally postulated: first, the increasing imposition of rules; second, an increasing level of sophistication (such as in tactics and the staging of games), and third, a decrease in the levels of violence amongst the players.

Prior to the mid 19th century, we are led to believe, football was a largely amorphous entity, a 'folk' game with few rules, no organisation and a propensity towards brutality and disorder.

Then came the Victorian modernisers, characterised by a coterie of ex-public schoolboys, who wiped the slate clean by devising new forms of the game.

The promoters of Association football, or soccer, with its accent on kicking, drew up their first agreed set of rules in 1863. Rugby football, with its emphasis on handling, responded by forming its own governing body in 1871. This was followed in 1888 by the formation of the Football League,

with its regular fixture list and professional ethos, echoed by the setting up of the Rugby League (originally called the Northern Union) in 1895.

So successful were these new forms of football that the urban masses in Britain's industrialised cities were drawn to these modern spectacles like ants to honey, while festival football, played mainly in small towns and villages, fell so far off the radar that it became virtually invisible.

Yet there is growing evidence to challenge a number of the assumptions on which this accepted narrative is founded.

Organised football, it can be demonstrated, played on a designated pitch by an equal number of players to an agreed set of rules, was patently not a new phenomenon in the mid 19th century. The notion of a club, or a representative team, was hardly new either.

Instead, in almost every aspect of the game the so-called pioneers of soccer and rugby drew on pre-existing practices and, in some cases, on traditions that were centuries in the making, not only in England but in Scotland and Wales too.

It is not the intention here to rewrite the history of football. That task is already under way in other quarters. Instead, in this chapter we will revisit the story of football to tease out those elements of festival football which, for a number of reasons, have either been lost or conveniently overlooked, or misinterpreted in previous mainstream studies.

To guide us on this journey, it is worth considering the different levels at which football is played.

At grass roots level there is the informal, daily kickabout, which might take place on a street, in a playground or park. Or in a field, as for example played by Alexander Barclay's 'sturdy ploughmen' in his poem of 1514 (see right).

At a second level there is what might be termed a regular fixture. Early examples would include weekly Sunday games played in churchyards in the Orkney Islands during the 18th century or, at the same period, in East Anglian camping closes (as explained on page 26). Nowadays the equivalent would be the Sunday leagues, or any league for that matter, the Premiership included.

Finally, at the third level, there is the one off match; in professional football perhaps a cup final or an international match, or at the Uppies and Downies level, a Shrove Tuesday or New Year's Day match.

The venues for any of these matches, at any level, are not important. Nor are the rules, since both teams agree to play at the chosen venue and to the same set of rules, whether it be on a local council pitch, at Wembley Stadium or in the streets of Ashbourne or Atherstone.

Looking back over football's history, it is apparent that all three types of game have existed for centuries, in one form or another, just as they do today. For that reason, we should be wary of trying to slot isolated snippets of historical data into an imagined, seamless continuum which leads inexorably from primitive football to Premiership football and the globalised game.

Instead, one snippet may lead us to a modern schools game at Eton, another to a scrum in a field in rural Leicestershire, and another to a harbour in Workington where a Downie throws up a ball three times to score in the early hours of the morning.

For readers conversant with football history, many of the references that follow will already be familiar. But in re-assessing them from the perspective of Uppies and Downies it is hoped that, firstly, a greater understanding will emerge of the provenance of those games that survive today, and secondly, that many of the negative interpretations that have arisen from the study of mass participation football will be properly redressed.

After all, no one would base any study of 20th century soccer solely on reports of hooliganism. That would be a distortion. So with festival football it is important to view the wider picture.

The Norman Conquest

The story of Uppies and Downies in Britain really starts in 1066, with the spread of Norman culture. One facet of this culture was the annual celebration of Mardi Gras, or Shrove Tuesday, and the possible introduction of a popular Breton game known as soule (also given as choule or cholle). »

▲ Dating from c.1350, these **ball players** feature among 58 scenes depicting domestic life, folk tales and sundry monsters, carved onto misericords in the choir stalls at **Gloucester Cathedral**.

Other scenes show wrestling, sword play, stag hunting, bull baiting, even gambling. And yet these carvings were largely for the delectation of monks, rather than laymen.

Further endorsement of the central role that games played in everyday life is found in Alexander Barclay's Fifth Eclogue, *Amintas and Faustus*, written c.1514.

Despite the continual prohibition of football during the medieval period, Amintas, a shepherd, speaks in glowing terms of the benefits to be accrued from playing the game, especially in winter.

*Eche time and season hath his delite
   and joys,
Loke in the streets beholde the
   little boyes,
Howe in fruite season for joy they
   sing and hop,
In lent is eche one full busy with
   his top,*

*And now in winter for all the
   greevous colde
All rent and ragged a man may
   them beholde,
They have great pleasour supposing
   well to dine,
When men be busied in killing of
   fat swine,
They get the bladder and blowe it
   great and thin,
With many beans or peason
   put within;
It rattleth, soundeth, and shineth
   clere and fayre,
While it is throwen and caste up in
   the ayre.
Eche one contendeth and hath a
   great delite
With foote and with hande the
   bladder for to smite;
If it fall to grounde they lift it
   up agayne,
This wise to labour they count it for
   no paine;
Renning and leaping they drive
   away the colde.
The sturdie plowmen, lustie, strong
   and bolde
Overcommeth the winter with
   driving the footeball,
Forgetting labour and many a
   grevous fall.*

» A frequently quoted passage, dated 1174, is from a work entitled *Descriptio Nobilissimae Civitatis Londiniae*, in which a Canterbury monk, William Fitzstephen describes this scene in London:

'Yearly at Shrovetide, the boys of every school bring fighting-cocks to their masters, and all the forenoon is spent at school, to see the cocks fight together. After the midday meal the entire youth of the city goes to the fields for the famous game of ball.

'The students of the several branches of study have their ball; the followers of the several trades of the city have a ball in their hands. The elders, the fathers, and men of wealth come on horseback to view the contests of their juniors, and in their passion sport with the young men; and there seems to be aroused in these elders a stirring of natural heat by viewing so much activity and by participation in the joys of unrestrained youth.'

Note that Fitzstephen does not use the word 'football', which has led certain historians to conclude that Shrovetide football was a later development. However, so many other later accounts also bracket cock-fighting with the playing of football by schoolboys on Shrove Tuesday that it would be fair to surmise that football was the ball game referred to in 1174.

Note also that Fitzstephen describes the game as 'famous', the implication being that it was already well established – this was more than a century after the Conquest – and was in itself a special occasion.

Nine of the 15 games of *Uppies and Downies* still played in Britain take place during Shrovetide, as did dozens more that would die out by the early 20th century. As detailed further in Chapter Three, Shrove Tuesday was, in many towns, also called 'Football Day'.

That is not to say that no football took place at other times of the year. Clearly it did. But the Shrovetide tradition patently has a pedigree that has endured for more than 900 years.

Throughout this book we learn of local legends that tell of ancient football games originating during the medieval period. For example in Atherstone, Warwickshire, a passage written in 1790 dates the town's Shrovetide game to the reign of King John (1199–1216). In County Durham, Sedgefield's game is said to have started in the mid 13th century when craftsmen working on the parish church challenged local farmworkers to a match.

No corroborative evidence survives for these and most other legends that inhabit the world of *Uppies and Downies*. Some may be the inventions of Victorian folklorists, seeking to defend their local games in the face of mounting opposition or, just as likely, as in the case of Hallaton and Haxey, to put a socially or religiously acceptable gloss on games that may have derived from less seemly or even pagan origins.

Yet as the 14th century carvings at Gloucester Cathedral and Alexander Barclay's poem of 1514 suggest (*see previous page*), football in one form or another was part of mainstream life in Britain in the period between the Conquest and the Reformation.

That we have come to view it as disruptive is largely because the authorities made repeated efforts at suppression, whether on Shrove Tuesday, Christmas or any other part of the year, and it is these surviving edicts which form the bulk of the primary sources available.

Thus the magic word 'football' first appears in a proclamation issued by the mayor of London, Nicholas Farndon in 1314, for the *Preservation of the Peace*.

This states that '...whereas there is great uproar in the City, through certain tumults arising from great footballs in the fields of the public, from which many evils may perchance arise... we do command and do forbid, on the King's behalf, upon pain of imprisonment, that such game shall be practised henceforth within the City.'

Note that the game itself was not necessarily violent. Rather that 'certain tumults' arose from it being played in a public area.

Numerous edicts were issued by the Crown or its agents thereafter, not least to ensure that men were not distracted from their patriotic duty to practise archery. In 1365, for example, Edward III decreed that in London 'every able-bodied man of the said city on feast-days when he has leisure shall in his sports use bows and arrows or pellets or bolts... forbidding them under pain of imprisonment to meddle in the hurling of stones, loggats and quoits, handball, football... or other vain games of no value.'

In 1496 Henry VII granted a minor concession by allowing artificers, labourers and servants to 'play' on Christmas Day. But this and other edicts were clearly as much honoured in the breach as they were observed, because they had continually to be reiterated.

One instance among many was in Chester, where in 1533 a banning order provides the first actual mention of Shrove Tuesday football in an official document (even though such games appear to have been popular since at least the time of Fitzstephen).

Apparently this order failed, because in 1540 the mayor, Henry Gee, tried a different tack. In this second edict it is proposed to substitute the Shrove Tuesday game of football with a running race on the Roodee (a large open space where horse racing, which continues until the present day, had been staged since at least 1511). Football, it was claimed, had been tainted by 'evil disposed persons, wherfore hath ryssen grete inconvenynce'.

What is interesting about the Chester edict is that it relates how every year on 'Shroft Teuesday, othewyse Goteddesday' the city's shoemakers had provided 'one ball of lether, cauled a fout baule', and that the 'value' of this ball was 3s 4d. This was not the cost of the ball, which would have been much less, but the prize money, handed presumably to the winning player (that is, either the scorer of the decisive goal or the last man to have possession at a certain time).

Once again, this practice of offering a monetary reward was common to several games of festival football, in which the ball, rather than scoring itself, was the ultimate prize. Indeed as we shall see, this remains the custom in Scottish Border games, albeit with now only token sums on offer.

(It cannot be a coincidence that during the same period in Chester a silver bell, also valued at 3s 4d, was offered by the Corporation for winners in the annual horse races, also staged on Shrove Tuesday.)

As the 1540 Chester edict makes clear, Shrove Tuesday matches were no ordinary kickabouts, but were sponsored by the city's drapers, saddlers and shoemakers, and had been 'always tyme out of mann's remembrance'.

This is another common factor in festival football, and one that in several locations would prove to be its saviour. Our story has many examples, continuing well into the 20th century, of where the authorities tried to ban festival football, only for prominent members of the community, property owners included – the drapers, saddlers and shoemakers of their day – to rally in support of what they considered to be 'the people's game' (see for example Ashbourne and Duns).

The supply of balls provides further evidence of how football enjoyed a measure of popular support. One Shrovetide tradition, especially in Scotland, was for married couples to donate a ball.

Yet in some quarters this went beyond custom and was used as a means of preventing other parties from supplying balls, thereby ensuring that games were played only on appointed days, and that the business (and profits) of ball making remained in approved hands. Thus in Carlisle in the early 17th century only the Chamberlain was permitted to supply a ball, and only members of the Shoemakers' Guild were allowed to make them. Journeymen or apprentices caught selling or playing with any other ball were liable to a fine of 7d, that is, the cost of a shoemaker's ball.

Thus far we have ascertained that football was played in many parts of the country – there were repeated bans also in Scotland during the 15th and 16th centuries – and that it was played on feast days, such as Shrove Tuesday and Christmas, as well as on a more routine basis.

But was it actually dangerous, as so often has been said of games of *Uppies and Downies*?

Certainly deaths from football were rarely reported. In 1303 »

▲ Written and illustrated by **Henry Peacham**, 'the country swaines at footeball' was published in 1612 in *Minerva Brittana*, the first ever English example of a genre that was popular on the Continent, known as an 'emblem book' (that is, combining pictures and prose or verse on matters of morality and manners). Peacham's theme is familiar; that life is like football, that our worldly wealth 'is tossed too and fro', and that in the game of life there are winners and losers. Note the mention of a 'goale' and the varying fortunes of each player.

In the margin, the short Latin verse by Valerius may be roughly translated as 'These frail and fragile things, akin to childrens' toys, which are called human strength and wealth.'

'Mr John Gray having laid down proper expedients to prevent riots and tumults within the burgh of barronie of Dunse, and particularly on the anniversary of Fasting's Even, when all the idle people in that burgh were usually conveened by touck of drum to play at the football, which did always end and determine in the effusion of blood among the inhabitants, and did in following out that just purpose order the drummer to bring the drum of that town to his house on the 18th of February last, being Fasting's Even, and yet notwithstanding of the said precaution, the persons above complained upon and manie others did gather themselves together upon pretence of playing at the football... and came up to the said Mr. John Gray, complainer, his house and insolently demanded of him that he should deliver up the drum to them, threatning and swearing revenge and mischief against him... and the said Mr. John Gray having in the maintenance of his authoritie not only refused to deliver up the drum, but likeways commanded the said persons to retire to their respective homes in a peaceable manner, they still persisted in their outrage, and went away together in a body to a place called the Cloack miln, where they played at the football. And when the game was over they did return to the Tolbooth stair, and the winners were then to shew the ball and proclaim the victory, certain particular persons, loosers in the game, opposed then therein and would not suffer the winners to get up to the Tolbooth stair to shew the ball unless they brought the drum alongst with them. Whereupon they fell a fighting and beating and blooding of one another, but att length went into one common concert to goe in a body and seize by force the drum in the said Mr. John Gray, his house.

And accordingly the persons above complained upon, with severall others their assistants in combination with them, came again to the said complainer's house, who att that time was expecting no harm, and whose authoritie in the burgh was sufficient to have defended him against anie insult, and they did then of new require that the drum should be delivered to them.

And not having all this time obtained their unlaufull desires, they did retire for a short space of time, and having gatherd together a body of no less than 2 or 300 persons, did once more return to the said complainer his dwelling place, where he and his family do reside, and did assult his house and endeavoured to break down the doors of entry to his house by throwing many heavy great stones att his doors, they broke down his windows and threw manie stones in at the said windows to the imminent danger of his own life and of those in his family; and during this time they used manie execrable oaths that they would destroy the complainer and bereave him and those of his family of their lives unless he would deliver up to them the drum, which was still refused by him in the just maintenance of his authoritie, ordering the persons above complained upon and those others who had joined with them in body to dismiss and retire to their respective houses. And they att length finding that their malitious attempts would prove unsuccessful, they went off for that night, cursing and swearing and reproaching the said complainer with many opprobrious names, and threatning to destroy him and his family.

Likeas upon Wednesday... one of the said persons above complained upon did come again to the complainer's house and did throw stones att his windows and broke severall... and the complainer having ordered the said... to be carried to the tolbooth by the town officers... as they were carrying her to the said tolbooth... who were ringleaders of the moab the night before... did of new attack the officers... and did rescue her and set her at liberty in manifest contempt of authoritie.

The trial of these persons is craved before the Lord Justice General or his deputes and a jury.

▲ Fasting's Even (or Shrove Tuesday) football was played in **Duns, Berwickshire**, from at least 1686. In 1724 the bailie (or chief magistrate) John Gray tried to stop the game by taking possession of the drum used to summon players, and ended up facing a riot. In his official complaint, Gray blamed William Home, shoemaker (and ball maker) for being the ringleader.

No doubt Gray felt he had a duty to save the town from disorder on football days, while Home was seeking to defend the citizens' ancient right to play ball. Either way, there is no record of a trial ensuing. However, by the following century, in Duns as in other Scottish towns, footba' had given way to handba', which causes much less damage to property.

at Oxford, Adam of Salisbury was killed by Irish students while playing ball in the High Street. Eighteen years later William de Spalding, the Canon of Shouldham, accidentally stabbed a friend with a sheathed knife as they tackled each other.

But these were isolated incidents. More often, the real fear of the authorities was that annual games which drew large crowds of players and onlookers would end in public disorder.

A typical case was in 1576 when, shortly after Shrove Tuesday, various husbandmen, yeomen, tailors and harnessmakers (who were probably the ball makers) from two neighbouring towns, Ruislip and Woxbridge (now Uxbridge), were accused 'with unknown malefactors to the number of a hundred' of assembling unlawfully to play football, as a result of which 'there rose amongst them a great affray, likely to result in homicides and serious accidents.'

Yet no homicides or serious accidents appear to have occurred.

Also significant is that only accredited tradesmen of a certain rank were summoned. Was this to make an example of them, or because they were more likely to be able to pay a fine?

There would be dozens of court hearings similar to this over the next three centuries, with even solicitors and vicars called to defend themselves for playing football in the streets.

Another frequent accusation directed at mass participation, festival footballers concerned the damage done to property in built up areas. Even today (as illustrated on page 13), arriving in some Uppies and Downies towns on the morning of a game, one sees boards and barricades protecting the windows of shops, offices and houses.

This was no less a concern in Manchester where, in 1608, 'An order concerning the ffootebale' stated: 'Whereas there hath bene heretofore greate disorder in our towne of Manchester, and the Inhabitants thereof greatelye wronged and charged with makinge and amendinge of theire glasse windowes broken yearelye and spoyled by a company of lewde and disordered persons usinge that unlawfull exercise of playinge with the ffotebale in ye streets of the said towne, breakinge many mens windowes and glasse at theire plesures, and other great inormyties, Therefore Wee of this Jurye doe order that no maner of persons hereafter shall playe or use the ffotebale in any streete within the said towne of Manchester sub pena to everye one that shall so use the same for every tyme 12 pence.'

The order was issued in October, so we cannot be sure which part of the year this annual affront took place. Perhaps the ban was timed to pre-empt a game at Christmas. But in any case it must have failed because in 1618 two 'offic'rs for ye ffootball' were appointed.

The Church and Puritanism
The role of the church in helping to form several of our most prominent football clubs in the late 19th century – the likes of Manchester City, Fulham and Barnsley – is well known. But long before this the church played a central role in supporting and nurturing popular games.

Many a festival football match started (and still starts) outside a church. At Sedgefield it was the duty of the parish clerk to provide the balls on Shrove Tuesday,

FOOTBALL, Played at the Market Place, Barnet.

while in Duns the kirk pulpit itself formed one of the hailing points.

Churchyards were also used for regular games of football on Sundays, for example amongst parishioners who preferred not to walk home in between matins and vespers. This practice often caused conflict, however. The Synod of Exeter tried to suppress it in 1287, as did the Bishop of Rochester, almost three centuries later, during the 1570s.

Sometimes, though, ministers sided with the congregation. In 1519 the curate of St Mary's in Hawridge, Berkshire, even lost his living after dashing to the church from playing football, without changing, then rushing through the service so that he could return to the game. »

▲ This engraving of football in an eerily deserted **Market Place at Barnet**, Hertfordshire, dated 1788, contrasts greatly with the extract below from the famously evocative poem, *Trivia: or, The Art of Walking the Streets of London*.

Written by **John Gay** in 1716, it appears to describe a typical Shrove Tuesday match, when the apprentices quit their work and snow lay on the ground. As Gay suggests in the penultimate line, street football also promised good business for canny glaziers.

Where Covent-garden's famous
*   Temple stands,*
That boasts the Work of Jones'
*   immortal Hands;*
Columns, with plain
*   Magnificence, appear,*

And graceful Porches lead
*   around the Square:*
Here oft' my Course I bend, when lo!
*   from far,*
I spy the Furies of the Football-War:
The Prentice quits his Shop, to join
*   the Crew,*
Increasing Crowds, the flying
*   game pursue.*
Thus, as you roll the Ball o'er
*   snowy Ground,*
The gath'ring Globe augments with
*   ev'ry Round;*
But whither shall I run? the Throng
*   draws nigh,*
The Ball now Skims the Street, now
*   soars on high;*
The dex'trous Glazier strong returns
*   the Bound,*
And gingling sashes on the Pent-
*   house sound.*

» Unsurprisingly the Puritans were hostile. In his famous tract, *The Anatomy of Abuses*, published in 1583, Philip Stubbes declared that, 'Any exercise which withdraweth us from godlines, either upon the Sabaoth or any other day els, is wicked and to be forbidden... For as concerning football playing, I protest unto you it may rather be called a freendly kinde of fight then a play or recreation, a bloody and murthering practise then a felowly sporte or pastime.'

James VI of Scotland (later James I of England) was equally scathing. Although we know that the king had watched football being played in Wiltshire, in *Basilikon Doron*, presented in 1599 as a guide for his son Henry, he described it as a game unfit for well-born men.

But some gentlemen found it amusing. In a letter dated c.1600, John Chamberlain invited Dudley Carleton to the Knebworth estate. 'You may do well, if you have any idle time, to play the goode fellow and come and see our matches at football, for that and bowling wilbe our best intertainment.'

Bowls was certainly fashionable at the great houses of Elizabethan England. So it would seem was football. In Thomas Dekker's play of 1607, *The Whore of Babylon*, a character called Plain Dealing remembers meeting some lawyers.

'I wondred what they were; I asked one of them if they were going to foot-ball. "Yes" said he, "doe you not see these countrey fellowes? We are against them."

In another play of the period, *Sir Gyles Goosecap*, written c.1602, the foolish knight Goosecap announces that he has decided to marry. His reason?

'Why madam, we have a great match at football towards, married

men against bachelors, and the married men be all my friends, so I would fain marry to take the married men's parts in truth.'

To which Hippolyta replies: 'The best reason for marriage that I ever heard, Sir Gyles.'

There is still one annual match played between married men and bachelors, at Duns in Berwickshire (*see page 132*).

At the same time there was also recognition that football could be character forming. Writing in 1581, Richard Mulcaster, the headmaster of Merchant Taylors' School in London, noted that 'footeball play... could not possibly have growne to this greatness, that it is now at, nor have bene so much used, as it is in all places, if it had not had great helpes, both to health and strength.'

Yet he had also to complain that the game had become debased by the 'rude multitude' who, by the 'bursting of shinnes, and breaking of legges' had made football 'neither civil, neither worthy the name of any traine to health.'

What was required, he went on, was for players to be attended by a 'traningmaister'.

Had Mulcaster visited Cornwall he might well have witnessed a handball game where many of the attributes he was espousing were on regular display.

Still played in its original form in St Columb Major (*see page 142*), Cornish hurling was a variant of *Uppies and Downies* played in two forms: hurling to goals (that is, to a specific point within a town or village), and hurling to country (in which the ball had to be carried further, perhaps over a parish boundary).

A full description of the game as written by Richard Carew in 1602 appears on page 139,

and is noteworthy for revealing a complex game whose rules predated certain basic conventions now applicable to all football codes, such as a set number of players and two goals; no forward passing (as in rugby), and the use of goalkeepers (as in soccer).

Two further references in the 17th century also show how alike football was then to the soccer we know today.

In *Vocabula*, a book from 1636 whose purpose would strike a chord with many a teacher today, David Wedderburn, a master at Aberdeen Grammar School, listed footballing expressions designed to encourage his pupils to learn Latin. These included 'We will pick teams: you choose your first team-mate... Come on, pass it here... You guard the goal... He is very skilful on the ball.'

Similarly, in the years shortly before his death in 1672, Francis Willughby, of Middleton Hall in Warwickshire, compiled a study of sports and pastimes, the *Book of Games*. One of them was football.

'They play in a long street, or a close that has a gate at either end. The gates are called Goals... The ball is thrown up in the middle between the goals... the players being equally divided according to their strength and nimbleness...

'They that can strike the ball through their opponents' goal first win. They usually leave some of their best players to guard the goal while the rest follow the ball. They often break one another's shins when two meet and strike both together against the ball, and therefore there is a law that they must not strike higher than the ball.'

The use of gates as goals may be characteristic of games of *Uppies and Downies* – and a gate still »

▶ One of the most extraordinary ball games ever played in Britain was **cnapan**, as graphically portrayed here by the *Badminton Magazine of Sports and Pastimes* in 1898, by which time this ancient Welsh sport had been all but extinct for a century or more.

Taking its name from the ball – a little larger than hand-sized, hewn from wood and boiled in tallow for at least 12 hours before games to make it extra slippery – cnapan shared several characteristics with other games, particularly Cornish hurling (*see page 138*) and with East Anglian camp-ball (*page 26*).

Played across country between representatives of specific parishes, hundreds or shires, its object was to convey the ball to one's home patch from a neutral starting point.

As in most other mass games, the teams consisted of those who contested and coaxed the ball in the pack (known as the 'hug' in Ashbourne), and those who ran with it following a breakaway.

Alas, apart from these somewhat lurid water colours, no images of cnapan have ever been traced, and we therefore depend for much of our knowledge on George Owen's *Description of Pembrokeshire*, dated 1603, and on more recent research conducted by Brian John (*see Links*). As will become clear, the *Badminton Magazine* artist also used Owen as his source.

Owen's account suggests that cnapan was different in three key respects. Firstly, there were no goals. Instead, the game ended once the ball had gone far enough towards one parish to make it impossible for the other side to win before nightfall.

Secondly, such was the robust nature of the contest that players stripped to the waist in order to avoid ruining their clothes (and no doubt allow them to display their virility). As Owen noted, 'It is a strange sight to see a thousand or fifteen hundred naked men to concur together in a cluster...'

He added, 'I have also seen some long-lock gallants, trimly trimmed at this game not by clipping but by pulling their hair and beards.'

Thirdly, and most alarmingly, the players on foot were accompanied by horsemen, who were allowed to attack each other with cudgels in order to gain possession.

According to Owen a horseman had to issue three challenges to his opponent to release the ball before striking him, and mounted players had to stay clear of those on foot. But as these conventions were largely ignored, games frequently descended into a free-for-all.

Owen claimed that despite this apparent savagery the players bore no grudges after the game (another characteristic frequently ascribed to *Uppies and Downies*).

Owen describes two types of game. The first, 'a settled or standing cnapan' was played on holidays. Five such games were known in Pembrokeshire: 'at the Bury Sands between the parishes of Nevern and Newport upon Shrove Tuesday yearly; the second at Pont Gynon on Easter Monday between the parishes of Meline and Eglwyswrw; the third on Low Easter Day at Pwll Du in Penbedw; the fourth and fifth was wont to be at St Meugans in Cemais, between Cemais men of the one party and Emlyn men (and the men of Cardiganshire with them) of the other party, the first upon Ascension Day, the other upon Corpus Christi Day.'

The last two encounters were apparently the most popular, 'for at these places there hath oftentimes

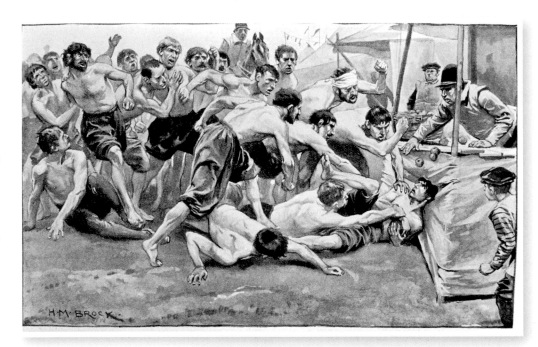

been esteemed two thousand foot besides horsemen.'

The second type of game was organised on holidays or Sundays between two gentlemen, who led teams representing larger areas. To these games were drawn 'divers victuallers with meat, drink and wine of all sorts, also merchants, mercers and pedlers would provide stalls and booths to show and utter their wares'. Note above, the player clutching the ball on the ground has crashed into one of these stalls.

'And for these causes, some to play, some to eat and drink, some to buy, and some to sell, others to see and others to be seen (you know what kind I mean) great multitudes of people would resort besides the players.'

But for all its popularity amongst onlookers, its violent nature led cnapan to die out by the 18th century. Since then, a revival was staged in Cardiganshire in 1922,

with goals located in churches eight miles apart, at Llandysul and Llanwenog. More recently a series of rather milder versions of the game were staged between 1985–95 (*see page 182*).

Otherwise, apart from the existence of a Cnapan Hotel in Newport, Pembrokeshire, little trace of this seemingly wild and fearsome game survives.

▲ A number of fields once used for camp-ball and marked as such on historic maps can still be identified. One is the former **camping land** at **Needham Market, Suffolk**, seen here adjoining Kings Head Meadow and Doctors Field on Pennington's map of 1772, but according to David Dymond (*see Links*), first recorded in 1476. The area is still in use for recreation today.

Other former camping lands or closes that survive as open fields are at Lakenheath, Shimpling and Swaffham (Norfolk), and at Bures, Hawstead, **Little Thurlow** (*see opposite*), Semer and Stanningfield (Suffolk). Other than Needham Market, all are located close or adjacent to the parish church, but are otherwise unmarked, an omission that should surely be addressed, at least somewhere in East Anglia (*see page 183*).

Meanwhile streets named Camping Close also exist in Haddenham, near Ely, and in Mattishall, Norfolk.

The word camp itself has no links with encampments, but derives from a Middle English verb *campen*, meaning to fight or contend.

» forms one of the goals in the Eton Wall Game (*see page 177*) – but otherwise Willughby's football appears to have a good deal in common with soccer.

Striking similarities between modern soccer and another form of football that originated long before the Victorian era are also to be found in East Anglia.

Camp-ball

Most popular in Norfolk, Suffolk, Cambridgeshire and Essex from at least the 15th to the mid 19th centuries, camp-ball, or camping, was, in certain respects, closer in form to modern rugby or soccer than any other variant of early football (some would argue closer still to American football).

Indeed in one reference from Littleport, near Ely, in 1638, a farm labourer used the name camp-ball to mean the same as football, while Shrove Tuesday football in Dorking, Surrey was also sometimes called camping.

As well as being played on commons, intriguingly, camp-ball was often played on fields specially set aside for the purpose.

In fact the sites of no fewer than 105 of these 'camping closes' or 'camping lands' – arguably Britain's earliest mapped football grounds – have been positively identified across Eastern England by historian David Dymond (*see Links*), and he believes there may be many more.

The earliest dated examples are from the late 15th century, but there is evidence of one from even earlier, in 1450.

The typical camping close was a level pasture, varying between half an acre and four acres, and either rectangular, square, or, as still seen in Little Thurlow, Suffolk, triangular (*illustrated opposite*).

These closes were mostly next to churches, and were equally used for popular gatherings and entertainments. Others, such as at Ixworth, Suffolk, in 1625, were on land owned by inns.

Some were specifically fenced or roped off to separate players from spectators. The camping close at Boxford, Suffolk, even had a stand, priced at 6d for entry in 1750.

Camp-ball's significance in wider footballing history has been the subject of some interesting recent debate amongst historians. But in the context of this book it is at least worth summarising its similarities with mass football, and also with Cornish hurling.

When played on a camping close, rather than across country (as explained below), camp-ball consisted of two teams of equal numbers. As in certain other games of *Uppies and Downies* these teams might be divided between married and unmarried men, or between men from neighbouring parishes. At Ashwellthorpe, south west of Norwich, those on one side of the road played those on the other. On a larger scale, Norfolk went up against Suffolk.

So demanding was camp-

ball that strict time limits were enforced, usually 30 minutes. At Boxford in 1750 a stopwatch and French horn were used for time-keeping. But writing in *Suffolk Words and Phrases* in 1823, Edward Moor describes games that ended only when one team had scored seven or nine 'notches' (as goals were called), which might take as long as two to three hours.

Moor was possibly the first person to record the use of 'jumpers for goalposts'. He writes:

'Goals were pitched at the distance of 150 or 200 yards from each other – these were generally formed of the thrown off clothes of the competitors. Each party has two goals, ten or fifteen yards apart. The parties, ten or fifteen a side, stand in line, facing their own goals and each other, at about ten yards distance, midway between the goals, and nearest that of their adversaries.

'An indifferent spectator, agreed on by the parties, throws up a ball, of the size of a common cricket ball, midway between the confronted players, and makes his escape. It is the object of the players to seize and convey the ball between their own goals.'

Note that scoring in one's own goal, rather than in one's opponent's, is also a common factor in *Uppies and Downies*.

Moor also describes two forms of camping. One was called 'civil' camp, in which players were not allowed to indulge in fighting. The other, in which players wore boots, was known variously as 'savage', 'rough', 'boxing' or 'fighting' camp. Also, if a larger ball was used, and therefore handling was less likely, the game might be called 'kicking camp'.

There also appear to have been two other distinct forms of camp-ball: that is, the game as played on a camping close, with strict boundaries, and a cross-country version. The former was played on a regular basis. One Suffolk man, DE Davy, wrote of his youth in the 1770s that 'the labouring youth' would play two or three times a week. The latter was a more occasional affair, perhaps even annual, and might involve many more players, ranging across a much larger area of open country. It was also more suited to those parts of East Anglia covered in heathland and open commons.

In this respect camp-ball exactly mirrored the two forms of Cornish hurling described by Richard Carew in 1602: hurling to goals and hurling to country. (Despite the distance between East Anglia

and Cornwall, hurling and camp-ball also shared certain rules, for example that any combat between players had to be one-on-one.)

Robert Forby, in his 1830 book *The Vocabulary of East Anglia*, wrote that camping always resulted in 'black eyes and bloody noses, broken heads or shins'.

Even worse was a comment by the Rev WT Spurdens, in a supplement to Forby's book, published in 1840. 'I have heard old persons speak of a celebrated camping, Norfolk against Suffolk, on Diss Common, with 300 on each side. The Suffolk men, after 14 hours, were victorious. Nine deaths were the result of the contest, within a fortnight.'

As ever, we need to treat such unsubstantiated recollections with caution. Then, as now, players in mass football games could be prone to macho exaggeration, especially when interviewed by sensation-seeking journalists. Asking a man about the dangers of his Shrove Tuesday game is like asking a fisherman about the one that got away.

Nevertheless, there can be no doubt that camp-ball's reputation counted against it, and by the start of the 20th century it was already a distant memory.

Meanwhile, elsewhere in Britain other forms of *Uppies and Downies* were also under threat. »

>> Of the 15 games featured in this book, sources confirm that at least nine were being played in one form or another before 1802.

These were St Columb Major (first reliable reference 1594), Kirkwall (1684), Duns (1686), Jedburgh (1704), Workington (1775), Alnwick (1788), Atherstone (1790), Hallaton (1796) and Sedgefield (1802).

Almost certainly, each one of these games predated those first references. For example, the report of Workington's Shrove Tuesday match that appeared in the *Cumberland Pacquet* of April 20 1775 described the game as being 'long contended'.

(Incidentally, this report is one of the earliest newspaper accounts of a football match anywhere in the world.)

How many other festival games were being played elsewhere at the start of the 19th century is much harder to state accurately.

What we can identify in detail, however, based on the increasing availability of newspaper reports from this period onwards, are those games which ceased to exist.

Victorian values

It would be tempting to conclude that the steady decline in *Uppies and Downies* was a direct consequence of the rise of both football and rugby from the mid 19th century

onwards. Yet this is not the case.

Firstly, in virtually every town where festival games survive there are also soccer and rugby clubs, and in many cases players from these clubs have featured prominently in games of *Uppies and Downies*. The two strands, played weekly and annually, can and do co-exist quite happily.

Secondly, in several of the communities where festival games came to an end they did so simply owing to declining support, for which there may have been a number of reasons; for example shifting demographics, changing social patterns and, not least, the inability of players to take time off work where Shrove Tuesday ceased to be a public holiday.

Thirdly, throughout the 19th century, opposition to all forms of what were considered immoral or disruptive activities hardened within the public realm. In the 17th century this trend was labelled Puritanism. In the modern era it is called political correctness. But in the early 19th century it was labelled by writers such as Pierce Egan (a real champion of bohemian lifestyles and especially boxing) and by the poet Byron, among others, as 'cant'.

'The English character,' warned Egan, 'may get too refined, and the thoroughbred bulldog degenerate into a whining puppy.'

Cant infected every aspect of public life in early 19th century Britain; the theatre, literature, politics, even the courts, where powdered wigs gave way to more sober fashions. On beaches, nude bathing was proscribed. Fun fairs were sanitised. There were campaigns to suppress horse racing. Bull baiting, that most ancient and bloodthirsty of popular entertainments, was banned in 1835. Cock-fighting suffered likewise in 1849 (though not fox hunting which, being an aristocratic pleasure, thrived).

Of course rumbustious sports such as camp-ball and cnapan hardly fitted into this new drive towards respectability either. After watching the hare pie scramble in Hallaton, Leicestershire (*see page 154*), John Britton wrote in 1807, 'How much more noble, and praise-worthy, would it be to encourage and reward some laudable competition, or instructive emulation; and, instead of sowing the seeds of discord and passionate contention, endeavour to cultivate the benign blessings of peace, brotherly love, and social harmony.'

But by far the most serious challenge to mass participation football was urbanisation.

It will be noted that by the early 19th century no mass participation games were being >>

▶ This lively but unsigned engraving of Shrove Tuesday football in the Market Place at **Kingston-upon-Thames** – one of the most familiar images of festival football from the 19th century – first appeared in the *Illustrated London News* on 28 February 1846, a time when festival football in Surrey was coming under increasing attack for the disruption it supposedly caused.

Not that this could be deduced from such a patently affectionate rendition. There appears to be no bad blood here, unless those two coves on the left are actually trying to pick the pocket of the unsteady gentleman in the top hat, rather than assisting him. But it is known that fights which broke out during the Kingston game were often settled by boxing bouts after it ended. And being so close to London, the game did attract considerable crowds, moreso after the banning of the Shrovetide games at Twickenham and Richmond in 1840.

In fact the Kingston game had already survived a banning order in 1799 (despite the reading of the Riot Act that year), and the game in 1840 – coincidentally the same year that the four-towered Guildhall seen here was completed – only went ahead after the Mayor resisted a motion by the Borough Council to ban it outright.

One factor in its survival, as the engraving suggests, was the participation of what the 1846 report called 'some of the wealthiest inhabitants' of the district, one of whom was William Wadbrook, a prominent maltster.

In his 1914 *Recollections of an Octogenarian*, GW Ayliffe also recalled how certain publicans would bribe players to kick the ball towards their own hostelry.

FOOT-BALL ON SHROVE TUESDAY, AT KINGSTON-UPON-THAMES.

One of these pubs, the Sun Tavern, is seen on the far left with its windows boarded up, on the High Street side of the Market Place. Another was the Griffin Hotel (not visible) a few doors south (and still extant), where pre-match pancake luncheons were served, and where tradesmen retired for supper after the game ended at 5.00pm.

Another key pub in the Market Place was the Castle. Play at Kingston was between residents who lived either north or south of this establishment. Their respective goals were Kingston Bridge (over the River Thames) and Clattern Bridge (over Hogsmill River), both also still extant.

Indeed one can stand on the very spot from which this tableau was drawn, with the Guildhall, now called Market House, still dominating the Market Place, and with All Saints Church visible to the right, exactly as in 1846.

Twenty years after this, a very different scene emerged. In 1864 the nearby game at Hampton was suppressed, followed by neighbouring Walton in 1866. The 1867 game at Kingston ended in a riot and numerous arrests. Councillors' homes were stoned.

The following year's game was, as a result, moved out to Fairfield Park, and although some defiant players tried to move play back into the town, their efforts were doomed. Once a stronghold of Shrove Tuesday football, only one game was now left in the entire county of Surrey, at Dorking.

» played in any of the nation's newly industrialised cities; not in Birmingham, Leeds, Manchester or Liverpool, where incoming workers left their rural traditions behind, and where so-called rational recreations, such as cricket, were more suited to the urban environment.

But even in smaller towns the pressure was starting to build.

In Scotland the need to limit damage caused by games of *Uppies and Downies* forced a gradual transition from footba' to handba'. In Alnwick, Northumberland, a petition from residents to the Duke of Northumberland in 1827 resulted in the Shrove Tuesday play being switched from the streets – where it not only threatened property but also held up through-traffic – to a field outside the town.

But the worst threat to festival football was yet to come.

The Highways Act of 1835 was ostensibly a direct response to the growing need to regulate traffic and ensure that roads be maintained. It formalised many of the measures that we still observe today, for example, the requirement to drive on the left, and not to obstruct the highway. But the Act also gave local authorities the power to fine anyone caught playing football on the public highway, up to a maximum of 40 shillings.

This was some 6-10 times the average weekly wage of a working man.

Combined with the growth of policing – following the formation of the Metropolitan Police in 1829 and the Police Act a decade later – the new highways legislation provided opponents of street football with just the ammunition they had been seeking.

Probably the first town to lose

its Shrove Tuesday game in this period was Barnes, in Surrey, in 1836. As we learned on the previous page, both Richmond and Twickenham followed in 1840.

Next came Derby in 1846.

With a population of 35,000, Derby was the largest urban centre where street football survived.

It was in Derby that one of the most celebrated comments on Shrove Tuesday football was made (according to Stephen Glover, writing in the *History and Gazetteer of the County of Derby* in 1831), by a passing Frenchman.

'If Englishmen call this playing,' the visitor was quoted as saying, 'it would be impossible to say what they call fighting'.

Derby also has the distinction of providing us with a sporting term that remains in common usage today. The two teams playing on Shrove Tuesday represented the parishes of All Saints and St Peter's (with Markeaton Brook as the boundary between them). Later in the 19th century, all football matches played between teams from the same town became known as 'derby' matches. (We can only presume that the name Derby was adopted, rather than, say, Dorking or Workington, because the town became an early soccer stronghold.)

As at nearby Ashbourne, where the festival game was similar in almost every respect, two games were played in Derby; an adult game on Shrove Tuesday and a boys' game on Ash Wednesday.

Stephen Glover described the games in some detail.

'The game commences in the market-place, where the partisans of each parish are drawn up on each side; and, about noon, a large ball is tossed up in the midst of them. This is seized upon by some

of the strongest and most active men of each party. The rest of the players immediately close in upon them, and a solid mass is formed.

'It then becomes the object of each party to impel the course of the crowd towards their particular goal. The struggle to obtain the ball, which is carried in the arms of those who have possessed themselves of it, is then violent, and the motion of the human tide heaving to and fro, without the least regard to consequences, is tremendous.

'Broken shins, broken heads, torn coats and lost hats are among the minor accidents of this fearful contest, and it frequently happens that persons fall in consequence of the intensity of the pressure, fainting and bleeding beneath the feet of the surrounding mob...

'Still the crowd is encouraged by respectable persons attached to each party, and who take a surprising interest in the result of the day's sport; urging on the players with shouts, and even handing to those who are exhausted, oranges and other refreshment.

'The object of the St Peter's party is to get the ball into the water, down the Morledge brook into the Derwent as soon as they can, while the All Saints party endeavour to prevent this, and to urge the ball westward. The St Peters players are considered to be equal to the best water-spaniels, and it is certainly curious to see two or three hundred men up to their chins in the Derwent continually ducking each other. The numbers engaged on both sides exceed a thousand, and the streets are crowded with lookers on. The shops are closed, and the town presents the aspect of a place suddenly taken by storm.' »

▶ A part of Britain where festival football was once common but where only one game now survives, at Kirkwall, (see Chapter 4) are the islands of **Orkney** and **Shetland**.

One unusual characteristic of festival football on these islands is that the games switched from fields and churchyards to the streets (rather than the other way round, as for example at Alnwick, Northumberland), at various points during the 19th century.

Kirkwall's New Year's Ba' can only be positively dated to the streets in 1830, while Stromness followed suit by the 1880s.

In the latter town, the teams were known as the **Northenders** and **Southenders**, as seen here, contesting the Ba' on Victoria Street, **Stromness**, on New Year's Day, c.1910.

In Stromness, as throughout the islands and several other regions of Britain, there existed a strong link between ba' games and weddings.

Orkney folklorist Walter Traill Dennison described the custom in 1880. 'If the bride and bridegroom belonged to separate parishes, the best-man had to provide the boys of one of the parishes with a football. The old rule gave this ball to the boys residing in the parish to which the bride belonged, but, in process of time, the ball was sometimes claimed by the youths of the bridegroom's parish, and in this case the dispute generally ended in a fight.

'Where the parties were stingy, the best-man sometimes refused to pay the "ba' siller", and in this case the wedding party was liable to an attack from the youths. The boys always met the wedding party as it issued from the church or manse, and loudly demanded the ba'.'

If a ba' itself was not given 'Ba' money' could be donated

▲ In the Orkney and Shetland Isles, certain place names are an indicator of where games were once played. As pointed out by Kirkwall historian John Robertson (*see Links*), names such as Lakequoy, Leaquoy and **Lyking**, as seen at this farm in **Sandwick**, are thought to derive from the Norse word *leika*, meaning to play. More obvious are those known as Ba' Field, Ba' Lea or Ba' Green (or Baa' Green, at Meoness on Fair Isle).

Football was not the only form of contest. To mark the monarch's birthday, in Kirkwall, Uppies and Doonies would fight over a pole placed in the centre of a bonfire. The teams had to drag the unburnt remains to their hailing point.

This last occurred in 1858, while a similar inter-district bonfire and log battle continued at Brough, Cumberland into the 1860s (latterly fought between pub factions, as at Haxey, see page 56).

In Stromness, on Christmas Eve, the Northenders and Southenders played out their own struggle with a tree trunk (but with no preceding bonfire). This custom lasted even longer, until 1936.

instead. Indeed coins, known as 'Ba' Money' are still thrown to youngsters after weddings in Stromness, even though no connection with the game remains.

Throughout the islands the style of play varied. In his undated work *Life and Customs in the Shetland Isles,* EW Hardy described the games thus: 'There are no goal-posts, no scientific play, no attempt at combination by the players, each plays for himself, and tries to score with a long, terrific drive.'

Yet on Whalsay, we learn, there were goalkeepers and the ball could be punched (perhaps in the manner of Australian Rules Football). A free kick could be awarded for a trip and the kicker was given "hailin' room" to take a shot at goal – a surprisingly modern feature.

Goals were called 'doors' and marked with stones on the ground. Honour also attached to the man who could kick the ball highest in the air, known as a 'pookie a' air'.

We also learn that Shetland play started after breakfast to make the most of limited daylight hours in winter. Players were roused by a call to the ba' on fiddles or horns, while games would be interrupted by the midday meal, and were followed by a dance in the evening.

Another variation was that whereas in Kirkwall only one ba' per game was played (that is, the game ended after the ba' was hailed), in Stromness several ba's were contested.

Also in Stromness, on Christmas Day 1910, there occurred a rare encounter between 'home' and

'away' teams. The latter consisted of trawlermen who happened to be in port that day. Another variation was in 1886 when Town played Country (as is still the case in St Columb in Cornwall).

The Stromness Ba' ended, as would so many other street games around Britain, over the issue of damages.

These had routinely been paid for by the rate-payers, until patience started to wear thin around the time of the First World War. Finally in 1924 the Town Council banned the game on the grounds that should any damage be caused to a particularly large plate glass window – newly installed at the café of Guilio Fugaccia on Victoria Street – it would not be able to afford a replacement.

» With the place names changed, this description could easily serve for some surviving mass games, especially Ashbourne, Workington and Kirkwall.

The first of several attempts to suppress the Derby game was recorded in 1731. But a century later the pressure mounted, led in the 1830s by a local trade union, which organised a rival attraction in a field in 1834, with hymns, speeches and refreshments. A thousand people attended.

Following the Highways Act the protests grew stronger in the 1840s. Prior to the 1845 game a petition was gathered, and funds raised to pay for alternative sports. The Mayor, John Moss, declared in the *Derby and Chesterfield Reporter* in February 1845, 'In former times, when the town contained but few inhabitants, the game was not attended with its present evils, but it was now a well ascertained fact that many of the inhabitants suffered considerable injury, in person as well as property, from this annual exhibition.'

In the event, a football was produced that Shrove Tuesday and the rival sports were cancelled. Meanwhile the town council voted to restart Derby races as an alternative attraction.

Finally, on Shrove Tuesday 1846, two troops of the 5th Dragoon Guards were drafted in from Nottingham, special constables were sworn in, and although some senior players capitulated and handed over the ball, another set of players defied the authorities and tried to play on.

In the resulting mêlée the Mayor was hit on the shoulder by a brick. The Riot Act was read. Numerous arrests were made, and after a similar outbreak of violence the following day, 20 men were fined

£20 each, a considerable sum, even if ten of them were tradesmen and businessmen. (Again the police focused on those who were more prominent and able to pay their fines.)

Sporadic attempts were made to play a ball in later years, notably in 1868. But Shrove Tuesday football in Derby effectively died in 1846.

There were alternatives, and not only at Ashbourne. In *Bell's Life* in February 1849 we read of a Shrove Tuesday match played eight miles from Derby involving '10 single men of Willington v. 10 single men of Egginton for £2 which was won by Willington, after one of the best games ever witnessed on the lawn of Egginton. It lasted two hours and 20 minutes and it was a fair kick and trip game.'

Great fun no doubt, but a small sided game on a lawn was hardly authentic Shrove Tuesday action.

Three years later *Bell's Life* carried a similar report, from Leicestershire. 'A match £5 a side, Shrove Tuesday. 15 a side Blaby Youth v Wygston Youth, in a field near to Countersthorpe, in the presence of several thousand people from two adjacent villages. The goals being pitched, the men stripped.'

Again, not a game of *Uppies and Downies* but more a precursor of a modern soccer match.

In Jedburgh, Scotland, defenders of their festival game were more successful. In 1849 the local authorities tried to impose a ban on the grounds that a cholera outbreak made it 'detrimental to the peace, order and good government of the Burgh...'

Yet amazingly, at a subsequent appeal by those players arrested for defying the ban, a judge in Edinburgh overruled the Jedburgh magistrates on a technicality,

adding the immortal words that 'I, for one, should hesitate to encourage the abolition of an old and customary game, which from time immemorial has been enjoyed by the community.'

Retreat in the south

Remarkable though the Edinburgh judgment of 1849 was, it proved a rare respite.

While in the Scottish Borders handba' street games continued in parallel with a rise in the popularity of rugby – where clubs in Melrose, Selkirk, Gala and Hawick took root – in another Shrovetide stronghold, Surrey, game after game was banned, leaving the whole region to rugby alone (as it has remained, with the likes of Harlequins, Richmond and Rosslyn Park based there).

Surrey towns where festival games have been noted but which failed to survive beyond the mid 19th century include – according to research by Matthew Alexander (*see Links*) – Cheam, Epsom, Ewell, Mortlake, Ripley, Thames Ditton and Weybridge. Another source mentions a game at Bushy in 1815.

These losses were followed by Molesey and Hampton Wick's festival games ending in 1857, then, as noted earlier, by Hampton and Walton's in 1864 and 1866, and Kingston's in 1867.

In almost every case the authorities made efforts to persuade the players to take their game out to parks or to outlying fields. But not one succeeded.

In a similar vein, in February 1864, *Bell's Life* noted that hundreds of people played Shrove Tuesday football in Battersea Park. A similar scene was played out by exiled Orcadians in Glasgow, on Glasgow Green.

But these games also proved to

be one-off experiments. Two years later Battersea Park would stage its first major soccer game, London v. Sheffield. The same code soon colonised Glasgow Green too.

Already festival football was becoming a rural curiosity, and more the passion of antiquarians – of whom there were now dozens poring over the games' origins – than of the new breed of industrial workers.

In the Midlands town of Nuneaton, the last festival match took place, it is thought, in 1881, leaving only Atherstone to fight on in Warwickshire, while in Northumberland the end of the Rothbury game in 1867 left only Alnwick surviving, in an area once thick with Shrovetide matches.

Even the players of Ashbourne – where the game enjoyed genuine popular support – became enmeshed in annual court battles.

In one sop to the authorities, in 1863 they agreed to let their game start in a field called Shaw Croft, just on the edge of the town, rather than from its customary place in the Market Place. But still the legal pressure hardly abated, not helped by a player drowning in 1878.

Damaging though this incident and the court cases undoubtedly were to the overall image of festival football – in 1884 the *Derby Mercury* described the Ashbourne game as being 'in a moribund state' – there is nevertheless a distinctly English sense of whimsy about some of the hearings. Among the Ashbourne players summoned in 1860 were a gentleman, a draper, a grocer and two attorneys. After being found guilty, one of the latter, George Brittlebank, hopped back into court in order to defend the grocer.

In 1891 one of the Ashbourne accused was the Rev Tomlinson. Before the game in which he had illegally participated, Up'ards and Down'ards gathered in Shaw Croft had sung *Rule Britannia*.

So these Shrovetide players were no revolutionaries. Rather, they were proud Britons, defending their rights against *petit-bourgeois* tradesmen and aldermen who sought to end centuries of tradition. In another age their struggle would have made perfect fodder for the Ealing Film Studios.

Nowhere was this spirit better exemplified than Dorking.

While in Ashbourne the 1890s signalled the cessation of legal challenges to the Shrove Tuesday game, in Dorking, the last bastion of festival football in Surrey, there would be no such let-up.

Dorking's game, oddly enough, was not of great antiquity. Indeed local historians have been unable to find evidence for it earlier than the 1830s. Nevertheless it rapidly assumed all the quirks of a classic Shrove Tuesday carnival, with processions and musicians preceding the game with mock pomp and ceremony (*see page 40*), and the whole town closing down once the 'pancake bell' (actually the bell of St Martin's parish church) had rung in the late morning, a custom which ended in 1862.

The game was played between Eastenders and Westenders, the dividing line being the passageway leading off the High Street to St Martin's. From the top end of this passage the ball was thrown up by the Town Crier, the aim being not to score but to retain possession in one's own side of town at a set hour (as was also the case at Chester-le-Street).

Three balls were contested, one by boys, thrown up at 2.00pm and two by adults, each coloured differently (*see right*). But the

third, golden ball was the main prize, and it was the fight for this, starting at 5.00pm, and ending an hour later, which in the end aroused the most concern amongst local traders.

According to Charles Rose's *Recollections of Old Dorking* (written for the *West Surrey Times* in 1876–77), until the 1870s the game featured some unsavoury practices.

'At that period, it was customary to make one or two bays in West Street, and into these were allowed to flow the blood and refuse from a neighbouring slaughter-house.

'Into this disgusting fluid the ball was kicked, and the players would go, and the more the latter were bespattered and saturated, the better it was liked.

'Another objectionable, and even more dangerous practice was then in existence, for in the midst of the game, the cry would be raised "The Brook, the Brook!" and thither the footballers would hasten, and while heated by the sport, would duck each other to their heart's content. It is needless to state that the results of this senseless conduct were most disastrous, for many, of course, caught severe colds, which in the case of one or two young men, who had previously been in the bloom of health, ended in a premature death. This deplorable issue had a deterrent effect, and the dangerous practice has now, for many years, been wisely abandoned.'

It was also common for the ball to be forced into one of the several pubs along the High Street for a drinks break, after which the ball would be thrown back into the fray from a first floor window.

Apparently the Eastenders were usually outnumbered and ⟩⟩

▲ The only tangible reminder of Shrove Tuesday football in **Dorking** is this simple pole, preserved at Dorking Museum and designed to carry the three balls played for in the Surrey town. No-one is certain what the inscription signified, the best guess being that it referred to the wind in the inflated balls and the water of the brook into which play frequently strayed. It is also known that in later years, before the game was banned in 1897, the inscription was prefixed with 'Kick away both Whig and Tory' (again, for reasons we can only imagine).

A photograph of the notoriously oddball musicians who bore this pole during the processions before matches can be seen on page 40.

The balls themselves are not the originals, and nor are historians sure of the exact colours used, since according to the recollections of locals they seemed to vary from year to year. In the final fateful year of 1897 the two side balls were painted black, as if in mourning. But the ball at the top – the 'five o'clocker' (that is, the final and most fiercely contested of the three) was always gold, as was also the case at Kingston.

Today at Duns, the three cushion-like balls are similarly colour coded (*see page 135*).

Drama in Dorking as police line the High Street before the 1897 Shrove Tuesday game. Yet far from menacing, the day turned into a rollicking farce, as the constables were forced to compete with the players in order to impound ball after ball. This they did to rounds of 'vigorous booing' according to the *Dorking Advertiser*, whose report was accompanied by these extraordinary photographs. Here are scenes that many a town had witnessed throughout the century, and yet ones that with true English phlegm seem invested with rage, resignation and general hilarity in equal measure.

» achieved only seven recorded victories. One was in 1866, when they were assisted by navvies building the London & Brighton Railway.

By that time opposition to the game had grown steadily, growing further in 1873 after passers-by, including a priest, were pelted with snowballs. Thanks to the railway, Dorking was now rapidly expanding, and the newcomers, many of them commuters to London, took a dim view of this apparently primitive escapade.

Nor did it help that the band of musicians who supposedly raised funds before the game to cover any damages usually ended up spending the proceeds on drink.

Nevertheless the Urban District Council continued to support the game. One councillor was even a keen participant, while the duty of throwing up the balls was taken on by a local antiquary, JT Maybank.

But in the end the views of tradesmen prevailed. In 1896 schoolchildren were no longer allowed a half-day holiday to watch or join in with the game, and the following year a petition was sent to Surrey County Council in Kingston, insisting on the enforcement of the Highways Act.

On the day of the match a crowd of 2,000 people gathered, but they were faced by a force of 50-60 policemen, some drafted in from Guildford and Oxted, lining the High Street (*see left*).

As per usual Mr Maybank threw up the first ball, but this was soon grabbed by the police.

Yet what could easily have turned into an ugly confrontation developed instead into an almost farcical game of cat and mouse, as the efforts of the police to intervene required them to join in with the game (*see left*), much to the amusement of the crowd, several of whom kept buying extra footballs from a local shop to keep the action flowing. The police even approached a gentleman who arrived in a carriage, thinking that he had concealed a ball under his overcoat.

In the end the names of 60 players were taken, and even the Urban District Council protested that the Surrey Constabulary had overstepped the mark. Meanwhile support, in the form of a Football Defence Association, attracted donations from no lesser figures than a local judge and Henry Attlee (father of Clement).

At the subsequent magistrates' hearing in March 1897, futile but unsuccessful attempts were made to verify the game's antiquity. At times there was much jollity in the proceedings.

But the outcome was serious enough. Fifty four men were charged with playing football in the streets, and although each one was fined only a token shilling, with 4s costs, the final curtain was now inevitable.

The following year 57 players were fined, one of them a local councillor, and despite further attempts to keep the game alive in subsequent years, when no-one other than 20 constables turned up on a wet Shrove Tuesday in February 1907, the Dorking game was well and truly up.

Since then two other major games have ceased, Chester-le-Street in 1932 (see right) and Hawick in 1939 (see page 102), while the outbreak of two world wars led to major concerns in several towns that the games would not survive the departure of so many of the regular players. In some locations, for example Hallaton, women kept the traditions alive by playing

the games, while in Ashbourne in 1943 Doris Mugglestone and Doris Sowter became the first females ever to score.

Increased traffic levels have also had an impact on Uppies and Downies, particularly at Ashbourne and Denholm, where roads are not closed for the games. Indeed, watching some games it seems fortunate that no players have ever been struck by passing vehicles.

In common with all traditional pursuits, the fate of the nation's festival games has always been subject to the vagaries of fashion and social trends. This may explain why, as will be seen in subsequent chapters, certain of the fifteen surviving games appear to have regained their sense of purpose in the latter years of the 20th century, while others have been forced to adapt to modern sensibilities and are only pale versions of the originals.

But whatever form they take, or may yet take in the future, the one lesson this brief historical account has surely given us is that, as their name suggests, Uppies and Downies have lived through many a difficult period during the last 900 years.

In today's feverish football climate they may not grab the same attention as the Cities and Uniteds, or the Harlequins and the Wasps of the professional leagues. But Uppies and Downies remain an intrinsic part of the same dynamic historical continuum.

Moreover, thanks to the efforts of a number of historians – the likes of John Robertson in Kirkwall, Lindsey Porter in Ashbourne, and the folklorist Doc Rowe seemingly everywhere (each of whom has contributed to this study, see Links) – we also now understand more than ever how important these games are to our national heritage.

▲ Water play in the Burn between Upstreeters and Downstreeters at **Chester-le-Street** c. 1920, one of dozens of postcards recording this famous game. As at Dorking there were no goals. Instead victory was achieved by retaining possession at the end of five hours play.

Chester-le-Street was Britain's last major game to fall foul of the 1835 Highways Act, in 1932, meaning that now only in Sedgefield is there now Shrovetide action in County Durham.

3. The Season

Snowball in Hobkirk, February 1989 – a time of year when the *Uppies and Downies* of Britain must brace themselves for all weathers. Unlike other forms of football, no pitch inspections are ever necessary, and so only if the players themselves are snowed in might a game not take place. Even then a sense of pride kicks in, so that despite the vagaries of the season, instances of cancellations or postponements in festival football are extremely rare, mainly confined to war time and outbreaks of foot and mouth.

In an age when soccer and rugby can no longer be described as purely winter games – having seemingly colonised almost the entire sporting year – the season for *Uppies and Downies* remains virtually unchanged, as it has done for centuries.

It is a short season, starting in Kirkwall on Christmas Day, and ending at Workington on the Saturday after Easter Tuesday.

There is one further game at Duns in July, but this is an exception, having been moved from winter to summer when it was revived in 1949.

Some might ask why other towns do not follow Duns' example and thereby seek to attract more attention. After all, it appears to have worked for Rugby League, which switched its fixtures to the summer in 1996.

But festival football by its very nature is not like other forms of the game. Each game is time specific. Each game stands alone; its own, self-contained local derby, played with no heed to the outside world. As we shall learn in Chapter 10, only in the Scottish Borders is there any meaningful interaction between players from neighbouring games, or any semblance of an agreed schedule.

Everywhere else acts in complete independence.

Because of this, the word 'season' when applied to festival football really refers to a time of the year from midwinter to spring, rather than to a set of fixtures drawn up by a governing body (of which of course there is none for *Uppies and Downies*).

Duns apart, there are currently 19 match days during this season, in 15 different locations.

This includes three match days at Workington and two each at Kirkwall, Ashbourne and St Columb Major.

Within that total there are also added boys' or youths' games, played in the hours immediately before the adult games at Kirkwall, Haxey, Jedburgh and Ancrum.

For ease of reference a calendar of games appears on page 188.

As can be seen from this list, there are two types of scheduling.

Four of the games take place on specific dates. For example Haxey's game (*see opposite*) is always played on January 6, the twelfth day of Christmas (unless that also happens to be a Sunday).

In contrast, the majority of other games are played on days set by the Christian calendar. For example, Hallaton's game is played on Easter Monday, which can vary from year to year between March 23 to April 25. Similarly, Shrove Tuesday, the busiest day of the festival football year, can range from February 3 to March 9.

To assist readers who wish to attend games, a year-by-year schedule is therefore available on the *Played in Britain* website.

As reflected in the following chapter order, the *Uppies and Downies* season is sub-divided into three short bursts: firstly Christmas and New Year, then Shrovetide, and finally Easter.

But why should football be associated with those particular festivals?

In one sense the answer is obvious. A Holy Day was, in many instances (though not all), a holiday. Thus football was played on Holy Days because that was

Has ne'er in a' this country been,
Sic shouldering and sic fa'ing,
As happen'd but few ouks sinsyne,
Here at the Christmas ba'ing...

Has ne'er in Monymusk been seen
Sae mony weel-beft skins:
Of a' the bawmen there was nane
But had twa bleedy shins...

Extracts from *The Monymusk Christmas Ba'ing*, Rev John Skinner 1738

when the general populace enjoyed free time. But we should not forget that religion and sport have long been linked. Most notably, the Olympiads of ancient Greece were in essence religious festivals with games attached.

Festival football is part of that age old connection.

Christmas and New Year
It may again be stating the obvious but another reason for playing football at this time of year was simply to keep warm.

As we saw in the previous chapter, William Fitzstephen wrote in 1174 of the 'stirring of natural heat' engendered amongst spectators at the annual Shrove Tuesday matches in London.

Alexander Barclay, in 1514 (*see page 19*) describes how 'in renning and leaping' the footballers 'drive away the colde' and thus 'overcommeth the winter'. He also alludes to the fact that in winter there was a ready supply of pig's bladders for balls, the 'fat swine' having been slaughtered in advance of the midwinter feast.

But there is another, more fundamental reason why games of *Uppies and Downies* should have been associated with the Christmas period, for this was a time in medieval Britain (and in many other parts of Europe) when the hierarchical order was briefly suspended and, in preparation for the festivities, a peasant or underling was appointed by his fellows as 'Lord of Misrule' (also known as 'King over Christmas' or Master of Revels, or in Scotland the 'Abbott of Unreason').

This custom had nothing to do with Christian beliefs. Rather it was a throwback to the Roman festival of Saturnalia, celebrated between 17 and 23 December,

in which slaves were served all the food they could eat by their masters. But whereas in Rome the Lord of Misrule paid for his brief period of power and excess by being sacrificed at the end of the festivities, in medieval Britain the Lord simply returned to his humble station.

John Beleth, a 12th century English writer on church liturgy, noted, 'now the license which is then permitted is called Decembrian, because it was customary of old among the pagans that during this month slaves and serving-maids should have a sort of liberty given them, and should be put upon an equality with their masters, in celebrating a common festivity.'

Henry VIII and later the English Civil War eventually put a stop to the appointment of Lords of Misrule in their various guises. »

▲ Britain's many folk traditions encompass all manner of strange rituals and ceremonies, most of which can be explained or at least linked to festive or pagan practices.

Not so the ritual of **'Smoking of the Fool'** which precedes the **Haxey Hood** game in Lincolnshire held on the twelfth day of Christmas, January 6. The character of the Fool is common enough, but not the smoking. Also unique is the Hood, held aloft by the Fool. This,

rather than a ball, is the object with which the Haxey game is played.

Another characteristic of Haxey is that some diehard locals still consider January 6 to be the true date of Christmas. Until Britain adopted the Gregorian calendar in 1752 that was indeed the case, and in Haxey – once an isolated community surrounded by marshes and water – as in other parts of the country, the new system was much resented as a foreign imposition.

» But the topsy-turvy theme would linger on for centuries in other forms; for example in parades of costumed pranksters with their faces blackened, performing songs and dances in return for coins or drinks – the original 'trick or treaters'.

Another manifestation of this licensed disorder was the playing of football in the streets.

Nowadays only the games of the Uppies and Doonies in Kirkwall survive on the actual day of Christmas. But it was once common throughout the Orkneys and Shetlands. In Wales, the renowned folklorists Laurence and Alice Gomme found whole communities in Cardiganshire who in the early 19th century would apparently turn out after Christmas morning prayers for epic mass football matches. In one, at Llanwenog near Lampeter the players, male and female, young and old, rich and poor, would divide into teams called Bro and Blaenau, their equivalent of *Uppies and Downies*.

Similarly in Kirkham, Lancashire, Christmas festivities in the 19th century included a mass game starting in the Market Place. This, it should be added, took place after the consumption of their Christmas dinners.

Another form of Christmastide encounter, similar to *Uppies and Downies* but without a ball, was the Twelfth Night custom known as Holly Night, in the Westmorland town of Brough.

Writing in the 1860s in *Bygone Cumberland and Westmorland*, Daniel Scott described this 'very ancient custom' as follows:

'There are two or three inns in the town which provide for the ceremony alternately, though the townspeople lend a hand to prepare the tree, to every branch of which a torch composed of greased rushes is affixed. About eight o'clock in the evening the tree is taken to a convenient part of the town, where the torches are lighted, the town band accompanying and playing till all is completed, when it is carried up and down the town, preceded by the band and the crowd who have now formed in procession.

'Many of the inhabitants carry lighted branches and flambeaus, and rockets, squibs, etc., are discharged on the occasion. After the tree has been thus paraded, and the torches are nearly burnt out, it is taken to the middle of the town, where, amidst the cheers and shouts of the multitude, it is thrown among them. Then begins a scene of noise and confusion, for the crowd, watching the opportunity, rush in and cling to the branches, the contention being to bear it to the rival inns,

'sides' having been formed for that purpose; the reward being an ample allowance of ale, etc., to the successful competitors. The landlord derives his benefit from the numbers the victory attracts, and a fiddler being all ready, a merry night, as it is called here, is got up, the lads and lasses dancing away till morning.'

Holly Night died out sometime between 1860 and 1899, but echoes of it can still be seen at Haxey, where rival pubs also form the competing teams.

The tradition also bears some similarity with the battle of the bonfires held in Kirkwall (*see page 31*) and Hawick (*page 100*).

Shrove Tuesday

For almost a millennium, the one day of the year most associated with mass football in Britain has been Shrove Tuesday, or Fastern's E'en in Scotland, celebrated in other parts of the world (famously New Orleans and Rio de Janeiro) as Mardi Gras, or 'fat Tuesday').

This was the day on which, as at Christmas, licensed misrule was tolerated as people indulged in a final orgy of consumption before the privations of Lent. As William Kethe described it in a sermon at Blandford Forum in 1571, the day was one of 'great gluttony, surfeiting and drunkenness'.

Nowadays, for most people the day is characterised by eating pancakes, a tradition which arose from the need to use up foodstuffs prohibited during Lent (although a more practical reason for the impending fast was to conserve stocks before they could be replenished in spring. Indeed the word Lent itself derives from the Old English or Tuetonic word 'lenct', meaning spring. Shrove, meanwhile, derives from the word shrive, to confess.)

As described by William Fitzstephen in 1174, before the Shrove Tuesday football match the day's sporting activities began with cock fights. Particularly popular among schoolboys this tradition continued until well into the 19th century,

As part of the reversal of the normal order, the masters – or as recorded in Pinner, Middlesex, the churchwarden – would supply cocks to the boys, sometimes at a penny per fowl, and then absent themselves. In Scottish schools, another name for Fastern's E'en was 'barring oot day'.

The boy whose cock triumphed would then be crowned 'King' and allowed to rule the roost, as it were, until the following day, Ash Wednesday. In Bromfield in Cumberland during the 18th century this period of misrule lasted even longer, with the school master excluded for three days.

The tenth hereof is Pancake Day,
Young fellows do at Football play.
'February' in Poor Robin, A New Almanack, 1730

'Pancakes and fritters,' say All Saints' and St. Peter's;
'When will the ball come?' say the bells of St. Alkmun;
'At two they will throw,' says Saint Werabo;
'O! very well!' says little Michael.
Rhyme inspired by Shrovetide in Derby. All Saints is now Derby Cathedral.

Violence and cruelty infected many a Shrovetide custom. Bull baiting, often subsidised by the local council, was common, as were dog-tossing and 'cock threshing', in which boys would peg a cock to the ground and invite passers-by to throw stones at it in return for pennies. In 1663 a Dutchman, William Shellinks, described also how in rural areas contestants, armed with a flail, were blindfolded and spun round before attempting to strike a cock that was buried in the ground up to its neck. But there were many other variations on this 'sport', involving cudgels, broomsticks, and the throwing of cocks too, until by the 18th century opinion turned against the abuses and more rational sports were encouraged instead.

We have already noted the efforts of Chester's lord mayor to instigate running races instead of football in 1540. Horse racing became a popular attraction from this period onwards, as did a variety of other sports and games, for example tugs-of-war in Ludlow and skipping in Scarborough. The custom of pancake races, now most famously staged at Olney in Buckinghamshire, is believed to go back to the mid 15th century.

Indeed the sounding of the pancake bell, usually at 11.00pm or mid-day, was generally the signal for the Shrove Tuesday holiday to commence. The bell was also, in those towns where football was played, the signal for the players to start gathering.

Nine of the 15 games still played in Britain are staged during Shrovetide, and within the tales that follow, we shall learn more about how they dominated local festivities in the hours before Lent heralded a new phase of the year.

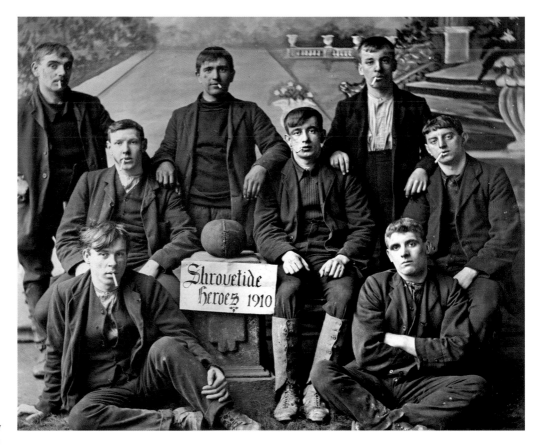

▲ Seemingly sponsored by a local tobacconist, the Shrovetide heroes of **Chester-le-Street** pose after the Shrove Tuesday game in 1910. There, as in many other towns, Shrove Tuesday was equally known as **'football day'**, as cited in this letter of 1815 (reproduced in William Hone's *Everyday Book*), from a correspondent called NS.

'Having some business which called me to Kingston-upon-Thames on... Shrove Tuesday, I got upon the Hampton-court coach... We had not gone above four miles, when the coachman exclaimed to one of the passengers, 'It's Foot-ball day;' not understanding the term, I questioned him what he meant by it; his answer was, that I would see what he meant where I was going. Upon entering Teddington, I was not a little amused to see all the inhabitants securing the glass of all their front windows from the ground to the roof, some by placing hurdles before them, and some by nailing laths across the frames.

'At Twickenham, Bushy, and Hampton-wick they were all engaged in the same way: having to stop a few hours at Hampton-wick and Kingston, I had an opportunity of seeing the whole of the custom, which is, to carry a foot-ball from door to door and beg money. At about 12 o'clock the ball is turned loose, and those who can, kick it... I observed some persons of respectability following the ball: the game lasts about four hours, when the parties retire to the public-houses, and spend the money they before collected in refreshments...

'I understand the corporation of Kingston attempted to put a stop to this practice, but the judges confirmed the right of the game, and it now legally continues, to the no small annoyance of some of the inhabitants, besides the expense and trouble they are put to in securing all their windows.

'I was rather surprised that such a custom should have existed so near London, without my ever before knowing of it.'

▲ Processions of pipers and drummers commonly preceded Shrovetide games, their purpose being not only to rally players and provide music and a sense of occasion, but also to solicit money to pay towards breakages.

Taken in 1895, two years before the game was banned, this is **Taffer Boult's Band** in **Dorking** on what is thought to have been their final outing.

Often described by 19th century observers as 'grotesquely' attired, the band members appear typical of various descriptions from other towns over the centuries, for example Duns in 1724 (*see page 132*). Some band members had their faces daubed with soot or red ochre. One, often dressed as a woman (as is the drummer above), would in some traditions, such as Yorkshire longsword dancing, circulate among the crowds, telling jokes in return for coins. Others wore brightly coloured rags and decorated hats (as still seen at Haxey). A drum, pipes, fiddle and a triangle were the usual instruments.

As seen here, in Dorking the procession was led by a man carrying the three coloured balls on a pole. This pole survives and is illustrated on page 33. Balls were also paraded on poles at Jedburgh and Alnwick (where a tin crescent topped the pole). At Hallaton, where there is still a pre-match procession, the corpse of a hare was used instead (*see page 154*).

Lively though these processions were, they often invited criticism however. In 1409 the Corporation of the City of London banned youths from collecting coins from passersby before the Shrove Tuesday cock fights. In Dorking, as elsewhere, there were also regular complaints that most of the money collected appeared to be spent on drinks during the post-match celebrations.

Another Shrove Tuesday custom frowned upon by polite society was one in which spectators, usually the better dressed ones, were pelted with soot or flour. This lingered on in Atherstone where only recently pea-shooters had to be ordered to desist. Even so, sporadic volleys of eggs and flour – the age-old Shrove Tuesday combination – are still part of the Atherstone experience.

Easter

Easter has long been a period of sporting activity, but less so when it comes to mass football. Today, only two such games survive at Easter, at Workington and Hallaton. But other Easter games have been recorded.

In Devon, for example, according to *Devon and Cornwall Notes and Queries* (for 1918–19), on Good Friday 'neighbouring parishes contested with each other in a very rough game of football across hedges and ditches and often with church towers as goals.'

Near Tiverton, Loxbear and Washfield challenged Calverleigh and Lurley annually, with a stream forming part of the playing area.

Of the other games played, in his *Everyday Book and Table Book* of the 1830s, William Hone mentions trap-and-ball at Bury St Edmunds, handball at Newcastle (where town officials occasionally participated) and stoolball, presumably in the south of England, where it predated cricket.

Other Easter Monday sports recorded include archery in 17th-century Chester, stag hunting in Epping Forest (eventually banned in 1847 because of the influx of unruly crowds from east London), and water fights in the Cotswolds village of Randwick (suppressed in 1892). Race meetings were also common, while running and jumping races played a key part in Easter fairs.

But only at Hallaton do we find specific elements of Easter being woven into the game. There, the consumption of food and ale hark back to much older customs, even if in every other respect the wonderfully titled Hallaton Hare Pie Scramble and Bottle Kicking is actually a classic *Uppies and Downies* encounter.

▲ Captured by a *Picture Post* lensman, members of the **Company of Freeman Marblers** dribble a football in the streets of **Corfe Castle, Dorset**, on Shrove Tuesday 1951, with the 11th century castle, now a ruin, in the distance.

There is no competitive element to this curious kickabout. Instead, it is the remnant of a ritual described as 'ancient' in the earliest known Articles of the Company, dated 1651, and which may well have originated in the 12th century.

Corfe Castle was once the centre of quarrying for Purbeck Marble, a form of limestone used in numerous buildings, not least the cathedrals of Salisbury, Lincoln, Westminster, Winchester and Worcester.

Membership of the Company, whose headquarters are in the tiny Town Hall on West Street – the smallest of its ilk in Britain – was originally confined to 'marblers' and their adult sons. However in the last century this was extended to outsiders, who pay £5 on top of the standard membership of 6s 8d.

Each Shrove Tuesday the guildsmen met at the Town Hall to agree a price for the stone, and to elect officials and induct new members. In addition, the last man to have married during the previous year had to provide a football.

After the meeting the men would kick this ball along the streets, and from there along a three mile route over Rempstone Heath to Ower Quay, an inlet in Poole Harbour, where the marble was loaded onto ships. Once at the water's edge the ball was kicked into the harbour.

The purpose of this symbolic jaunt was – rather in the tradition of beating the bounds – to assert the marblers' right to use this route for the transportation of their stone.

As part of this rite, a pound of pepper was also handed to the tenant at Ower Farm, which formed part of the Rempstone Estate (hence part of the way became known as Peppercorn Lane.)

In 1860 Ower Quay was superceded by Swanage as the main port. But the Shrove Tuesday football custom survived, to be joined by another ritual in which new members are challenged to carry a quart of ale from the 16th century Fox Inn (on the opposite side of West Street), to the Town Hall, while the rest try to make them spill it. Conveying the beer in bottles is therefore the preferred method, but even then members do their utmost to impede the initiate.

Today only one quarry survives in the area, so that the Shrove Tuesday kickabout is now a modest affair, confined to a brief foray into West Street. But visitors might still wish to visit the small museum in the Town Hall, where there is more on the ancient Company and its curious footballing tradition.

Christmas and New Year

4. Kirkwall, Orkney Islands

The Reverend Bill Cant throws up the ba' to start the men's game at Kirkwall on New Year's Day, 1987. In the background is his place of work, St Magnus Cathedral, which that year was celebrating its 850th anniversary. The ba' game is a more recent innovation, being a mere two or three centuries old. The men's game on both Christmas Day and New Year's Day starts as soon as the cathedral clock strikes 1.00pm. Two hours later it starts to get dark.

The Orkney Islands, an archipelago of some 70 islands and rocky outcrops with a total population of only 20,000, may seem an unlikely location for one of the most vigorous games in Britain. The hotbeds of soccer and rugby are a long way from here. So, seemingly, are the *Uppies and Downies* traditions found on the mainland. Moreover, when Orcadians say they are going to the mainland they do not mean Scotland. To them, the mainland is the Orkney island on which the two largest towns, Kirkwall and Stromness, are situated.

Here, therefore, is an outpost of Britain, proud and independent in spirit. And yet the islands form a vital part of our story.

Over the centuries dozens of football games of various forms have been recorded as taking place in communities spread around the Orkneys, and on the neighbouring Shetland Islands (*see page 31*). Stromness hosted its own festival games until 1924. But now, in terms of *Uppies and Downies*, only the Christmas and New Year games in Kirkwall survive.

The word 'survive' is rather an understatement, however.

The Kirkwall ba' is currently in robust health, and continues to play a vital part in local life. Native born Orcadians will travel hundreds of miles to see the games, while it is often said that ba' is the first word many local toddlers learn.

Kirkwall is additionally important because its ba' games have been so well documented. For this we are indebted to John Robertson CBE, whose wonderful 2005 history *The Kirkwall Ba'* (an update of his earlier study – *see Links*) forms a seminal text.

A focal point for the Kirkwall ba' is St Magnus Cathedral, midway between the two goals. It is from the Mercat Cross, in front of the cathedral, that the ba' is thrown up to start the game. But St Magnus also defines the division of the town into rival factions.

When work on its construction started in 1137, it was then located on the edge of the old Viking town. The land to the south, up the hill, known as the Laverock, fell under the control of the cathedral and its bishops, while to the north, around the harbour, the Burgh stayed in the hands of the earls.

Nearly 900 years later that division still determines the make-up of the two sides playing ba'. The Uppies are known as the Up-the-Gates, the Downies as the Doon-the-Gates. (Gates, in this context, derives from the Old Norse word 'gata', meaning street.) In modern times the border is marked by Post Office Lane, running west from the Mercat Cross, across Broad Street.

Readers need therefore to bear in mind that in Kirkwall playing Up means going south (that is, up the hill), while Down means going north, down to the harbour.

The New Year's Day Ba' in 1930 – one of many photographs of the Kirkwall game taken by Tom Kent (1863–1936) during the early 20th century and now held at the Orkney Library and Archive. Kent studied photography in Chicago and was also a contributor to *Country Life*.

Returning to St Magnus, the earliest reference to football in Kirkwall is an entry in the Cathedral's Session Book of December 7 1684, in which, 'It was intimated that ther is non in toun and paroch that marries but shall pay a foot-ball to the scholers of the grammour school.'

This custom of married couples paying for the provision of balls is found in many other parts of Britain. Grammar schools also play a part in the Shrovetide football traditions at Ashbourne and Jedburgh. But the custom does not necessarily relate to the playing of *Uppies and Downies* as we know it today. At Kirkwall, for example, the schoolboys played their football not on the streets but on common land known as Ba' Lea (or Ball Field), which was also used for golf and which lay south east of the town, beyond the present day Dundas Crescent.

As the common became progressively enclosed, by the late 18th century games had moved further into the town centre to Kirk Green, directly adjacent to the cathedral. Here the games were played mainly on Sundays and holidays, with the teams now being divided into Up-the-Gates v. Down-the-Gates.

That by the early 19th century these games had spread beyond Kirk Green and into the streets is confirmed by an edict drawn up by the Town Council, almost certainly aimed at suppressing the New Year's Day game of January 1826.

Apparently the result of a petition from 'Burgesses and other Inhabitants', it reads: 'Whereas sundry Idle and disorderly persons have occasionally disturbed the public peace of the Burgh of Kirkwall by playing at football through the Streets and liberties

thereof whereby the Inhabitants and Community have been much annoyed and molested, and their persons and property hurt and endangered, Notice is hereby given that all and every persons are strictly prohibited and discharged from such practice in time coming.'

As in other towns, this ban appears to have been ignored. For example, a private letter from the parents of Henry Leask to their son in London, dated 18 January 1830, includes the comment, 'their is bein a Great struggle about the foot Ball this year on the Broad Street – nearly four hours – at last carried up-street.'

Ten years later another letter, to the *John O'Groats Journal*, published on January 24 1840, informed

readers that 'Yesterday was held as old-new-year's day. Men, women and children, turned out to a man, to witness or assist at playing the foot-ball. The "down the gets" won the day after a short struggle. The shops were all shut after 1.00am and the people were on the whole very orderly and sober.'

(Note that at that time New Year's Day was celebrated in Kirkwall on January 13, the islands having failed to introduce the Gregorian calendar, adopted elsewhere in Britain in 1752.)

Orderly and sober the people may have been, but in January 1841, as again reported in the *John O'Groats Journal*, the magistrates made a further attempt to halt play, only for their warnings to be drowned out by the players. »

Local businessman Archie Spence throws up on New Year's Day 1958, when relatively few turned out in the snow. The honour of throwing up for the men's game is usually given to a leading local figure, who also pays for the ba' itself. Women are more often chosen to throw up for the boys' ba', held in the morning.

▶ The **Uppies'** goal is the gable end of a house, variously known as Mackinson's, Sandison's or the Long Corner, opposite the Catholic church, where Main Street joins New Scapa Road (once regarded as the southern extremity of Kirkwall).

Some maintain that, to score, a player must touch the ba' against the wall. Others say that reaching the corner is sufficient in itself.

Other goals used by the Uppies in the past include various points on Wellington and High Streets, and in the late 19th century, a location called Burgar's Bay.

The **Doonies** score by wetting the ball in the sea, at any point along a stretch from Shore Street to Ayre Road, either side of the harbour. The Uppies consider this flexibility to be an unfair advantage as it is much harder for them to defend. Generally though, the Doonies end up dunking the ba' in the inner Basin, near the Corn Slip.

Wetting the ba' in the Peerie, or Peedie Sea, does not count.

Linking the two goals, with St Magnus forming roughly the midpoint, is a winding way, particularly narrow along Victoria Street, en route to the Uppie goal, and Albert Street, en route to the harbour. The scrum often spends an uncomfortable hour or even longer in either street, although once again the Doonies may be said to have the easier route in

Victorious Doonies emerge from the harbour at the conclusion of the New Year's Day Boys' Ba' in 1950. For the Doonies to score the ball must enter the water.

that Albert Street is more easily accessed off Broad Street. To force the ba' onto the wider Junction Road the Uppies must also go along Tankerness Lane.

But there is also a warren of alternative passages and closes to choose from, and no limits on where the play may roam.

U Uppies goal
   (Mackinson's Corner)
D Doonies goal (in the water)
1 St Magnus Cathedral and
   Mercat Cross
2 Post Office Lane
3 St Ola Hotel
4 West End Hotel
5 Burgar's Bay

≫ As the report noted, 'The game has been played in Kirkwall on such occasions for time immemorial, and some folks will have it that there was no good reason for attempting to put it down.'

Four years later the authorities tried another method, when Sheriff Substitute C Gordon Robertson put forward a proposal to prettify the Kirk Green with flowers and trees, on the understanding that the ba' game would be banned. On hearing this, an even greater crowd than usual turned up on New Year's Day 1846, openly defying the judge's threat of imprisonment. Even the Town Clerk, John Mitchell, made a stand, telling the judge that if one player was sent to prison then 'You'll need to put us all in jail.' Mitchell then promptly plunged into the scrimmage from which, according to one account, he would later emerge with only one tail of his coat intact.

Mitchell's stand was all the more remarkable given that, as Town Clerk, he had signed the banning order of 1825, twenty years previously. Either he had signed that under duress or the ba' had won him over.

Unable to stop the game outright, Robertson next proposed that it should be relocated to 'some more suitable locality', away from the town centre (as had happened at Alnwick in 1828, *see page 92*).

In January 1855 *The Orcadian* (published in Kirkwall) endorsed this idea. 'We have always regarded this uproar on the streets as most indecorous and absurd, and we would recommend that a piece of ground be given for this holiday sport, and players absolutely prevented from disturbing the town.'

Still nothing was done, and so the criticism continued, unrelenting. In January 1863, the *Orkney Herald* declared, 'Really it is high time that our citizens, young and middle-aged, should bethink themselves of some more rational amusement. It is as barbarous as the Christmas diversion of the young Shetlanders, who drag a burning tar-barrel through the streets of Lerwick.'

Regarding Christmas – which was not deemed a holiday – there is evidence of ba' games also being played on that day in Kirkwall. For example, a letter in *The Orcadian* of December 29 1855 lamented, 'Christmas Day has passed over; but how changed! Not the slightest difference could anywhere be observed in town – not even the usual game at football.'

From footba' to handba'

As also occurred in the Scottish Borders (*see page 99*), at some point during the 19th century the Kirkwall ba' evolved from a predominantly kicking game to a handling one (although kicking would still be allowed).

A correspondent called 'Granpa', writing in *The Orcadian* in January 1889, remembered how the game had been played in the 1840s. At that time, he wrote, one of the leading players, an Uppie called James Mowat, could kick the ba' the length of Broad Street, and no-one would try to pick it up. Granpa added that the modern ba' game had become 'a rush, push, tumble, smack-your-neighbour, go-as-you-please free-fight, and brute force generally wins.'

In *Kirkwall in the Orkneys*, published in 1900, BH Hossack made a similar point when recalling how the game was played before 1850.

'In those days to have lifted the ball would have been very risky for the lifter; the ball was kicked or dribbled but never held, so it went all over the street or green.'

By the 1870s, as Kirkwall became more built up, handling assumed a greater importance. Mainly it reduced the potential level of damage to properties, but it also gave players more control over the ball.

Even so, the shift was not universally accepted. On New Year's Day 1875 the Uppies' tactic of smuggling their way to victory – a classic manoeuvre of the handling game – attracted criticism, and in 1888, in an attempt to reduce handling, the ba' was made larger, and therefore harder to hold. But apparently the players soon learnt to adapt.

As opposition to the ba' continued throughout the 19th century, in the local press at least, there were periods when it looked as if the Kirkwall ba' would die out altogether. According to the *Orkney Herald* 'only a small number took part in the scuffle' on New Year's Day 1861. There was no game at all on Christmas Day 1872.

Then, on Christmas Day 1875, at the very time the street game would normally start, 1.00pm, Kirkwall Football Club organised a game of rugby at Soulisquoy. According to *The Northman* newspaper, the Uppies triumphed by a goal to a try, in a game it called 'more civilized' compared with 'the usual street riot'.

And that might well have been the end of the ba'. After all, the increased use of handling in the street game was not so different from rugby, itself an emerging code in the 1870s – the Rugby Football Union was formed in 1871 – while there would have »

In the days of sailing ships the Doonies would signal victory by 'trucking' the ba from the tallest mast in the harbour. This image, by Tom Kent, shows Doonie boys climbing the mast of the *Mary Ann* on New Year's Day, 1906. The earliest record of this practice is from 1856. In 1878 the ba' even sailed to the island of Shapinsay, tied to the mast of the *Klydon*.

▲ Kirkwall shoemaker Jim Harrison stitches up one of the ba's to be used over the winter of 1947–48.

The **Kirkwall Ba'** looks much like a soccer ball from the 19th century, but instead of a bladder it is stuffed with cork dust and hence weighs around 1.4kg (that is, three times heavier than a soccer ball, even though its diameter is only marginally larger, at 22.6cm).

The boys' ba's are slightly smaller, weighing on average 1.3kg and measuring 19cm in diameter.

Each ba' takes as long as four days to make, one factor being that the cork dust must be allowed to settle, and then be supplemented, so that no bulges or soft spots

occur after stitching. Using cork helps to ensure that the ball will float should it be thrown into the harbour for a Doonies' score.

As of 2007 there are three ba' makers. George Drever, ba' maker since 1983 and otherwise employed at an oil terminal in the Orkneys, makes two per year, with his familiar diamond pattern around the buttons. The brothers Sigurd and Edgar Gibson, who work at the BBC in Glasgow, make the others. Their father Gary made ba's from 1966–95.

Although each maker has his own style, none deviates from the standard scheme of alternating panels in brown and black.

» been many a local seafarer, and visiting sailor, who had played rugby on the mainland. Kirkwall was by no means an isolated community.

But instead of accepting such a radical change, and perhaps even rallied into action by the 1875 experiment, supporters of the ba' resolved not to let their old game be further diluted. The following year it was back to normal.

Nor was there any support for a proposal published in The Orcadian in 1883 to limit the teams to their best twenty men each, move the play to a park and appoint umpires.

Boys' and Youths' Games
Since 1911 there has been a set pattern of a boys' and a men's ba' each being played on Christmas Day and New Year's Day.

The boys' game, perhaps following on from the tradition of ball games at the grammar school, appears to have been established on New Year's Day by the 1830s, and on Christmas Day by the end of the 1870s.

But it was never easy to stop older youths and men joining in with their younger counterparts.

In 1882 the Town Crier announced that the age limit for boys would be set at fifteen. Still, as reported in the Orkney Herald in 1885, when apparently the boys' game was 'interfered with by old boys with beards', this proved hard to enforce.

To avoid this, a third game, for youths, was introduced some time on or before New Year's Day, 1892; youths being classed as aged 14–21. This required the boys to start much earlier, on one occasion as early as 8.00am. But they clearly took it seriously, for there is evidence of boys at the grammar

school, from the late 19th century until World War Two, practising beforehand using turnips as balls, both in the playground and the streets.

The youths' game followed later in the morning, followed by the men's starting at 1.00pm.

Inevitably, however, this made for a long day for all concerned, making it even more common for adults to get involved in the youths' game, particularly on New Year's Day 1902, for example, when the men's game finished before the youths'.

Three games in a day also tested the patience of local residents and businesses. As a result, some time between 1892 and 1910, a petition was circulated.

It stated, 'Complaints having from time to time been made regarding the annoyance and damage to property caused by the playing of three foot-balls on Xmas Day and the like number on New Year's Day, the magistrates have thought proper to invite as they hereby do, an expression of opinion on the part of occupants of property along the route of said Balls whether or not the playing of them on the public streets should be henceforth discontinued.'

There were 107 signatures altogether, of which only 24 voted for a complete ban. But of the 83 who voted in favour, 12 wished to see a reduction in the number of ba's played for, and it was their view that was subsequently carried by a large majority at a public meeting in November 1910.

From then onwards, only two ba's per day were contested, with the youths' game being dropped.

Not that this prevented men from interfering, so much so that, in 1913, bouncers were called upon to weed out the interlopers. »

The Christmas Day Ba' in 1953, as recorded by **Bob Johnston**, known as Spike, a regular contributor to the *Orkney Herald* until its demise in 1961. (Readers of the *Aberdeen Press and Journal* knew Johnston as Donovan Smith.)

As the cartoon suggests, the Kirkwall ba' can be a rough and tough affair. Even hardened rugby players have found the game to be harder than their own code.

Yet this seldom prevents older spectators joining in for a few minutes when the urge strikes, often with no thought as to the damage this invariably causes to their clothes. Nor is it unusual to see respectable professionals from the town suddenly getting down in the scrum alongside labourers and dock workers.

Famously, one local doctor, a winner of the ba' in 1895, handed his tile hat and malacca cane to a spectator before plunging into the action in his frock coat. When subsequently a fellow player broke a leg, the doctor emerged, made the man a splint, and then instantly rejoined the struggle.

John Robertson, the esteemed historian of the game, won the ba' himself in 1966.

Only one death has ever been recorded, when on New Year's Day 1903, Captain William Cooper, a Doonie in his forties, suffered a fatal heart attack.

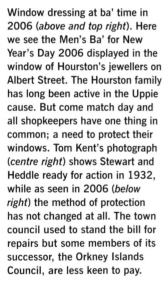

Window dressing at ba' time in 2006 (*above and top right*). Here we see the Men's Ba' for New Year's Day 2006 displayed in the window of Hourston's jewellers on Albert Street. The Hourston family has long been active in the Uppie cause. But come match day and all shopkeepers have one thing in common; a need to protect their windows. Tom Kent's photograph (*centre right*) shows Stewart and Heddle ready for action in 1932, while as seen in 2006 (*below right*) the method of protection has not changed at all. The town council used to stand the bill for repairs but some members of its successor, the Orkney Islands Council, are less keen to pay.

Notable incidents

Over the years Kirkwall has seen plenty of unusual and clever moves of the type which do so much to enliven and enhance games of *Uppies and Downies*.

Bob Nicolson, an Uppie, won the day at New Year 1901 by pretending to be injured and retiring to a doorway on Broad Street. Of course he had the ball secreted in his coat all the time.

After waiting for the scrum to move on, Nicolson then walked straight to Mackinson's Corner, to score unopposed. (The 1943 Haxey Hood was won in a similar fashion, *see page 67*.)

Another famous play took place on New Year's Day 1936. This time a Doonie managed to grab the ball on Victoria Street and throw it to a waiting colleague. From there, runners were ready to relay the ball via Junction Road and West Tankerness Lane to the Peerie Sea.

Instead of heading straight from there to the harbour, two Doonies then waded across to Pickaquoy with the ba', before turning north.

By now some of the Uppies had arrived on the scene, but before they could make a challenge, one of the Doonies managed to throw the ba' into the sea, from where it was picked up by more Doonies stationed in a small boat. They then rowed back to the basin – the Doonies' goal – and scored.

As a counter to those who see only chaos in 'mob' football, this type of elaborate 'set-piece' move would be worthy of the Superbowl.

The New Year's Day game of 1966 culminated in an even bigger twist than that summer's World Cup final at Wembley, when West Germany equalised in the last minute against England.

The Doonies manoeuvred the ball to the harbour in the gloaming at 4.30pm, when the ba' was then dropped over the edge for its clinching salt bath, and the game appeared to be over.

But even at this late stage, a well-positioned Uppie, on his knees in the scrum, was able to reach out and catch the ba', then quietly slip away to a car which took him to the Uppie goal for an unopposed hail.

He and his companion then drove back to the harbour where the remaining players were still in action, including several searching for the lost ball in the water.

Another notable year was 1881, when on New Year's Day two ships, the *Paragon* and the *St Clair*, were spotted, becalmed in Kirkwall Bay, as the throwing up time of 1.00pm approached.

As the Doonies were often supplemented by crew members from whichever vessels happened to be in port, some of their number on shore deliberately hid the ball and announced that the game would be delayed until 2.00pm.

According to the *Orkney Herald* this unprecedented ploy resulted in one of the keenest games ever.

Outraged by their opponents' 'cheatriness', the Uppies started at 1.00pm, using an ordinary football. Then at 2.00pm the real ba' was produced, setting off an epic struggle amongst a now seething crowd of some 500 men.

But as the Uppies seemed to gain the advantage by forcing the ba' to Clay Loan, a detachment from the *Paragon* finally arrived, turning the game in the Doonies' favour. The game ended with the ba' being trucked up the mast of the *Paragon* as darkness fell.

Ba' players have long memories, and trickery of any sort is never forgotten, although in the spirit of the game, it is usually forgiven.

Raising funds

Since the demise of sailing ships, the trucking ritual at Kirkwall has ended. But only a few of the other traditions associated with the ba' have changed.

One concerns the raising of money for the game.

As mentioned earlier, as early as the 17th century newly married couples in the town were expected to donate.

By the early 19th century that meant a payment of 1s 6d per couple, collected by the Session Clerk. One ball was provided for the grammar school, another for the men on New Year's Day.

These collections ended with the passing of the Registration Act of 1855, after which a simple collection was made in and around the town. However it was often suspected that more was raised than was actually required and that the surplus was spent on drink.

In 1910, therefore, two official collectors were appointed and the maximum donation set at 6d.

From this practice there emerged the beginnings of a fully-fledged Ba' Committee, an idea eventually formalised in 1949.

Numbers have fluctuated over the years but nowadays the Ba' Committee comprises five Uppies and five Doonies, a mixture of current and former players.

Their responsibilities include the selection of prominent individuals to throw up the ball, representing the views of players and supporters to the authorities and, increasingly, explaining the game to film crews and journalists.

The Committee also arranges for the ba' to be taken to the house of the thrower-up, where there will be drinks on the eve of the game, and where the ba' will spend the night. »

▲ Orcadian women are amongst the most vociferous supporters of the Ba', and not always from the sidelines. One incident in particular has passed into folklore.

In the late 1860s a distaff Doonie apparently caught the ball from the throw-up and managed to elude the crowd as she headed down towards the harbour. There she was finally caught and knocked into the sea. But by that very act a Doonie victory was assured.

A 1920 poem by David Horne, written to commemorate the restarting of the Ba' after World War One included this stanza:

And then I think o' women's rights,
And women's votes and a'
And wonder dimly if next year
We'll hae a Ladies' Ba';
And certies! if they try the ploy,
They'll stand their ground as
weel's a boy!'

Horne thought of a Ladies Ba' as 'but a silly dream'. Yet at times during the 1920s there were more girls than boys in the boys' game.

A dedicated women's Ba' did become a brief reality after the Second World War.

Two games were held, on Christmas Day 1945 and New Year's Day 1946.

The first was marred by the theft of the ball from the scrum, either in protest at the event or as a prank.

Eventually it was found in the Cathedral graveyard, only for a Doonie to run with the ball to her house, where she was robbed by Uppies, one of whom, Violet Couper, was declared the winner.

The Uppies also won the second game, in just four minutes.

But the *Orkney Herald* noted that 'there was considerable opposition to the holding of this game, on the grounds that it would prove to be an undignified exhibition,' and the experiment has not been repeated since.

▶ One of the rituals at Kirkwall is the pre-match procession of the two rival factions from their prospective heartlands to the Mercat Cross. For the **Doonies** (seen right on Broad Street in 2006) this takes them from their headquarters at the St Ola Hotel, on the harbour, via Albert Street, just visible in the distance.

For the Uppies, the route goes from the West End Hotel on Main Street, via Victoria Street.

On arrival, the teams exchange handshakes and friendly banter, before those who have chosen to contest the Ba' in its earliest phase – a matter of tactics usually decided at a meeting held the night before – will group with their backs to the Town Hall (*below right*).

Meanwhile the majority of other players await the throw up standing on the side furthest from their respective goals.

Note how neither side wears any distinguishing clothes or colours.

In former times when Christmas Day was not a holiday, more players arrived when work was over. Today most are present throughout.

There is no time limit to the game – some have gone on as late as 8.00pm, as on New Year's Day 1975, won by the Uppies. The shortest game, on Christmas Day 1952, won by the Doonies, lasted only four minutes.

The game today

As tradition requires, two ba's are played for on both Christmas Day and New Year's Day, unless either falls on a Sunday, in which case the games are staged a day later.

The Boys' Ba' starts at 10.30am, followed by the Men's at 1.00pm.

Any reader wishing to attend should note, however, that transport links to the islands are suspended on holidays, so that 'ferryloupers', as visitors are known, need to plan on staying for a few days at least.

Needless to add they should also take warm clothing and book well in advance. Many an exiled Orcadian returns for the games, and hotel beds are at a premium.

Both games commence with a throw up outside St Magnus, at the Mercat Cross. (The cross is actually a replica of the 1621 original, which is now exhibited inside the cathedral.)

The teams

In the past, the factor that decided who played Up-the-Gates or Down-the-Gates was one's place of birth, north or south of Post Office Lane, an alley running west from the Mercat Cross.

Nowadays, to ensure a balance between the two sides, birthplace is no longer decisive. This is because the construction of the Balfour Hospital after the Second World War has meant that most locals would automatically qualify for the Uppies.

Also, as Doonie territory is naturally limited by the harbour, and therefore the town can only expand inland to the south, Uppie households have multiplied.

As a result, many an inhabitant of Uppie territory chooses to play for the Doonies, according to their family's origins. »

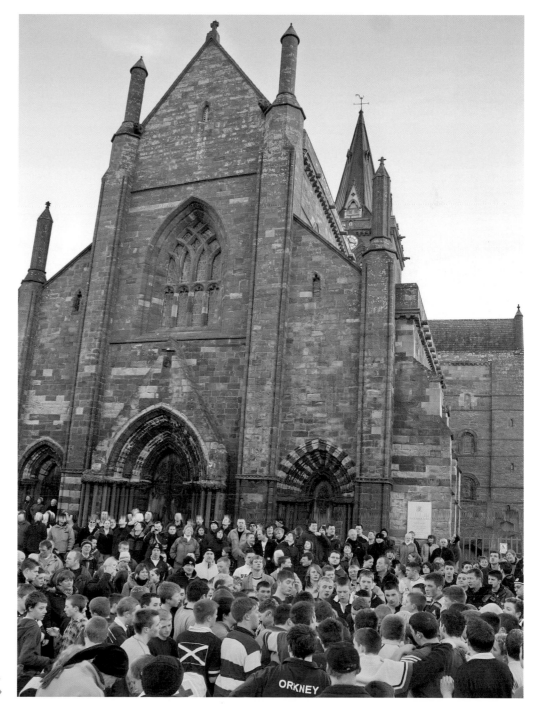

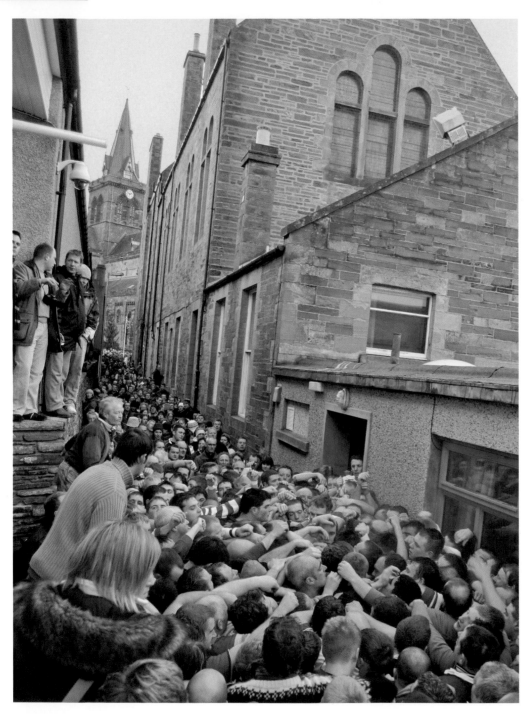

>> Incomers, meanwhile, may choose allegiance by their point of entry to the town. Arriving from the airport or Scapa makes you an Uppie. Driving in on the Ayre Road, from the Stromness ferry, makes you a Doonie.

For the Boys' Ba', teams of around 50 per side are typical. But this is no sanitised version of the main event. The enthusiasm of those as young as six or seven years old can be quite startling. And when one hears an adult crying 'Get back in there son!' it might easily be his mother egging him on.

Certainly the boys' game can take as long as the men's, and on occasions even runs into the afternoon, so that there may be two scrums, junior and senior, just a few yards apart.

However, the adults have needed to stamp down on certain juvenile practices. On New Year's Day 1998, the ba' was dropped down a drain, then hidden in an attic. From there a number of boys managed to take the game up onto the roof of a warehouse, causing several hundred pounds worth of damage, before the ball was spirited into a home and a long stalemate ensued.

Since then, members of the Ba' Committee have visited local schools in advance in order to emphasise respect for the spirit of

A concerted pile up in the narrow confines of Post Office Lane, west of the cathedral, during the New Year's Day Men's Ba' of 2006. Once trapped in a situation like this, it becomes almost impossible to withdraw. Play can remain stationary for as long as an hour with spectators blocking the escape routes.

the game, if not for the rules, of which, of course, there are none.

The men's game in the afternoon is a larger affair than the boys', involving around 75–100 players per side at any one time. But these numbers fluctuate throughout the game, as spectators – who typically number between 1-2,000 – drop in and out of the action.

Many older players, for example, will wait on the early exchanges before adding their weight as matters proceed.

This blurring of the line between playing and spectating is one of the distinguishing features of mass football, and adds considerably to the atmosphere engendered.

The terrain

Nowhere is out of bounds, not even the cathedral graveyard.

But once the ba' is forced from the more open spaces of the aptly named Broad Street in front of St Magnus's – roughly half way between the goals – both sides have the option of either taking the more direct route down narrow, winding streets, or of trying to reach the wider, north-south route of Junction Road.

If the former, for the Uppies this means heading into the narrow mouth of Victoria Street . For the Doonies the aim is Albert Street.

It is often said, however, that the longer the ba' stays in Broad Street, which can mean hours, the more likely it is to go Doon.

But it is just as likely that the ba' will be forced down one of the many alleys which run off the main thoroughfare. These passages are particularly tight and the scrum can be wedged in for a long time.

Should it then emerge onto Junction Road, the potential

for sudden escapes increases considerably.

A further factor is the failing light. As darkness falls, around 3.30pm, the situation invariably becomes more volatile should the ba' be released into more open ground. In such circumstances it only takes a second or two for someone to seize the opportunity to escape down a side street, over a wall or even onto the rooftops.

Tactics

At Kirkwall moving steadily and staying upright are key concerns. Control of the ball is paramount and can easily be relinquished if players grow impatient.

Moreover, unlike the games staged in the Scottish Borders,

only the weaker of the two sides will try a smuggle to win.

Above all, the Kirkwall Ba' requires a mixture of abandon and restraint. Anyone who enters the scrum must accept that bruises and sprains may result, and that at the very least the forces at work in the centre, combined with the obstacles present on the edge, make a degree of pain inevitable.

But the participants do not charge in like madmen. Rather, the most common instruction heard from experienced players directing their men is to 'lie on' – that is, to push from the rear.

To control the ba' at the centre, it is argued, is the key, while applying gradual but concerted pressure from behind. »

Steaming in – a classic Kirkwall scene captured during the Christmas Day Men's Ba' in 2002. As bodies press together in the cold afternoon air, their combined heat releases clouds of vapour above – a phenomenon often witnessed, but rarely captured with such drama.

▲ A ba' is not just for Christmas. Here, displayed permanently in typical Kirkwall style in the window of stalwart Uppie **Gary Gibson** – a member of the Ba' Committee and a former ba' maker himself – is the boys' ba' from Christmas 1985 and the men's ba' from Christmas 1999, won by Gary's sons **Sigurd** and **Edgar Gibson** respectively.

Also in the window are two other ba's won by Gary, as a boy on New Year's Day 1949 and as a man on Christmas Day 1967, plus a fifth that Gary's father Edgar won on the same day as his son in 1949.

Meanwhile fellow Uppie **Raymie Stanger**, a 37 year old joiner from Kirkwall, seen opposite on Christmas Day 2005, keeps his prized possession well polished in a display cabinet in his sitting room.

》 To counter this tactic, players will occasionally get on the 'wrong side' of the ba', in an attempt to disrupt their opponents. But as this ploy is frowned upon it can lead to the interlopers being pulled bodily out of the throng, usually by their collar or shoulders.

Half throttled in this way, an isolated man may resort to a swinging punch as he is ejected. As Spike's cartoons in the *Orkney Herald* highlighted, brief fist fights are common at Kirkwall.

Yet rarely does anyone dwell on these fleeting spats, for the focus returns swiftly to the whereabouts of the ball.

Deciding the winner

Undoubtedly the most perplexing aspect of the Kirkwall Ba' for the inexperienced spectator is the struggle which occurs at the conclusion of each game.

Once the ba' is hailed, players from the same side will then fight or argue amongst themselves to be declared champion and claim the ultimate prize, the ba' itself.

Instantly, team spirit evaporates as a knot of senior players, who will have fought hard for their team over many years, and who may have particularly distinguished themselves on the day, form a mini-scrum.

This part of the game can be frantic and last several minutes. This is especially true if one side has gone a long time without a win, as the Doonies did from 1997 to 2006.

Not everyone in the splinter group may be too concerned with winning. Some will be laying down a marker for the future; establishing their *bona fides* as it were.

But finally, as shown opposite, one man will wrestle the ba' into his own hands and raise it above his head, to the cheers of his supporters. It is he, and not the scorer, whose name will be entered into the records, and he who will get to keep the ball, for life.

The winner is also expected to host a party at his home that same night, a potentially expensive celebration that can go on for days, and is open to players from both sides, many of whom will in any case be friends, workmates or even relatives. One winner was said to have spent nearly £1,000 on his victory party.

The Future

To those born and bred in Kirkwall, the Ba' is of supreme importance.

However, not everyone in the town is a native, while a shift of political control from Kirkwall Town Council to the larger Orkney Islands Council, effected in 1974, has given a greater say to people further afield. Not all, as might be expected, approve of the Ba'.

Nor does the Ba's timing help the local economy much. Few extra tourists visit over Christmas or New Year.

Kirkwall is a long way from losing its Ba', however. The game is now stronger than it has been for some time. Both match days are public holidays, and Christmas dinner in many households still has to fit in around the Ba'. Indeed, some families delay the meal until Boxing Day.

For the Ba' Committee there remain ongoing concerns that the disapproval or antipathy of incomers might eventually bolster attempts to sanitise their game, and thereby sacrifice the very traditions that have helped to make the Orkneys such a unique place to live.

If you love a democratic, acrobatic, half-aquatic
Game of football, with ten rules, or none at all,
Then you'd better take a train, then a boat to cross the main,
And land on New Year's Day at Old Kirkwall.

Put on your cast-off clothes, and if you love your toes,
A pair of seaboots helps in the stramash;
Throw all your dignitee away into the Peerie Sea;
Don't bring your watch, though none will steal your cash.

Then take your proper place, minus frock-coat and sleek 'lum',
On Broad Street nearing one, and keep an eye
Upon the crawling clock; when it rings you'll get a shock!
Up leaps the Ba', and then it's do or die!

For the game may last an hour, yet it's far beyond the power
Of mortal man to give an estimate;
It may run for half a day, or ten minutes end the fray
In favour of the Up- or Down-the-Gate.

Extract from The Ba', David Horne Snr (1923)

Christmas and New Year

5. Haxey, Lincolnshire

Read all about it – but do not expect to unravel the mystery. Seven hundred years of tradition there may be, according both to legend and the local newspaper, but despite the probings of dozens of historians, no-one knows for certain how or when the extraordinary game of Haxey Hood came into being. In 1840 the *Stamford Mercury* described it as a 'foolish, wicked and utterly useless custom.' As Hood regulars would jest, perhaps that is the real secret of its success.

Our second featured game takes place on the twelfth day of Christmas, January 6.

It is contested between four factions from two neighbouring villages, Haxey and Westwoodside, each competing not for a ball but for a 'hood'– except that it is not a hood at all but a leather cylinder, 24 inches in length and three inches in diameter, inside which is a length of thick rope.

Presiding over this struggle are twelve 'boggins' dressed in scarlet, two of whom wear extravagantly decorated hats, and a thirteenth, the Fool, dressed in rags, who has just survived a ritual smoking in front of the parish church.

The hood in question is thrown up on Haxey Hill, an open expanse of farmland which lies between Haxey and Westwoodside, in an area known as the Isle of Axholme. Each faction seeks to direct the hood towards its own village, and from there to the threshold of one of four pubs.

In short, no ordinary game, in no ordinary part of England.

Yet despite its singular character and the week long ritual which precedes it, on its day the Haxey Hood has much in common with other games of *Uppies and Downies*. Rival communities engage in hours of scrimmaging on a late afternoon in midwinter, sandwiched between concerted bouts of drinking and singing in local hostelries.

What therefore does it matter that in the sweat and heave of the 'sway', as the Haxey scrum is called, the prize is a leather cylinder rather than a sphere?

But why call it a hood?

This question has been picked over by a succession of historians, including, most recently, Hood chronicler Jeremy Cooper, and by the folklorist, Venetia Newall, whose article in *Folk Life*, 1980, is recommended to anyone wishing to delve deeper into the tangled mysteries of the game (*see Links*).

Jeremy Cooper speculates that the word hood could derive from the Old English 'hude' (or 'huid' in Danish), meaning the hide of a cow. If so, could the game be a throwback to a pagan midwinter ritual in which, following the sacrifice of a cow, rival factions fought to bring the hide (or even the head of the beast) back to their fields, where it could be buried in the hope of bringing fertility and abundance? After all, before each game, by tradition the Fool makes a jocular speech in which he speaks of the slaughter of 'a bullock and a half'.

Or does 'hood' have a sporting origin, as in the 'hot', or scrum at Winchester College (*see page 175*), or as in 'hold' meaning a wager?

We will return to this question later. But for now the most frequently aired explanation for the hood game is a local legend.

It goes as follows.

One day during the 14th century – given as 'Old Christmas Day' in one account (as January 6 was before the Gregorian calendar was adopted in 1752) – Lady de Mowbray, wife of the Lord of Epworth Manor, was riding across Haxey Hill when a gust of wind carried away her scarlet riding hood. Thirteen farm labourers chased after the hood, until finally, with the men repeatedly thwarted by the heavy soil, one managed to grasp it.

Just as he was about to hand back the hood to the Lady, however, he was overcome by shyness, and so one of his fellow workers handed it to her instead.

The Lady thanked this man and said that he had acted like a Lord. The shy one she called a Fool.

The story then goes on to claim that Lady de Mowbray had been so amused by the chase that each of the thirteen men was granted a strip of land, to be known as 'hoodland', on condition that they re-enacted the tussle over the hood every year thereafter.

It seems an unlikely tale and might well have been concocted in the 19th or early 20th centuries as a way of romanticising the game, which had plenty of critics.

One piece of evidence has been put forward as corroboration for the legend, however.

After the Battle of Hastings the Mowbrays, originally de Monbrais, were rewarded for their valour with extensive gifts of land. These included the Isle of Axholme, with the family seat at Epworth.

Shortly before his death in 1361, John de Mowbray, the 3rd Baron Mowbray of Axholme, angered his tenants by infringing their ancient rights to use the 'wastes', or uncultivated commons, which bordered their tenements. These rights included grazing animals, collecting wood and fishing.

In order to restore these rights, on May 1 1358 a group of five holders managed to extract from de Mowbray a deed acknowledging that which had been theirs 'time out of mind', in return for various commitments to manage their livestock and maintain certain structures.

Could this deed, perhaps seen as a major victory for the people, have formed the basis for some sort of celebration, from which the hood game evolved? Would a scarlet hood have been used in »

Thought to date from the 1890s, this is the earliest known image of the gathering that precedes the Haxey Hood game, in which the Fool stands on top of the Mounting Stone in front of the Church of St Nicholas in the centre of Haxey.

The current 'Smoking of the Fool' ceremony – in which the Fool delivers a speech from the Mounting Stone (*see page 61*) – dates only from the 1940s. But the role of the Fool is much older.

As is the Mounting Stone itself. It is the remnant of the base of a medieval cross, which may originally have been positioned inside the church yard.

Whether or not there is any truth in the connection between the Haxey Hood game and a 14th century noblewoman, Lady de Mowbray – possibly the wife of the 3rd Baron Mowbray of Axholme, or his daughter in another version of the tale – there can be no doubt that Axholme was once Mowbray territory. This Mowbray coat of arms on a medieval cross was originally sited near Idlestop, where Cornelius Vermuyden diverted the River Idle as part of his controversial drainage works. A fragment was broken off, apparently after the Civil War, and this now stands on Greenhill, in the centre of Haxey.

» the annual chase, or hunt of the 'beasts of commoners' for which the 1358 deed makes allowance?

And were the supplicants named on the deed the original boggins, as some have claimed?

Alas there are too many inconsistencies between the legend and the actual deed for the story to have much credence.

The deed concerned eleven supplicants and related to an area of some 13,000 acres, whereas the legend as handed down in various versions speaks of eleven, twelve or even thirteen men, and claims that each was granted a portion of 'hoodland' amounting to 6.5 or 40 acres, depending on whose account one reads. It is true that there was a variable measurement of land called a 'hide' (which has led some to suggest that this too might be the origin of 'hood'). But however this measurement is calculated and split up between the men, the figures cannot be made to match up even closely.

But in any case, no evidence exists to show that land was granted in any other way other than as specified in the 1358 deed.

One issue is clear, however. We cannot equate the Haxey of the 14th century with the village we see today. As mentioned earlier, the village lies within the Isle of Axholme. This was indeed an island, surrounded by water and with its own distinct identity and way of life.

Until that is 1626 when a Dutch drainage expert called Cornelius Vermuyden struck a deal with Charles I whereby, in return for reclaiming Axholme's boggy fenland, he and his mainly Dutch backers, and the king, would each share two thirds of the resultant new acreage, leaving the rump to the locals. Amid violent and ongoing protests over the next century or more, the drainage scheme changed not only the landscape but the entire economy and social structure.

On one side were the local Commoners. On the other were the Participants, those who signed up to benefit from Vermuyden's efforts. This being a period of civil war, however, the conflict soon evolved into a battle that went beyond land rights. It also engendered bitter antipathy between the English Commoners and those Dutch workers and speculators who were drawn to the area. Thirty-one pitched battles erupted between 1655 and 1714, resulting in hundreds of deaths and widespread destruction.

But of most interest in relation to the Haxey Hood game was a development earlier in the campaign, in 1636, when the Participants were instructed to pay the Commoners £400 in compensation, this to be used for the improvement of the local textile industry. Specifically, as explained by Venetia Newall, the money was to be spent on 'sackcloth and cordage'.

In today's Hood game there are two elements. First, the 'Running Hood' has youngsters in the area chasing after twelve rolled up sacks. Then, in the main game, the teams contest the 'Sway Hood', which as mentioned earlier, consists of a thick length of rope encased in leather.

In other words, 'sackcloth and cordage.'

Even more persuasively, another word used for homespun cloth at that time was 'hoddin'.

So could this token offer of compensation lead us to the true origin of the Hood game?

Certainly the Commoners would have been infuriated by the Participants' attitude, and may have later woven the events into their game.

One further question concerns the origins of the 'boggins'.

Again, various theories exist. One has it that the word boggin derives from a dialect word for marsh fairies. Similarly, when people get clogged up in the area's heavy soil it is said that they have become 'boggined' (as in bogged down). But another theory is the word may be linked with begging.

In Lincolnshire as in several other counties there existed from the 15th century a rural custom whereby on Plough Monday (the first day of the ploughing season, usually the first Monday after the Twelfth Day of Christmas), farm boys would drag a plough through villages begging money from locals, often with menace.

'If you refuse them,' complained one man in Derbyshire in 1762, 'they plough up your dunghill.'

As opposition to their methods grew, increasingly the 'plough bullocks' (as they were known in Lincolnshire) would embellish their entreaties with songs, rhymes and, in time, well worked plays. As in the tradition of the Mummers they would dress up in distinctive clothes, blacken their faces with soot, and one of them always played the Fool.

Could it therefore be that the Haxey Hood legend somehow evolved from a Plough Monday play, aimed at an audience keen to reinstate its links with a more innocent past? Might even the game have been a playful invention of the plough bullocks?

This link between 'plough bullocks' and 'boggins' was aired in the earliest known reference to Haxey Hood, written by William

Peck, from Epworth, in his *Topographical Account of the Isle of Axholme*, published in 1815.

In a chapter on Sports and Pastimes, Peck wrote that the twelfth day 'is devoted to throwing the hood: an amusement, tradition reports, to have been instituted by one of the Mowbrays.'

Note he made no mention of the legend of the Lady's hood.

'A roll of canvas, tight corded together, weighing from four to six pounds, is taken to an open field and contended for by the rustics, who assemble together to the number of many hundreds; an individual appointed, casts it from him, and the first person that can convey it into the cellar of any public house receives a reward of one shilling, paid by the plough-bullocks or boggins. A new hood being furnished when the others are carried off, the contest usually continues till dark.

'Many of the candidates for athletic fame, receive great injuries by falls, bruises, &c. The evening is usually commenced with mirth and glee, at the place where the victor has deposited his prize, and concluded, in general, with quarreling and drunkenness.

'This rustic amusement is only observed at Epworth and Haxey: at the latter place, the day is kept as a feast by the inhabitants, who have their friends and acquaintances to visit them.'

(The Epworth hood game was last recorded as being played in 1932, while one at Belton, north of Epworth, appears to have ceased after the 1890s. But both were considered as only imitations of the original at Haxey.)

Peck further noted that Haxey's festivities continued on January 7, when the boggins, now yoked to a small plough, went round each

house crying out 'largus', hoping to solicit gifts. These might be monetary or in kind, such as sacks of flour. (Largus, or largesse, was apparently a common begging term in eastern England.)

To conclude the day, the plough was dragged three times around the Market Cross as the boggins tried to throw their fellows over. The strongest boggin then made off with the plough to a pub, where he was rewarded with a shilling.

None of these plough rituals survive. But Peck did mention that the boggins were 'habited similar to the morris-dancers' and were joined by a fool called Billy Buck, 'dressed like a harlequin, with whom the boys make sport'.

Significantly Peck made no reference to the Haxey ritual known as 'smoking the fool'. »

▲ The Haxey Hood game is one of only three games featured in this book that is monitored by men we may loosely call umpires – the others are at Duns and Alnwick.

Above are the **Haxey Hood boggins** from the mid 1920s.

The **Fool**, with his blackened face, patchwork trousers and goose feathered hat, carries both the hood and a stick with a small stuffed ball attached. In earlier times, when the fool was also an integral figure in Plough Monday plays, this would have been a pig's bladder. (The Latin root for the word fool, *follis*, means bellows, or a windbag.) This he uses to punish anyone caught misbehaving during the Hood celebrations, small boys especially.

To the left, the **Lord of the Hood** carries his staff, or wand of office, comprising 13 willow sticks,

gathered from the banks of the River Idle – where it runs into the River Trent – and tied by 13 pieces of willow, each wrapped 13 times around the wand. One of the sticks is shorter, to represent the Fool.

No reference to such a wand has been found before 1904, so this, like so many of the Haxey customs may have been a later addition, (albeit one that celebrated the Isle of Axholme's natural habitat).

The two other figures are the **Chief Boggin** and one of the ten ordinary boggins. Only the Lord, Chief and Fool wear decorated hats, and all but the Fool are dressed in scarlet, a mode that is first recorded in a description of 1828.

Today's leading boggins wear the scarlet coats of the Grove and Rufford Hunt.

To be a boggin requires immense stamina, a strong bladder and an even stronger set of lungs. Gathered here in the Duke William – one of four pubs that compete for the hood – are the boggins of 2005, led by Chief Boggin, Ian Dawes (*second left*) and the Lord of the Hood, Philip Coggon (*second right*). Coggon is only the third Lord to have served since 1941, having first taken the role in 1990. Dawes joined him in 1994. Note that both officials wear scarlet jackets and decorated hats, while the remaining boggins wear red sweatshirts. Only after a week of singing and drinking does the Haxey Hood game commence.

» As illustrated opposite (*and on page 37*), this strange and seemingly unique ritual – not seen or known of in any other context – takes place in front of the church before the Hood commences.

According to another 19th century antiquarian, the Rev WB Stonehouse, writing in the 1850s, smoking was then used as a form of initiation ceremony for boggins.

In later accounts from the 19th century we read of only the Fool being smoked, not on the day of the Hood but on January 7.

Apparently the poor man was hung upside down by a rope from a tree, and swung through smoke rising up from a burning pile of straw. Just before he suffocated he was cut down and expected to make his escape.

This continued until the end of the century or into the early 20th century until one year, the Fool only narrowly escaped death from this ordeal and the ritual promptly came to an end.

Only in the 1940s was it revived in its current form, and in rather safer conditions for all concerned.

That the Haxey Hood itself has survived at all into the modern era is no mean feat.

An observer in 1896 predicted that it would soon die out, as there were seldom enough boggins to make up the full contingent.

The game also struggled after it was suspended throughout the First World War, until the local vicar, JW ff Sheppard, offered his endorsement and support, not least by inviting the Bishop of Lincoln to attend in 1924.

Four years later Sheppard wrote the first brief history of the game, and this, combined with growing interest from folklorists, and in the post-war years from broadcasters and the media generally, helped to ensure the game's continuation.

Inevitably it has had to adapt to changing circumstances and fashions, as it appears to have done throughout its life, or at least since William Peck's first account in 1815.

The itinerary for the day has also evolved, being shaped into its current format in 1994.

But since the days of the plough bullocks the Haxey Hood has always been more than just a game played on one single day.

Pre-match rituals

The build-up actually begins seven days earlier on New Year's Eve, when the thirteen boggins meet in the pub that won the Hood the previous year.

The Hood is taken down from above the bar where it has been displayed all year, at which point the boggins sing three traditional songs, *Farmer's Boy*, *John Barleycorn* and *Drink Old England Dry* (also known as *Cannons*), before handing round the Fool's hat to collect money for local charities.

From there, and over the five dark nights that follow, whatever the weather and however tired they get, the boggins embark upon a marathon tour of local pubs, businesses, private houses and nursing homes, repeating the same three folk songs, and on occasion, having to offer encores.

Overall they can visit up to 40-45 different locations.

That adds up to a lot of singing, and a great deal of drinking.

Hood Eve

As the great day nears, the Lord of the Hood completes the binding of his willow wand (*see previous page*). Meanwhile, the Chief Boggin and his helpers tie up twelve sacks that will be competed for the following afternoon by younger players

in the Running Hood game, a prequel to the main event.

For the boggins there is no early night before the game. Hood Eve starts at 6.00pm with yet more visits, culminating in a final round of the three folk songs at each of the four pubs that currently compete for the Hood. These are identified on pages 62-63.

The final port of call is the pub where the celebrations began on New Year's Eve. Here the singing and carousing continues until after midnight. Yet still the boggins' work is not done.

Haxey Hood Day

Anyone intending to watch the Haxey Hood should note that if January 6 happens to fall on a Sunday, the game will take place on the previous day. And when Saturday is the day, the crowds can number 2,000.

The day commences around 11.30am when the boggins meet up for one last pre-match tour of the four pubs, starting at the most westerly, the Carpenters Arms in Westwoodside.

Here, around midday, the Fool has his face daubed with burnt cork by the Lord of the Hood (a practice found in other traditions, such as the Britannia Coconut Dancing at Bacup, Lancashire).

The Fool – a role performed by Dale Smith since 1994 – wears a patchwork of rags, with the initials HH on his chest, and a hat decorated with feathers, flowers, badges and assorted baubles. In return for being marked out in this way, the Fool may hit anyone with his stick and ball (now a stuffed stocking) and kiss any woman he chooses.

From the Carpenters Arms the boggins and Fool drive a mile and a half to the pub furthest to the

east, the Kings Arms, in Haxey. Outside stands the Buttercross, where the gang will stop, as they have done every year since at least the 1930s, for a group photo.

From there they continue back towards the church, first stopping at The Loco, then at the Duke William, for the final tot of rum or port before the next phase of the day.

This entails a short procession from the Duke William towards the church – a procession that used to be accompanied by the ringing of the bells when the boggins came into view – until suddenly the Fool makes a break for it, dashing up the street, only to be caught by his fellow boggins and manhandled onto the Mounting Stone in front of the church, to the cheers of the crowd.

There, around 2.00pm, the Fool begins his customary speech, welcoming all and alluding to the feast days of old. He says 'We've killed a bullock and a half'. Could the hood represent the half that is still running out in the field?

As he speaks, smoke rises up around him as damp straw is lit by the boggins, and it may be only a minute or so before he is forced to jump down to avoid his trousers catching alight.

But not before he calls out:

Hoose agen Hoose,
Toon agen Toon,
If a man meets a man
Knock 'im doon
But don't 'urt 'im.

(The final line, it is said, was added by the Rev ff Sheppard in the 1930s in an attempt to make the game more acceptable.)

At this the crowd cheers again, and starts to wend its way to Haxey Hill for the game to start, at last!

Smoking the Fool in 2006. A number of historians have offered explanations for this unique ritual, among them that it is an echo of a pagan midwinter practice in which human sacrifices were smoked as an act of purification before being slaughtered. Another account from 1877 mentions the hood itself being smoked by the fireside of a local pub, and then basted in ale.

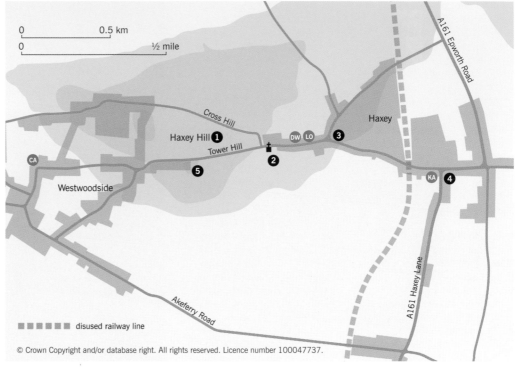

0   0.5 km
0   ½ mile

▪ ▪ ▪ ▪ ▪ ▪ disused railway line

▲ Four pubs currently compete for the **Haxey Hood**, three in Haxey, and one in Westwoodside, the Carpenters Arms. This imbalance suggests, and the roll of honour confirms, that it is relatively difficult to get the hood westwards to the Carpenters, and so they have on occasions solicited outside help – in 2007 for example from members of Doncaster Rugby Club.

The action starts on Haxey Hill, when the hood is thrown up just below the brow of the hill on the Haxey side. This presents the Westwoodsiders with an immediate uphill challenge. Their easier route is not via the road but behind a bungalow on the brow of the hill, where the incline is less severe. On the rare occasion when they gain the vital first 100 yards, it is downhill all the way home.

The Haxey contingent work collectively to 'sway' the hood back into their village, but once there split into rival factions in an attempt to reach their own favoured pub. Nearest are the Duke William and The Loco, yet the Kings Arms still wins more often than might be expected, given its position.

We know from William Peck's account that inns formed the goals in 1815. Of the current pubs, both the Duke William and Kings Arms have been licensed since 1852, while the Carpenters Arms dates from at least 1874. The Loco, a more recent addition, entered the fray in 1985.

Participation is open to others though. In 1948 a marathon sway took the hood south to the Great Northern Hotel in Graizelound, across fields and dykes.

Key:
CA   **Carpenters Arms**
DW   **Duke William**
LO   **The Loco**
KA   **Kings Arms**

1   **Starting point**
2   **Church of St Nicholas, Haxey**
3   **Mowbray Cross**
4   **Buttercross**
5   **Water Tower**

▲ And still they sing – boggins and friends stop for what has become an annual photo opportunity at the **Buttercross**, opposite the Kings Arms, Haxey, in 1948.

On the left, **Church Street** on game day 2007, with The Loco on the right. Not seen, just further on, is the Duke William.

The Loco (previously a fish and chip shop) became involved in 1985, when only the Carpenters Arms and the Kings Arms remained in competition.

Four years prior to that the Duke William had dropped out from contesting the Hood when its landlady preferred to protect her new carpet from the ravages of so many muddy boots. The pub returned to the fold in 1991, however, and nowadays sheets of plastic are rolled out to protect the furnishings.

In the distance, the concrete water tower looms surprisingly large behind Haxey Church, even though it is actually located some 500 yards to the west.

Built in 1935 to ensure a reliable supply to the parish, the tower provides a useful landmark during the Hood game, as well as enabling Westwoodsiders to boast of their generosity in allowing water to flow down to their rivals in Haxey.

Of the 74 victors of the Hood recorded since 1931, the Duke William has won 25 times, second only to the Kings Arms with 35 victories. By comparison, the Carpenters Arms – facing the greater weight of the Haxey contingent and the rigours of that initial uphill struggle – has won on only ten occasions, four of those during the 1980s, while the Duke William was *hors de combat*.

Only twice, in 1998 and 2005, has The Loco been triumphant.

It is often said that entering the Sway offers an ideal opportunity for people to settle old grudges, a suggestion that not even Lord of the Hood Stan Boor would deny when interviewed in 1979. But the crucial thing, he also insisted, is that the parties would have to share a drink afterwards.

As to which pub an outsider should choose to play for – and outsiders are welcome – Boor felt the best choice would be the one that served your favourite beer.

Unlike in the adult game, running with the hood (*above*) is the norm in the children's version which precedes it. Each hood is made from a piece of sacking – flax was an important crop in this part of Lincolnshire for centuries.

The Running Hood

After the smoking of the Fool, the assembled make their way to Haxey Hill, where, as shown in 2007 (*left*) they may find a rain-sodden field, or as in 1979 (*below*) more wintry conditions.

Beginning at approximately 2.40pm, the Running Hood game is now restricted to children but it was once contested by adults.

Twelve hoods are thrown up, the first by the Lord of the Hood.

Those who gain possession must attempt to elude the boggins, who patrol the edge of the field. If a child gets past the cordon, he or she wins £2. If a boggin manages to stop them – a touch of the hood is enough – the hood is thrown up again.

With plenty of tripping and rugby-style tackling by the older children, the Running Hood game is rough enough.

But it usually takes no more than half an hour for all twelve hoods to be won, so that by 3.15pm the main event can begin.

The Sway Hood

Dusk is now rapidly approaching as an invited guest throws up the thirteenth hood – the much coveted Sway Hood.

Immediately, a large scrum of bodies forms, to cries of 'C'mon Haxey' or 'C'mon Westwood'. At this stage, village solidarity takes precedence over inter-pub rivalry. The main concern is to push, or sway, the hood in the right direction, east or westwards.

At this early stage, the numbers of both players and spectators are at their highest, with a little daylight remaining to assist organisation of the effort. There may well be some girls and women adding their weight at the back of the sway.

Although there are no written rules, it is the convention at Haxey that no-one should run with the hood, or throw it. Instead, it should be steadily swayed, as seen above.

Shouts of 'Old 'er up!' are heard as experienced players apply pressure to one side of the mass, steering it in the desired direction.

But as is the case at Hallaton, younger players can be impatient and charge into the rear, knocking those in the centre down to the ground like dominoes, as often as every minute.

'Man down!' goes the cry whenever this occurs, at which point the pushing stops and everyone tries to make room while the fallen get up, assisted by the ever watchful boggins. The Lord raises his wand in the air until the game can recommence.

The shortest Sway Hood ever recorded was in 1953, when it took only 40 minutes to sway the hood from Haxey Hill to the Duke William (the nearest pub). Mostly it takes hours, and for those in the midst of the pile, it can be arduous in the extreme. It was known in the past for bystanders to be »

>> deliberately swept up by the sway and and charged half a crown for their release.

Once off the hill and into either village the playing area narrows dramatically and the atmosphere changes. Everyone is now funnelled together. Steam billows from the sweating mass.

If in Westwoodside, victory can be swift, as once over the brow of Haxey Hill, it is downhill all the way to the Carpenters.

If we are in Haxey, tension rises between regulars of the three competing pubs.

Being nearer the Hill, the Duke William and The Loco seem to be favourites, yet if the sway can just be eased past their doors, downhill momentum along Church Street is often enough to carry the hood to the junction at Greenhill, beyond which resistance is usually token and the Kings Arms is soon within reach.

Victory is achieved when, amidst heaving crowds, the pub landlord, with his feet inside the threshold, manages to touch the hood with his fingers. This signals the end of that year's struggle and sparks off a round of cheers that echoes across the village.

For the winning pub, however, victory can prove rather expensive as, according to tradition, free drinks should be provided for one and all.

In the sway of things, from 2006 (*above and left*), where players in a fetching range of attire attempt to push the scrum away from the church wall. On Hood days no laws of trespass are recognised, but the players do their best to avoid damaging cars and fences. Those on the outside of the sway will steer it all the way down the street.

Haxey tales

Haxey *whodunnits* are part and parcel of the Hood's folklore.

In 1943, for example, it was suddenly realised that the hood had disappeared from the sway. News later emerged that it had been smuggled away to the Red Lion at Owston Ferry, three miles to the east. Sam Scott from Thorne, a friend of the Red Lion's landlord, was apparently the culprit. As a letter to the *Epworth Bells* in 1985 recalled, 'How he secured it was a work of art. He and a party, including two soldiers home on leave, arrived at the ceremony, and one of the soldiers dropped the hood.

'Mr Scott urged the surging crowd to keep away, saying the soldier had broken his leg. While tender hands were lifting him, Mr Scott succeeded in getting the hood and secreting it down his trousers. He walked down the main street with two policemen who were not aware they were so near to the priceless possession, through a backyard and across a field, where a lorry was waiting.'

(The Red Lion is one of only two pubs outside Haxey and Westwoodside to which the hood has been taken in modern times. The other was the Great Northern Hotel in Graizelound in 1948.)

On one occasion, in 1976, the hood was stolen from behind the bar of the Kings Arms and a ransom demand for £500 sent from Lincoln. As the hood was worth only a fraction of this the demand was refused, however, and the hood was later found abandoned under a children's slide in the Haxey playground.

Another act of smuggling – a tactic admired in many games of *Uppies and Downies* but not so in Haxey – occurred in 1984, when two men spirited the hood out of the scrum and carried it to the Kings Arms. Debate raged about whether to restart the game but in the end the result stood.

During the 1985 Haxey Hood, worse happened. The scrum had moved over Cross Hill into a leek field where it was realised that the hood had been snatched. The Lord toured all the local pubs in his car, to no avail, forcing the game to be finished using a sack hood as a substitute.

Police were then called in and the story ran and ran. According to the *Epworth Bells*, folklore experts from Sheffield University made inquiries as far afield as Darlington, Chester, Leicester, Huddersfield and London.

In fact, as only revealed during research for this book, it had been taken to Scotland in a daring manoeuvre, requiring a new hood to be provided the following year.

Since, as they say, 'There's no law in Haxey on Hood Day', the risk of someone taking that phrase literally must always be there.

The future

Whatever its origins, the appeal of the Haxey Hood game appears to be as strong as ever. The advent of mobile telephones now means that reinforcements can even be summoned into action whenever one side or the other appears to be in the ascendancy.

'Respect for the game is the most important thing,' says the current Fool, Dale Smith.

Others have described it as the world's most energetic drinking game. As one-time Lord Stan Boor told the *Epworth Bells* in 1986, 'You just need tolerance, fortitude and a capacity to drink beer.'

Many a professional sportsmen would no doubt nod to that.

The landlord at the Carpenters Arms reaches out to 'tig', or touch the Hood at the end of the game in 2007 (*top*). Once inside, as above at the Kings Arms in 1983, the hood is hung over the bar, where it will remain until the following New Year's Eve. Local tradition dictates that any visitor subsequently asking 'What's that hanging there?' should buy a round.

Shrovetide

6. Ashbourne, Derbyshire

Patriot games – the Ashbourne ball for the 1981 Shrove Tuesday game. Ashbourne is the only game of *Uppies and Downies* to bear the title Royal Shrovetide Football. On two occasions the game has been started by a Prince of Wales, in 1928 and 2003, and every game is preceded by communal renditions of *Auld Lang Syne* and the National Anthem. In 1915 the ball (seen on the front cover of this book) was decorated with portraits of Lord Kitchener and Admiral Jellicoe.

Of all Britain's festival football games, those at Ashbourne, where the Up'ards take on the Down'ards twice each Shrovetide, are probably the best known and most widely recognised as part of our national heritage.

Patronised by royalty, regularly covered by the media and, partly owing to the town's central location, enjoyed by large crowds of locals and visitors – even school holidays in the area are scheduled to allow children to attend – the Ashbourne experience represents a high point within the festival football season.

Uniquely, and exhaustingly for the participants, games are played on two consecutive days, Shrove Tuesday and Ash Wednesday. (The locals say 'Tuesday's for tourists, Wednesday's for us'.)

But by no means has this popularity come about by re-packaging the game for modern consumption. Far from being tamed or tarted up, with the goals three miles apart and divided by terrain that would challenge an infantry battalion, Ashbourne is as gruelling as festival football gets.

It is also extremely well chronicled, thanks to local author Lindsey Porter (*see Links*) to whom we are most indebted.

That said, as with so many other festival games, references to Ashbourne from before the mid 19th century are few and far between (and alas a fire destroyed many of the game's records during the inter war period).

The earliest appears within a wintry poem, *Burlesque on The Great Frost*, written in 1683 by Charles Cotton, a Derbyshire writer and friend of the great angler, Izaak Walton (*reproduced below*). Although Cotton does not mention a specific location, Lindsey Porter believes that the two towns mentioned were Ashbourne and Compton.

Forty years earlier, as the poem begins, these neighbouring towns, on either bank of the River Henmore, had been the scenes of skirmishes during the Civil War. The 'Rolle-rich stones' referred to are probably the Rollright stones on the Oxfordshire–Warwickshire border, said by legend to be a king and his soldiers turned to stone, rather like the Hurlers of Bodmin

Moor (*see page 138*). Aganippe is a fountain and source of poetic inspiration in Greek mythology.

Since the 19th century Compton has been absorbed by Ashbourne, but the areas still form the basis of the rival teams; Ashbourne, north of the river being 'up', Compton, to the south, being 'down'.

After Cotton the next detailed reference dates from 1821, when Ashbourne football was referred to in a comic song delivered in the town's theatre, possibly by the actor and dramatist John Fawcett. Later reproduced in a London journal, *The Reliquary*, in 1867, its second verse begins:

Shrove Tuesday, you know, is always the day / When pancake's the prelude and football's the play / Where Uppards and Downards men ready for fun / Like the French at the battle of Waterloo run.

Later verses cite the involvement of players from Mappleton, Mayfield, Okeover and Thorpe (who 'furnish some men that nothing can whop'), and from Bentley, Tissington, Clifton, Sturston, Snelston, Wyaston and Shirley.

Two Towns, that long that war had waged,
Being at Foot-ball now engaged
For honour, as both sides pretended
Left the brave tryall to be ended
Till the next thaw, for they were frozen
On either part at leest a dozen;

With a good handsome space between 'em,
Like Rolle-rich stones, if you've seen 'em,
And could no more run, Kick or tripye,
Than I can quaff of Aganippe;
Til ale, which crowns all such pretences,
Mull'd them again into their senses.

Burlesque on The Great Frost, Charles Cotton (1683)

The ball maker Paul Getliffe is also mentioned, as is another local character, Luke Faulkner, portrayed in a painting of 1862 (*see right*).

The fourth verse continues:

The ball is turned up and the Bullring's the place | And as fierce as a bulldog's is every man's face | Whilst kicking and shouting and howling they run | Until every stitch of the ball comes undone | There's Faulkner and Smith, Bodge Hand and some more | Who hide it and hug it and kick it so sore | And deserve a good whopping at every man's door | In the neat little town of Ashbourne.

Waterplay, still very much a feature at Ashbourne, was also common at that time:

Then into Shawcroft where the bold and the brave | Get a ducking in trying the football to save | For 'tis well known they fear not a watery grave | In defence of the football at Ashbourne.

Several of the places mentioned in the song remain familiar today, such as The Park (the grounds of the late Georgian mansion, Ashbourne Hall), Shaw Croft (where the game now starts), and Church Street, where it was joked that the game would halt while players refreshed themselves at the White Hart or the Wheatsheaf:

For from tasting their liquor no man can refrain | Till he rolls like the football in Warin's tear-brain.

A third reference to Ashbourne football appears in Stephen Glover's *History and Gazetteer of the County of Derby*, published in 1831.

After describing how the game was played in Derby (*see page 30*) – a tradition that Glover suggests may have dated back to the Roman occupation, and which bore similarities to Shrovetide games in Scotland – he describes the Ashbourne game as being 'of a modern date'.

▲ Ashbourne's **Market Place** depicted in **1862**, the last year that Shrovetide games were started by the bull ring. In the centre, holding the ball, and with the bull ring at his feet, is the strongest player of the period, Luke Faulkner.

Thought to be either the landlord, or the son of the landlord of the Durham Ox pub (no longer extant), Faulkner held the dubious distinction of being the last man in Britain to provide a bull for baiting, in 1841, six years after the practice had been banned. As the magistrate commented when Faulkner was summoned, a town so reluctant to relinquish bull baiting would no doubt fight hard to stop its football being banned (as happened in Derby five years later).

To the immediate left of Faulkner stands John Whieldon, father-in-law of the licensee of the Green Man Hotel. It was Whieldon who, in 1863, allowed the ball to be

But if the game dates back to the 17th century, as suggested by the Cotton poem, why call it modern?

Glover may have described it thus because apparently the game had only recently been refashioned (or possibly revived) in the 1790s, with the play switched to an east-west axis and the goals being fixed at two mills, Clifton and Sturston (where they remain to this day).

Previously, it is thought, the play had been north–south, which would have been more logical for a straight fight between Ashbourne and Compton. Moreover, before the mills were selected, the goals were moved from location to location, each year.

(Further evidence for this switch to east–west comes in an article by the Rev JF Tomlinson, in the *Ashbourne News* in 1909, relating the memories of his grandfather, Thomas, born in 1789 and once resident at Sturston Hall.) »

turned up in his field, Shaw Croft, after the Market Place was ruled out. This not only helped save the game but was also the beginning of a long relationship between the Green Man and Shrovetide players (no doubt to the chagrin of the George and Dragon, seen on the left and still extant).

On the far right stands Betty Blore, who sold oranges on match days, a common Shrovetide custom.

The painting is in the Victorian narrative style perfected by William Powell Frith, whose *The Derby Day* was exhibited in 1858.

Of the artist we know only that his name was Day, and that having failed to find a buyer he raffled the painting. It was last in the possession of a local dentist but has not been seen for years. However a copy is on display at the Green Man, where hearty pre-match luncheons still form part of the Shrovetide tradition.

▲ Nowadays most spectators arrive in Ashbourne by car. But the arrival of the **North Staffordshire Railway** in 1852 transformed Shrovetide football from a parochial event to one visited by literally thousands of day trippers. The downside was that the station master had to cope with mass trespass every time play entered the station or crossed the tracks. Nor was it unknown for trains to be held up by the action, or for spectators to nip onto the train to Clifton, four minutes down the line, to catch up with a Down'ard breakaway.

More recently the Up'ards used a motorbike to cross the fields to Sturston in 1952, followed in 1956 by the Down'ards hitching a ride in a car from the Market Place to Clifton.

Both actions were deemed contrary to the spirit of the game and in 1957 a ban on the use of 'any form of mechanical propulsion' was instituted.

≫ Glover's account of 1831 mentions games only on Shrove Tuesday. However a second game was being played on Ash Wednesday by at least 1859. We know this because that year one of several attempts was made by the local authorities to move the game out from the town centre.

Knowing that they had the sanction of the 1835 Highways Act, magistrates posted a warning that street play would no longer be tolerated, while the vicar, Rev Errington, proposed moving play to Ashbourne Green, a mile from town. He also proposed switching the two matches from Tuesday and Wednesday to Monday and Tuesday.

But when a poster to this effect was put up, offering an additional incentive of £5 to the goalscorer, diehards responded angrily.

'No Bribery' was the heading of their bill stated, 'Men of Ashbourne, the old game of football will be played in the old way, the ball will be thrown up in the old place, and the old goals will be used. Signed, My Old Great Grandfather.'

And so it was, until the following year when the police hardened their approach.

In a letter to the *Derby Mercury* on the day after Shrove Tuesday's game in 1860, Superintendent James Corbishley explained:

'Upon two persons appearing in the Market Place with the ball, I informed them that if the game were played in the streets to the annoyance of passengers, proceedings would be taken against those who joined in it; that I should not attempt to interfere with the play, but simply take the names of those who took active part in it. I also informed them that Capt Holland (owner of

Ashbourne Hall) had authorized me to say that the ball might be thrown up in his park.'

Once again, however, the ruling was ignored. The ball was thrown up in the Market Place.

In total 54 men were summoned to the Magistrates Court, while a collection to pay for their defence raised £60. And although no passengers (or passers-by) had actually complained, five of the accused ended up being fined, as the Highways Act allowed, 40 shillings each, plus costs.

The identity of the five accused reveals much about the strength and nature of the opposition. There was a gentleman, a draper, a grocer and two attorneys, one of whom, George Brittlebank, having been found guilty, then represented the grocer.

More fines were imposed a year later, yet still the games went ahead, as well as late night music and dancing in the Market Place.

But the following year, 1862, the authorities' resolve appeared to have more effect. Many players stayed out of the fray until the ball left the town centre, while five men later prosecuted for playing in the streets were persuaded to sign a pledge in lieu of fines:

'We, the undersigned, having been summoned for a breach of the law by playing the game of football in the streets of Ashbourne, do hereby engage and bind ourselves, severally, not to offend in like manner for the future, and promise that we will not join in playing any game of football that may or shall be turned up in any other place than the outskirts of this or any other town, and also that we will severally use our best endeavours to discourage others from again offending in like manner as we have done.'

Before the following Shrove Tuesday in 1863 copies of this pledge were circulated around the town, while instead of the ball being turned up at the Bull Ring, as of old, the game was started on a field called Shaw Croft, courtesy of the landlord at the Green Man.

At the same time the new owner of Ashbourne Hall, a Mr RH Frank, granted permission for the players to continue using The Park.

And so for the next few years, Ashbourne football settled down into its new regime, although, despite police blockades, play still entered the streets from time to time, resulting in further prosecutions in 1872.

Then in 1878 tragedy struck. James Barker, a 19 year old carter, drowned at Clifton Mill during the Ash Wednesday game, while another player, Jimmy Harrison, had to be rescued from the water.

At an inquest held at the Cock Inn, Clifton, it was stressed that Barker was not drunk and knew the depth of the pool – after all, he worked at the Mill.

Nevertheless, both days that year had been marred by violence. The *Derby Mercury* reported that 'men and women vied with each other in fighting in a brutal manner,' leading to several being fined for disorderly behaviour.

Somewhat presumptuously a *Mercury* editorial stated, 'It is gratifying for us to receive the assurance that this unmannerly custom, which has so long been perversely persisted in by some and indulgently tolerated by others – in spite of the better judgement of all – has been observed for the last time, and by common consent will in future be forever abandoned.'

Backing the newspaper's stance was a petition signed by 232

people, while various landowners, including Mr Frank, resolved to deny access to their estates on future match days.

So, before the 1879 games, Frank hired Shaw Croft for the week in order to prevent players from using it. He also closed The Park, threatening imprisonment to anyone who trespassed. (This was particularly provocative to the Up'ards, as it ruled out their most direct route to goal at Sturston.)

Yet still Ashbourne's players were undeterred. Despite the presence of 50 policemen, they managed to throw up a ball on Shaw Croft, only for it to be promptly confiscated and cut up. Soon after, another ball was turned up in Compton and goaled at Clifton. But as a third ball was being played in the streets, the police intervened once more.

As tensions mounted, stones were thrown. Then Luke Faulkner assaulted Inspector Hollingworth (whose great grandson, ironically, would goal for the Down'ards in 1983). In response, the police hit out at the crowd with staves as Faulkner's arrest was effected.

Similarly ugly scenes followed on the Wednesday, when play was started provocatively from the old turning up point in the Market Place. Once again the police seized the ball and cut it up, although later the legend grew that it had been filled with horse dung.

Chief Constable Parry, on horseback, then marshalled those playing a second ball towards Clifton. Instead of creating further disorder, however, this helped to diffuse tension.

Overall that year, eleven men were convicted of being drunk and disorderly, 21 for playing football in the streets, and a further 19 were warned for trespassing.

And so it went on, leading to an all-out propaganda battle. After further prosecutions in 1880 an anonymous handbill was circulated, concluding with this strident, if crude attack on Frank (who also acted as a magistrate):

'Now Men of Ashbourn about the real disturber of the Peace.

'Who is he? A Gentleman. No. A Liverpool Tradesman, who has a share in the business still, having 200 acres of land, thinks he will rule Ashbourn with a rod of iron.

'Will you stand this? By whose right does he bring the police here to protect private property?

'Is it Law? the people do not want to play in the Street, but they will play over the Old Ground.

'Mr Fraks (sic) can leave Ashbourn, it will be no loss, but the old Game will & shall be played. You people of Ashbourn, if you let a man like Fraks ride you down you are not fit to bear the proud name of Englishmen.'

The bill was signed 'an Ashbourn Tradesman'.

To calm matters, Joseph Simpson, owner of Mayfield Mill near Clifton, offered the use of his fields, and even pledged a bond of £100 against encroachment by the players on streets and private land.

But his faith was misplaced. Once again the following year the ball was carried onto Shaw Croft and Sandy Lane, with the police now acting as marshals; not so much stopping play as removing the ball to less sensitive areas.

Thus the game soldiered on into the 1880s, but with much less excitement than of old, and with the Frank estate being patrolled along its boundaries.

In 1884 the *Derby Mercury* described the game as being 'in a moribund state'. »

Suited and booted the men of Ashbourne tussle in the Henmore on Shrove Tuesday, 1928, watched from a specially erected bridge by the Prince of Wales, who had just turned up the ball. Aptly, it was eventually goaled by an Up'ard by the name of George Waterfall. Ashbourne football has long been a favourite draw for the media. Gaumont and Paramount sent film crews in 1933, followed in 1935 by the BBC, while several clips from Pathé newsreels, dating back to the 1920s (some shot from the bridge seen here), can be viewed on the British Pathé website (*see Links*).

Only in Ashbourne is there a purpose-built platform to start the game, erected in 1998 on Shaw Croft. On the side of its plinth are the words to the *Shrovetide Song*, penned in 1891 by George Porter, who had lost an arm playing the game some years earlier.

There's a town still plays this
  glorious game,
Tho' tis but a little spot,
And year by year the contest's fought
From the field that's called Shaw Croft,
Then friend meets friend in a
  friendly strife,
The leather for to gain,
And they play the game right manfully,
in snow, sunshine or rain.

For loyal the Game shall ever be,
No matter when or where
And to treat that Game as ought
  but the free,
Is more than the boldest dare;
Through the ups and downs of its
  chequered life,
May the ball still ever roll,
Until by fair and gallant strife,
We've reached the treasur'd goal.

It's a good old Game, deny it who can,
That tries the pluck of an Englishman!

》 But not for long. In 1891 a turning point was reached.

One factor was the decision to invite a guest to turn up the ball at the start. For years prior to that, the *de facto* Down'ard captain, Alfred Hall, had thrown up the ball on Shrove Tuesdays, followed by Charles Coxon, an Up'ard, on Ash Wednesday, whereas thereafter, a local dignitary (and in later years the odd celebrity) was invited to perform the honours and make a short pre-match speech.

To demonstrate that the footballers were loyal citizens, *Rule Britannia* was also sung.

Nonetheless, that year the police once again took the names of players in the streets, leading to the summons of 74 men, the Rev Tomlinson included.

Yet this only had the effect of galvanising support.

A protest attended by an estimated 7-800 people, carried this resolution: 'That this meeting of the inhabitants of Ashbourne desires to press its emphatic condemnation of the action of the police in summoning a large number of persons for playing football in the streets, such action being entirely opposed to the wishes of the large majority of ratepayers, and trusts that the magistrates will see their way to dismiss the summonses.'

Now, seemingly, the whole town rallied behind the footballers.

A concert, organised to raise money for the players' fines, sold out and had to be repeated. During this concert was performed the *Shrovetide Song*, written specially by former player George Porter (*reproduced left*), which has since been sung before every game.

At the subsequent hearings, defence solicitor Mr Mathews argued that the Shrovetide games

at Atherstone and Nuneaton were not hindered by prosecutions.

It was also noted that other gatherings which obstructed the highway, such as election hustings and meetings of the Meynell Hunt, escaped legal censure.

Meanwhile the local council railed at the expense of bringing in policemen from outside the town, especially when so many of the players summoned appeared happy to have their day in court and be martyrs to the cause.

Faced with these arguments, at last the authorities ended their campaign. There would be no further prosecutions after 1891.

In return, the players took on more responsibility by forming a game committee.

Life was also made easier when Mr Frank's widow died and Ashbourne Hall became a hotel in 1898, followed a year later by the restoration of access to The Park, which would in any case soon be turned into a public park.

20th century

Since the uncertain years of the late 19th century, Shrovetide football has come to be seen as part of the mainstream culture of Ashbourne; a custom to be nurtured by the authorities (and the police), rather than stymied.

At the same time, the players and the game committee have made great strides in emphasising the good intent of the participants.

Much of this goodwill was secured during the First World War, when leading Shrovetide players were among 75 Ashbourne men who left for France with the Sherwood Foresters in February 1915. Among the volunteers was Joe 'Ninety' Burton, who goaled a record seven times in all for the Up'ards (once in a boys' game).

Burton survived the trenches and lived until the age of 96. (The 1915 game is featured on the cover.)

In 1920 the *Ashbourne News* noted a renewed enthusiasm. 'Such a happy state of affairs has not always existed, and we have more than once referred to the fact that organised opposition had the effect of giving to the ancient custom a new lease of life, rather than bringing about its suppression.'

Only twice since has the game failed to take place, both owing to outbreaks of foot and mouth disease. In 1968, a milder game was played on the recreation ground. In 2001, the usual songs were performed at the plinth but no balls were turned up.

Apart from the construction of this plinth, in 1998, and of purpose-built goals in 1995, there have been only two other changes.

In 1967 the deadline for scoring was brought forward from midnight to 10.00pm, and in 1991 a rule was introduced whereby the game is judged void if the ball goes missing for more than an hour (partly to prevent smuggling, a tactic which is much less popular in Ashbourne than for example in the various Scottish games).

But make no mistake, the Ashbourne game is still as tough as ever. Since James Barker's drowning in 1878, two other players have died. William Tunnicliffe was found dead from hypothermia in a field at Clifton on Ash Wednesday, 1906, while in 2007, 51 year old David Johnson, died from a heart attack.

Compared with the casualty figures in mainstream sport this is still a remarkable record, however, and is testament to the excellent spirit in which Shrovetide football is played.

▲ Shown here on the 1992 ball is **Clifton Mill**, goal for the Down'ards before its demolition in 1967. As is customary, the ball also features a Union flag and the Imperial State Crown.

Although dimensions have varied, modern Ashbourne balls are slightly larger and flatter than a standard football (in festival football only Atherstone's are larger). Each consists of one rectangular and two circular panels. To give strength and buoyancy the case is stuffed tightly with cork shavings.

Should the decoration rub off during play, which happens less since modern paints were introduced, they can be handed back to the artist to be repainted.

Three balls for each day are produced. However not since 1967 have more than two been played on one day, and one is the norm.

▶ Well worth a visit during the Shrovetide period are the displays of historic Ashbourne balls, dating back to the 1890s, above the bar of either the **Ex-Servicemen's Club** in the Market Place (*as seen here*), or the **Wheel Inn, Compton**, a favourite haunt of the Down'ards.

Each ball is loaned by its owner, who might be either the scorer (or his descendants) or, if the ball was not goaled, the guest who threw it up to start the game.

Ashbourne's current ball maker, John Harrison, an Ashbourne resident, is only the fourth to have taken on the role during the past century. One of his longest serving predecessors, until 1948, was John Barker, brother of the ill-fated James, who drowned during the 1878 game.

After the ball has been stuffed and sewn, it is handed to a local artist (currently Tim Baker) who applies signwriter's enamel paint to create a unique design that reflects the career or interests of the invited guest, together with the guest's name and the date.

Thus each ball tells its own story, providing a vivid reminder of past triumphs and memorable moments.

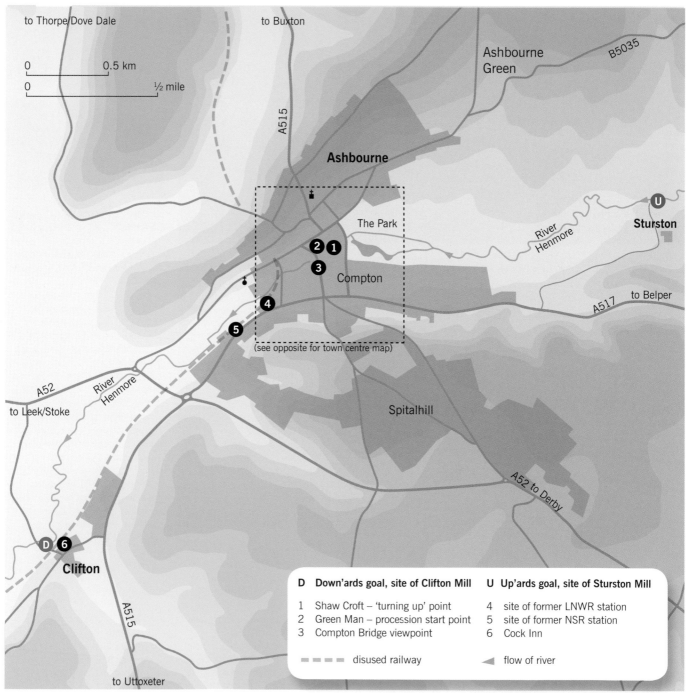

to Thorpe/Dove Dale

to Buxton

B5035

Ashbourne
Green

0   0.5 km

0   ½ mile

A515

Ashbourne

U Sturston

The Park

River Henmore

2 1

3

Compton

A517 to Belper

4

5

(see opposite for town centre map)

A52

River Henmore

to Leek/Stoke

Spitalhill

to Uttoxeter

A52 to Derby

D 6

Clifton

A515

D	**Down'ards goal, site of Clifton Mill**	**U Up'ards goal, site of Sturston Mill**

1	Shaw Croft – 'turning up' point	4 site of former LNWR station
2	Green Man – procession start point	5 site of former NSR station
3	Compton Bridge viewpoint	6 Cock Inn

- - - disused railway   ◄ flow of river

◀ The terrain makes **Ashbourne** the Paris-Dakar rally of festival football. Three miles separate the Up'ards' goal at Sturston Mill from the Down'ards' at Clifton Mill. From the streets of the town, the play can and often does pass down narrow alleyways (known as jitties), across car parks and busy roads, through parks and playing fields, out to open country, criss-crossed by hedges, ditches and a winding river.

As can be seen, the valley of the River Henmore forms the main east-west axis of the course.

To advance across such mixed and sapping ground requires perseverance and stamina, moreso considering that committed players turn out twice on consecutive days.

After the procession from the Green Man (*see below*) and the turning up of the ball at Shaw Croft, early skirmishes are often inconclusive, as the huge crowds and the freshness of the players conspire to make significant breaks less likely. Indeed the first hour may conclude with the ball back where it started, at Shaw Croft.

From Shaw Croft the Up'ards

face a short distance to the open ground of The Park. There, players may sometimes show their nerve by swimming across the Fish Pond – formerly the ornamental lake of Ashbourne Hall – before heading out across country.

In the Down'ards' favour is the flow of the Henmore, which makes waterplay their favoured tactic (as is also the case for the Downies in Workington). They can also take advantage of the network of jitties

and lanes in the town, spreading confusion amongst their opponents. With so many people about, few defenders know which way to turn when a runner takes possession.

So beware of following someone simply because they are running. They may have no more idea where the ball is than you do.

Scoring in Ashbourne is now a quite different affair than in the past. As seen at **Sturston Mill** in 1952 (*above left*), Up'ard Bill Allen poses stiffly for *Picture Post* photographer Bert Hardy, to demonstrate how goals were scored by entering the wheel-house and tapping the ball three times against the mill wheel. Only a few other players would have been able to witness the act.

Today's goals are, by contrast, out in the open air. After both mills were demolished (Clifton in 1967, Sturston in 1981) the arch of each mill bridge served as the goal.

However, as seen above at **Sturston**, the current goals, erected in 1995, are purpose-built stone plinths, with a circular target, as the goal, representing the mill wheel. (Clifton's goal is identical.)

Scoring from the riverbank is not permitted. Instead, the scorer must be standing in the river. But as illustrated later, that is no simple task, given the throng of players gathered around the goal, including last-ditch defenders doing their utmost either to win back possession or prevent a goal before the 10.00pm deadline.

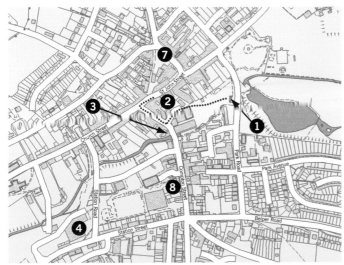

© Crown Copyright and/or database right. All rights reserved. Licence number 100047737.

Ashbourne town centre

•••••••••••• procession route

1 Shaw Croft – 'turning up' point
2 Green Man – procession start
3 Compton Bridge viewpoint
4 site of former LNWR station

7 Market Place – site of bull ring and ex-Servicemen's Club (display of Shrovetide balls)
8 Wheel Inn

▲ The **Prince of Wales** holds up the ball, and is himself displayed on Ash Wednesday, 2003. Tradition requires that the guest be hoisted onto players' shoulders for the benefit of photographers before the procession continues to Shaw Croft.

In 1928, in a more deferential era, the Prince's great uncle, the future Edward VIII, was allowed to forego this ritual.

Contrary to popular belief, the title of **Royal Shrovetide Football** was not granted as a result of that first royal visit, but six years earlier, when the committee sent a specially decorated football to London to celebrate the marriage of Mary, (daughter of George V), on Shrove Tuesday, February 1922.

Over the years a number of soccer stars have turned up the ball: Steve Bloomer in 1920, Billy Meredith (1925), Stanley Matthews (1966) and Brian Clough (1975). Other guests have included John Roberston, the Kirkwall Ba' historian (1986). But no women have turned up the ball since 1860 when Elizabeth Woolley eluded the police by hiding the ball in her skirt. She is said to have thrown the ball out of an upstairs window.

Pre-match

Match days at Ashbourne start with up to 400 committee members, guests, players and supporters squeezing into the Green Man for the official lunch.

Strictly speaking the pub's full name is The Royal Green Man and Blackamoor's Head Commercial and Family Hotel, a result of the merger of two adjoining inns during the 19th century. Visitors cannot miss the place. Its pub sign, said to be the longest in the world, spans the entire width of St John Street.

After lunch the guest of honour is called on to make a speech. The Shrovetide song is then sung, and shortly before 2.00pm the procession leaves for Shaw Croft.

It is a stirring sight (and photo opportunity too), and a perfect way to build the tension.

Alas Shaw Croft, once a bucolic pasture, is now rather less fetchingly a public car park behind a supermarket. But at least the elevated plinth allows the crowds, usually numbering in their thousands, to witness the prelude to the game.

Up the steps climb the guests, the committee chairman and three individuals whose task it is to lead the singing. The chairman then addresses the massed ranks of players standing before him, reminding them of their need to behave and to stay out of the churchyard, the cemetery, the town's memorial gardens and all private gardens.

'Look after it; it exists. Don't look after it, it doesn't,' is his simple warning.

There then follow the customary renditions of *Auld Lang Syne* and the National Anthem, after which, at last (*as seen on page 1*), the ball is tossed into the waiting throng.

The game

Though never quite as lawless as its reputation, Ashbourne football only has a few rules. For example, if the first ball is goaled before 5.00pm, a second one is turned up at Shaw Croft. If this too is goaled before 5.00pm – a rarity not seen since 1967 – a third ball is played.

But in any case play must cease at 10.00pm, so that any ball not goaled by then is declared void – an occurrence that has become more common in recent years owing to the growth in numbers and the relative parity of the two sides. From 1990–2004, of 33 balls turned up, eight were not goaled.

The usual description of the Ashbourne game is 'hug ball', reflecting the way in which the ball is carried around amidst a large pack. As shown in these action shots from 2006 (*top*) and 1983 (*below*), the ball is also tossed and tipped in the air. But old style kicking does still take place, especially when a break is made into open country.

Jack Hawksworth, secretary of the committee from the late 1890s, wrote to the *Ashbourne Telegraph* on this very topic in 1934.

'It is up to those who take an active part in the game to assist in keeping our traditions as of old: by playing the game, I mean 'football' not 'hugball'.

'Let us have a good kicking, good play with good fellowship... Let us see more of the ball and give the visitors a chance to see that the leather, as Ashbournians know, will stand the punching... it does not require cuddling like a child three weeks old.

'Give it plenty of boot,' he urged.

But that is easier said than done. Current players prefer to keep possession of the ball, so that if »

» they are not actually in the hug they may choose to climb up onto a bank, a vehicle or a wall, or even up a tree, in order to be in a better position to have the ball passed up to them from the mass of bodies below. From their elevated spot they can then throw it in the desired direction to a teammate or at least gain valuable ground.

In such a way it is therefore common to see the sides at Ashbourne make progress back and forth in quick succession.

Unlike Scotland, where smuggling is more common, spectators at Ashbourne also get to see much more of the ball. Above the heads of the players, its whiteness, bright decoration and size make it easily visible.

As in all festival games where the numbers of players is greater, there is some differentiation of roles. Faster players stand off the hug on both sides, either to sprint away if the ball is thrown out to them, or to guard against a similar break by the opposition.

As the *Ashbourne News* noted in 1929, 'all the outlets had their sentinels, and the cross roads were strongly guarded'.

Recent years have seen the Up'ards dominate the scoring, partly thanks to players from the Ashbourne Rugby Club, whose teamwork, fitness and strength have tipped the balance.

The future

Given the level of opposition to the game between 1859–91, the survival of Shrovetide football at Ashbourne is testament to the doggedness of its supporters.

While the nearby games at Derby and Nuneaton, and also those at Dorking and Chester-le-Street succumbed to concerted pressure from the authorities, Ashbourne men refused to let their traditions die.

Now, typified by Prince Charles's appearance in 2003, the Ashbourne game has achieved a level of acceptance and respectability that has led to sustained levels of participation and media interest.

Crowds of up to 4,000 are still common and the number of players involved can reach hundreds per side. Even more remarkably, the same players turn out on both days, clocking up 12-15 hours of action over a 32 hour period in often adverse conditions. In such gruelling circumstances cuts re-open, bruises get knocked and sprains multiply.

And yet the spirit amongst the players remains positive, suggesting that if only more towns had fought harder to preserve their own Shrovetide matches, the Ashbourne experience would be the rule today, rather than the exception that it clearly is.

Action from Shrove Tuesday 2006, showing an Up'ards break across The Park and out towards the open fields where, en route to Sturston, a series of hedges and the River Henmore have to be negotiated; barriers that require careful co-ordination and passing strategies between team members (as at Hallaton, *see page 159*).

▲ Nowadays every **Ashbourne** match is followed by a posse of video cameramen. Indeed the resultant DVDs are often well worth watching. Yet because goals are usually scored after dark, images of the actual moment of scoring are rare. Taken by Lindsey Porter, this dramatic shot shows Up'ard Kirk Maskell scoring at **Sturston** on Shrove Tuesday, 2002.

The quickest goal ever recorded took 30 minutes in 1959, but more often it takes hours to reach this point. Maskell's goal came after 7 hours and 20 minutes play.

Even at the goal, it can take an age for a scorer to emerge, as defenders gamely continue their rearguard action, if only to hold on until 10.00pm. Meanwhile the attackers may debate amongst themselves as to who should have the final touch. They might even draw lots before, often without warning, the one who is chosen applies the *coup de grâce*.

And so the game ends with a white flash from an alert photographer fleetingly illuminating the seething, soaking mass of winners and losers, crammed into the cold, dark waters below.

Shrovetide

7. Atherstone, Warwickshire

The 1922 Atherstone winner poses with the ball, which appears to be a larger version of an old-style panelled football. Today's balls are cheese-shaped, akin to the Harrow ball (*see page 172*), and are made by the Warwickshire firm, Gilbert's of Rugby, better known as makers of rugby balls. As shown right in 2007, the ball is 27 inches in diameter (68cm) and weighs four pounds (1.8kg).

After the marathon cross country match at Ashbourne, the Shrove Tuesday game at Atherstone is a quite different affair, confined solely to the streets, with no goals, no teams and a strictly enforced time limit.

It is also, unfortunately, poorly documented prior to the 20th century, leaving large gaps in our knowledge of how it came into being and how much it might or might not have changed.

Until the late 20th century the market town of Atherstone, close to the border with Leicestershire, was best known for its hat making industry, now extinct. At its peak in the 19th and early 20th centuries Atherstone hats, belts and braces were said to have been worn by armies all over the world. Mining, brewing and, in Roman times, brick making have also been important local industries, while Atherstone is now a recognised book town, offering a wealth of second-hand bookshops.

But perhaps the town's most significant role has been as a stopping-off point on the Roman road of Watling Street. In modern times this route has become better known as the A5, which although now by-passing the centre, continues to make town a major distribution hub.

The original route of Watling Street still runs straight through Atherstone, however, from east to west, with the section in the town centre known as Long Street.

It is on Long Street that most of the Shrove Tuesday action takes place; a street once lined with coaching inns, though still with sufficient watering holes to allow for a truly staggering pub crawl.

Most accounts of the game state that it dates back to the reign of King John (1199–1216), a claim based upon one snippet, written in 1790, by Ralph Thompson of Witherley (a village on the opposite bank of the River Anker, which forms the border between Warwickshire and Leicestershire).

Thompson wrote: 'It was a Match of Gold that was played betwixt the Warwickshire Lads and the Leicestershire Lads on Shrove Tuesday; the Warwickshire Lads won the Gold. It was in King John's reign... Atherstone being the nearest town to the place where they play'd it, it is and has been a custom to turn a Foot Ball up at Atherstone on Shrove Tuesday every Year since that time.'

If this story were true, it is likely that the game was centred around the River Anker, with one of the bridges forming the starting point.

But alas no written evidence to back up Thompson's claim exists.

For sure, there is William Fitzstephen's account of Shrove Tuesday football in London in 1174 (*see page 19*), and plenty of other uncorroborated material suggesting that mass Shrovetide games took place elsewhere before the 18th century.

But none make any reference to matches being played between Atherstone and Witherley.

Nevertheless, modern day Atherstonians are content that the

Thompson quote is sufficient, and in 1999 went so far as to celebrate the game's 800th anniversary, even though Thompson did not actually mention 1199 as the date of the Warwickshire v. Leicestershire encounter.

Moreover, to be absolutely strict, King John did not accede to the throne until April 6 1199; that is, shortly after Shrove Tuesday.

But whatever the truth, clearly the game was regarded as an established custom by 1790, which is provenance enough in the context of other games played around Britain.

In the century or so following 1790 coverage of the game in local newspapers remained disappointingly absent.

Then, in 1901, a report appeared that the police intended to enforce Warwickshire County Council by-laws which, under the 1835 Highways Act, prohibited the playing of football in the streets.

According to the *Atherstone News*, however, the local parish council had other ideas. While the council chairman, Mr C Orton, said that it was their duty to protect town property, it was also argued that 'the custom had been observed so many years that it had become to be looked upon as a kind of charter by the working classes, and not only by them but by others as well...'

Another defender of the game, Mr HE Vero, was reported to have said that 'he did not approve of these old customs and usages of the town being abolished.

'The reason that football kicking had been stopped in other towns was because tradespeople objected to it, but in Atherstone they did not...'

The meeting concluded with the chairman hoping 'that members

of the Parish Council would assist any working men who might be summoned before the Magistrates.'

After a debate, the Council also resolved to continue with their normal practice of removing the glass panes from the town's gas lamps to protect them from damage by the footballers.

And so the 1901 game went ahead, against the wishes of Warwickshire County Council.

(A similar stand off between a county council and a local council threatened the Dorking game in 1897 – *see page 35* – only in that case the county eventually prevailed.)

Since 1901, as far as can be ascertained, only two major developments have taken place.

In 1974, for the first time, an organising committee was formed, and the action, which once roamed freely around the town, particularly towards the Coventry Canal, was confined to Long Street only.

After a particularly boisterous game in 1986 it was furthermore decided, following a heated public meeting, that experienced players would act as stewards to clamp down on excessive behaviour.

Given how close the game had come to extinction in 1901, and again in 1986, these measures have proved a small price to pay for maintaining public support.

Indeed having been played without break throughout both world wars, the only year when it looked as if no play would take place was during the foot and mouth outbreak in 2001.

But even then permission was granted at the last minute because, unlike in places such as Ashbourne and Hallaton, the game at Atherstone is well and truly an urban affair. »

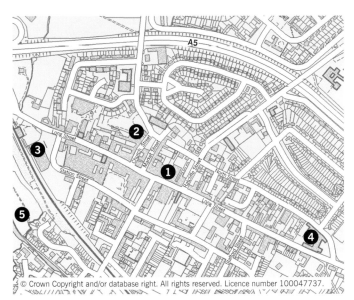

▲ Since 1974 play at Atherstone has been confined to **Long Street**, an historic thoroughfare lined with interesting shop fronts and buildings, and which is mostly level until rising at the eastern end, towards the old grammar school.

The school, at the junction of Long Street and North Street, also used to form the eastern extremity of the game.

Nor does play extend any more to the Coventry Canal or the station, whereas prior to 1974 it was common for the ball to enter the canal for bouts of water play. Earlier, it was also kicked around

the yard of the workhouse (now a retirement home).

The unofficial headquarters of the game are the Angel Inn, Market Square, outside of which labourers used to stand on hiring day, hoping to be taken on for the next year.

Various buildings on Long Street have been used for the throw up, with, since 1981, Barclays Bank being the current choice.

1 **Starting point (Barclays Bank)**
2 **The Angel Inn**
3 **Railway station**
4 **Atherstone Grammar School**
5 **Coventry Canal**

▲ Over the years a number of windows and balconies on **Long Street** have been used to throw up the ball, though few as seemingly precarious as this narrow ledge at the **Blue Bell** pub in the 1930s.

The Blue Bell succeeded the Hand and Bottle Inn, demolished in the 1920s. Then, after the Blue Bell also closed the Three Tuns took over, followed by a shop called Cooke and Ryders. When this too closed there were fears that no other premises would be available, until in 1981 Barclays Bank stepped in to save the day.

The honour of throwing up the ball is usually reserved for a celebrity. Footballers have often featured, from Aston Villa's Pongo Waring in 1934 to Gordon Banks, once of Leicester City, in 1995.

Stars performing at the Coventry Hippodrome were also regularly summoned, including George Formby, Beryl Reid, Mike Yarwood and (*lower left*), **Edwin Starr** in 1994. Just after **Ken Dodd** performed the honour in 1970 (*top left*) the scaffold under the balcony gave way, forcing him, the mayor and their companions to nip hastily back through the window.

Pre-match build up

Shrove Tuesday celebrations in Atherstone start at 1.00pm when the committee and guests meet for lunch at the Angel Inn, the game's *de facto* headquarters in Market Square.

Then around 2.30pm, children and youths gather below the upper storey window of Barclays Bank, on Long Street, from where a golden penny is tossed out by the guest of honour, along with hundreds of sweets. As pupils at the Queen Elizabeth High School (successor to the Grammar School founded in 1573) are given a half-day holiday, that means plenty of takers (though in keeping with the times, many of the sweets are hurled back, with interest).

After a scramble, one lucky child will claim the golden penny and in return receive a cash prize (£10 in 2007). Meanwhile, the composition of the crowd rapidly alters as older players start to gather – many emerging from the nearby pubs – for the main event.

The game

Atherstone is a game of two uneven halves. The first 90 minutes are essentially ritualistic, followed by a final 30 minutes of highly competitive action.

The game commences at 3.00pm when the guest of honour reappears at the window of Barclays Bank with the ball. By now as many as 2,000 players and spectators fill Long Street, which remains closed to traffic throughout the game.

Since the mid-20th century, ribbons have been attached to the ball, as is also the custom in the Scottish borders (*see page 98*). At Atherstone they are red, white and blue. Once the ball has dropped into the crowd, each ribbon torn from the ball and handed in to the organisers yields a prize of £10.

Occasionally, black ribbons are added as a mark of respect on the death of a notable player or supporter of the game, or to mark a major loss of life further afield.

Otherwise, for the next hour and a half the ball is punted up and down Long Street, covering three lengths of the route between two extremities: to the east, the Old Swan and the Black Horse pubs; to the west, the Wheatsheaf.

Throughout most of this first phase the kickabout is reasonably friendly, with children and women being invited to have uncontested kicks (*as seen right in 2007*), and only an occasional scuffle for the honour of catching the ball and sending it on its way again.

In this respect it is similar to watching a series of marks being contested in Australian Rules Football, albeit with the odd burst of eggs and flour filling the air, in an echo of the traditional custom of Shrovetide mischief-making. (Peashooters also used to be in evidence, before they were banned a few years ago.)

In common with Sedgefield (*see page 91*), the game at this stage has no objective other than to give as many people as possible a touch or kick of the ball. The only real excitement is when someone punts the ball high enough for it to become stuck on a roof or balcony.

Then, as 4.30pm approaches, the mood changes palpably, until one of the stewards sounds an air horn to signal the final phase.

Non-players step back, small children are herded to the sides, the stewards in their fluorescent jackets take their positions, and the ball suddenly disappears under a pile of bodies.

Game on!

Atherstone punters in 2007, when for once the ball was filled purely with air. In other recent years water has been added, making it heavier to kick and easier to control. In case of an accident a spare ball is always provided, though in 1975 it had to be called into action after the original ball was spirited away in a car and held to ransom.

▲ In Atherstone, with no goals and a strict time limit, possession is everything. During this frenetic, heaving **final half hour** it is not uncommon for the ball to be spiked or cut, making it far easier to grip.

As seen here at the climax of the 2007 game, experienced players usually seek out a protected place up against a wall, or even better, in a corner, while their cohorts climb up above the crowd to ward off body-surfing rivals.

Thus friends and family members press and push and strive together against the crush to ensure that once held by one of their own, the ball does not leave their possession before the air horn sounds again at 5.00pm.

Only at the death do the stewards and police then move in to escort the tenacious winner away from the throng and shepherd him and the deflated ball back to the gateway of the Angel Inn (*above opposite*), where free drinks and a round of interviews with the local media await.

He will then tour the town with the ball for days afterwards, collecting money for a charity of his choosing.

The future

Atherstone's Shrove Tuesday football, in its final stages, appears a brutal trial of strength, almost primaeval in its intensity.

Some of the tactics employed in protecting the ball-holder would even be considered over-zealous in the more expansive and longer lasting games at Workington, Ashbourne and Kirkwall.

Yet there is also a sense that Atherstone's game provides an interesting model of how mass football has been adapted and reworked to suit the strictures of the modern world.

Its double bill of friendly, ritualistic play for everyone, followed by feverish competition for the few, all within a single hour and within a tightly confined and highly controlled space, has a definite popular appeal.

Spectators can watch from start to finish, without walking too far and without waiting for too long.

Was this perhaps how mass football was played, in the tight streets and alleyways of medieval towns and cities, hundreds of years ago?

Whatever, and whether or not the game is 800 years old, Atherstone football appears to be well supported, much enjoyed, and, just as importantly, well able to sustain itself for many more years to come.

Shrovetide

8. Sedgefield, County Durham

According to the *History, Topography and Directory of Durham* in 1894, the Sedgefield parish clerk 'is obliged to furnish a football on Shrove Tuesday, which he throws into the market place, where it is contested for by the mechanics against the agriculturalists...' Shown here is a ball won by Tommy Johnson in 1942, one of a record seven he won altogether. He gave one to his brother but still treasures the rest. Made of hand-stitched saddle leather covering a cork or softwood core, the standard Sedgefield ball is only a little larger than a cricket ball, needing to be small enough to pass through a four inch diameter bull ring in the town centre.

Legend has it that the Shrove Tuesday game in Sedgefield originated some 750 years ago, when craftsmen working on the construction of St Edmund's parish church, between 1246–56, issued a challenge to local farmworkers. At noon the rector threw a ball from the church tower to start the game, and although the play turned rough, tempers were later soothed with beer served from four-gallon casks.

It is a charming tale, but not until February 1802 can any written record of Shrove Tuesday football in this delightful town be found, and only a passing mention at that, in a London publication, *The Sporting Magazine*. (Sedgefield was a great hub of sporting activity at this time, with a racecourse, still extant, and a prized reputation for hunting with foxhounds, hence its nickname 'Melton of the North'.)

William Parson and William White's *History, Directory and Gazetteer of the Counties of Durham and Northumberland*, published in 1827, adds more colour, referring to the Shrove Tuesday game as 'an ancient custom' in which 'the parish clerk is obliged to find a ball for the use of the townsmen and the country people, who assemble for the purpose of playing a game at football, after which the victorious and the vanquished resort to the public houses where they generally "drink deep e'er they depart".'

Post-match libation is of course a staple element of festival football, but so too are other characteristics of the Sedgefield game; the fact that it is played on the streets, that both kicking and handling are allowed, that both goals – known as alleys in Sedgefield – were originally water features, and that the number three plays a part in the ritual.

Sedgefield may therefore lack the scale of Ashbourne or Workington, but it represents the essence of British festival football.

The teams and alleys

Until the 1920s players were divided into Town and Country, a division also found at St Columb Major in Cornwall (*see page 142*).

The Country goal, or alley, was a pond at North End, a few hundred yards north from the town centre, in front of a blacksmith's.

Five hundred yards to the south, on the other side of Sedgefield, the Town alley was a stream, running along the southern boundary.

That the Country alley was located closer to the centre than the Town goal seems odd. However one possible explanation, if the antiquity of the game is to be believed, is that many of those working the common land around medieval Sedgefield would still have lived inside the town, where they enjoyed the protection of the town walls (parts of which are still visible at East End). Only after the common land was enclosed in 1636 were farmhouses built further out. In other words, countrymen were as much townsfolk as the townsmen, apart from their place of work.

Compared with festival games elsewhere, reports of the Sedgefield game are short on detail. But the general pattern appears to have been as follows.

At midday on Shrove Tuesday a bell rang to warn housewives that they should start preparing

When with pancakes you are sated,
Come to this ring and you'll be mated.
For there this ball will be upcast,
May this game be better than the last.

Traditional Shrove Tuesday rhyme inscribed on the Sedgefield ball

pancakes. Then, with the players having enjoyed their fill, at one o'clock the rector threw down the ball from the tower of St Edmund's, for play to begin.

The aim of each team was to be the first to reach its own alley and immerse the ball.

Once this had occurred the next stage would commence. Whoever from the scoring team managed to retrieve the ball from the water would carry it back to the Town Green, where it would be passed three times through a bull ring embedded in the ground opposite the Black Lion pub. After this the winner could keep the ball and be acclaimed as the champion.

This additional element – of a winning player within a winning team – still forms an integral part of the games at Kirkwall, Ashbourne and Workington.

If neither side managed to alley before 6.00pm, the ball became the property of the clerk (thereby saving the expense of providing a replacement the following year).

Owing to the small size of the ball, the Sedgefield game could be a punishing affair. As an account of the game in 1894 reported, 'The liberal use of sheet iron leg guards is not merely a precaution but an absolute necessity, for no sooner does the ball touch the ground than the most indiscriminate kicking begins and continues throughout the game.'

Two years later the *Yorkshire Post* of February 19 1896 reported a crowd of 2-3,000 watching a short game of 40 minutes, started by the parish clerk, Mr Webb. 'The countrymen had the game well in hand throughout, being decidedly stronger numerically than their opponents, and succeeded in landing the ball in their alley – the North End pond.   »

Action on the Town Green from Shrove Tuesday, 1919, one of the last Sedgefield games played between Town and Country. The game was won by Raymond Iceton, whose family name features often on the roll of honour displayed in the Hardwick Arms pub. An Iceton first won in 1878, and most recently in 1996. Taken from the Cross Hill Hotel, this postcard shows the late 15th century tower of St Edmund's, a Grade 1 listed church. To the left is High Street. To the right, where the ball appears to be heading, is Rectory Row.

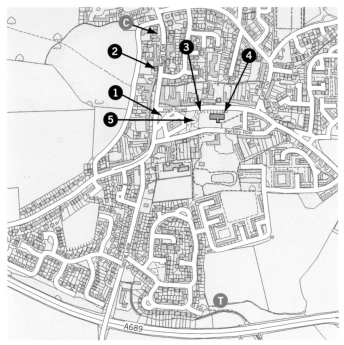

Most of the action on Shrove Tuesday takes place within the centre of Sedgefield, although abductions of the ball to outlying villages, such as Fishburn, two miles to the north, have formed a regular part of recent games. A short distance to the south west lies Sedgefield Racecourse.

Key:
C site of former Country alley (*see below right*)
T Town alley
1 Bull ring
2 Hardwick Arms
3 Millennium sculpture
4 St Edmund's Church
5 Cross Hill, former market place

Photographed in c.1910, this is the pond next to the blacksmith's on North End, which until filled in during the 1920s formed the Country alley. A modern garage now occupies the site. Seen on the opposite side of the road is the White House (actually a pair of houses, taller than their neighbours), dating from the 1790s and now listed Grade II.

'The ball was secured by B. Hart, who was carried shoulder high in his dripping clothes up the North End to the bull-ring, where the ball was again passed through the ring and handed back to Hart.'

The report concluded, 'There was less rough play than usual.'

Soon after the First World War this established pattern of play came to an end, when the pond which formed the Country alley (*see below*) was filled in and the blacksmith's converted into a petrol station and garage.

Yet possibly owing to the lack of any suitable water feature in that part of the town, or perhaps because of declining interest in the game, instead of simply choosing another goal the pattern of play was changed thereafter to its current form, in which only the Town alley is used, and players are no longer split into two teams.

Regrettable though this is, at least the Sedgefield game survives. Not so the other famous Shrove Tuesday football game played in County Durham, at Chester-le-Street, some 20 miles to the north.

As explained earlier (*see page 35*), this died out in 1932 after several players were fined for obstructing the highway, which happened to be the old A1 from London to Edinburgh.

In this respect, the compact nature of Sedgefield's townscape and its focus around the Town Green has enabled it to live on.

The game today
Having consumed their Shrove Tuesday pancakes, crowds gather opposite the Black Lion at 1.00pm, to witness the passing of the ball three times through the bull ring. This ceremony is performed by a guest of honour, usually a senior resident whose identity is kept a secret until the big day.

The ball is then thrown up in the air to begin this fast-moving game.

As stated earlier, since the loss of the Country alley in the 1920s there are no teams.

Instead, individuals and groups compete for possession, moving this way and that across two open spaces; a triangle of ground by the bull ring, and the green on the east side of the Cross Hill Inn, facing the church.

Although there is plenty of open space to exploit, several »

▲ Sedgefield's **bull ring** is located on the corner of High Street and North End, where it might well have been used not only for tying up animals for sale, but also for bull baiting. A market was held in front of St Edmund's from 1312 until 1918 on an open area of land known as Cross Hill, although the market cross itself was removed in the 19th century.

On the left, **Draycott Norman**, landlord of the Nag's Head in Darlington, demonstrates the ritual passing of the ball through the bull ring before the Shrove Tuesday game in February 1968.

By tradition the responsibility for providing the ball lay with the verger at the parish church. But as that position had remain unfilled since the year before, local licensees stepped in to save the day. As Morgan told the *Northern Echo*, 'This is just too valuable a hit of old England to allow to fade away for the want of a ball.'

Note the inscription of the poem on the ball (*reproduced on page 86*). This was added by local signwriter Leslie Butler, while the ball itself was made by a Darlington saddler, Richard Marshall. Instead of using a cork or softwood centre, Marshall used an old polo ball as the core, stitching the leather around it, a method which has remained in use until the present day.

Spot the ball – it is just about visible in each of these images of action from the Shrove Tuesday game at Sedgefield in 2006. They show the main elements of play: contesting the ball in classic *Uppies and Downies* fashion, scrimmaging, running and kicking.

windows are boarded up in case, and not all local residents look on in favour.

But the ball game is hardly one of the most physical. While rugby-style tackling is common, heavyweight pile-ups are rare, unlike in other festival games, and the ball is more often picked up and thrown than kicked.

Nor are referees or stewards needed to oversee the action. Largely the players are self policing and accidents are rare.

There being no need to gain ground towards a goal at this first stage, the aim is simply to win possession of the ball for a precious moment or two, especially for younger participants (remember the poem, 'come to this ring and be mated').

Occasionally players will even hand the ball to small children or elderly spectators so that they too may have a touch or a kick for luck.

And so for an hour or more the game darts about the town, the pursuing crowd turning and swooping like a flock of starlings at dusk, following the ball.

But then at any moment the game may take an unusual turn, as a group of players suddenly secrete the ball and speed off in a car to a neighbouring hostelry. Others follow in their wake, as anyone in possession of the ball is entitled to a free drink.

These excursions – a more recent twist to ancient customs – typically occur twice during the afternoon, each lasting about half an hour. The Beehive pub and the Social Club in Fishburn, two miles up the road but still within the parish, are favourite destinations, though the ball has also been taken as far as Ferryhill and Thorpe Thewles (five miles to the north west and south east

respectively). In this sense the game echoes the ancient practice of beating the bounds, in which residents toured their parish, often kicking a football as they went. Such ceremonies survive in a few places, for example Bodmin.

Meanwhile the rest of the crowd stays in Sedgefield to enjoy local hospitality and await the ball's return, for the last time, around 4.00pm. It is at this point that the players move down to the Town goal, a stream a few hundred yards south of the church, close to the A689. Once this was open country. Now the players must go through a housing estate or take a path from Rectory Row.

Once at the stream the ball is alleyed, or dunked in the water, after which the players return en masse to the green.

As at Atherstone, the most competitive element of the game is kept until last. A ferocious struggle now takes place for possession, the day's champion being the player who manages once more to pass the ball through the bull ring, three times. This is not a task to be accomplished alone, so allies are vital to offer protection.

For spectators it is virtually impossible to see exactly what is going on amid the heap of bodies, but after a few minutes one player invariably emerges triumphant.

He then heads for the pub where, as in 1802, the players generally "drink deep e'er they depart". The winner also keeps the ball as a trophy, and has his name inscribed upon the honours' board at the Hardwick Arms.

The future
In its modern form the Sedgefield ball game is a blend of ritual, playfulness and competition, the result of years of adaptation to

changing circumstances. For this reason there is little reason to fear for its future. Indeed in recent years it appears to have grown in popularity, despite antipathy from sections within the community.

It may have lost one of its goals, and the age old division of its players too. But it remains at the centre of the town's being, in all senses of the word.

Unveiled on the north west corner of St Edmund's churchyard as part of Sedgefield's Millennium celebrations, this fine, 3m tall bas relief sculpture – carved in Dunhouse Buff sandstone by Darlington stonemason David France – was designed by a local artist and teacher, Brian Sutherland.

Shrovetide

9. Alnwick, Northumberland

Since 1933 Alnwick's game has been preceded by a throw-off by the Duke of Northumberland, or his representative, from the barbican of Alnwick Castle (as shown here in March 1938). The ball used is a standard soccer ball. Unlike in other games, this part of the proceedings is ceremonial only. The ball is not contested but simply caught and then taken in procession to the field of play, on the north side of the River Aln.

In a region once regarded as a thriving centre of festival football, Alnwick (pronounced Annick) hosts Northumberland's sole surviving Shrovetide game.

Albeit its modern form is much altered – resembling soccer in several respects – the setting is magnificent, and the traditions surrounding the game can be traced back to at least 1788.

Alnwick is of course dominated by its Castle, the second largest inhabited castle in England (hence Alnwick's nickname as the Windsor of the North). Since 1309 this has been home to the Percys, the earls and dukes of Northumberland, who have long been patrons of the game (as the Hays family is of handba' in Duns, 40 miles to the north).

Unusually for a festival football game, the Alnwick game features goalposts, called 'hales' (spelt as 'hail' in Scotland, meaning goal).

Also unusually, there are three written rules.

The festivities are characterised by three main stages. First there is the ceremonial throw-off from the Castle barbican (see left), followed by a procession; then the game itself, and finally a contest to 'claim' the ball by carrying it to the opposite bank of the River Aln.

Local legend has the Shrove Tuesday game beginning in 1762. But the first account is by John Brand, writing in 1788. 'The waits (or musicians) belonging to the town come playing to the castle every year... at two o'clock pm when a foot-ball was thrown over the castle-walls to the populace.'

George Tate, referring in his *History of Alnwick* (1868–9) to 'some forty years ago', confirmed Brand's account, adding that the ball was kicked into Bailiffgate. From there, 'the young and vigorous kicked it through the principal streets of the town, and afterwards into the Pasture, which has been used since time immemorial for such enjoyments.

'Here it was kicked about, until the great struggle came, for the honour of making capture of the ball itself; the more vigorous combatants kicked it away from the multitude, and at last some one, stronger and fleeter than the rest, seized upon it and fled away pursued by others; to escape with the ball, the river was waded through or swam over, and walls were scaled and hedges broken down. The successful victor was the hero of the day, and proud of his trophy.'

So the old game had two parts, in the streets, then on the fields.

As would occur in many towns, opposition to mass football and its effect on traffic using the main road leading north through Alnwick to Scotland led to the prohibition of street games under the Alnwick Improvement Act of 1822. This Act provided for the 'lighting, paving, watching, cleansing and generally improving the town.' Under the Act bull-baiting, cock-throwing, bonfires and football were all outlawed.

However this ban was not enforced until after the 1827 Shrove Tuesday game, when the Duke of Northumberland (who had paid for the damage caused by the footballers), received a petition from residents, demanding action.

Consequently the Duke gave his consent for all the action to take place on the North Peth of Alnwick

Pastures, on the far side of the River Aln. On February 16 1828, three days before Shrove Tuesday, the magistrates cautioned that anyone playing football in the streets would be fined. Meanwhile the Improvement Commissioners issued notices announcing: 'To promote the diversion of the day, the Duke will give a football, in the Pasture, for the Non-Freemen at 2 o'clock; and also a Football for a regular match, between the married and unmarried Freemen, with a prize of Five Sovereigns for the Winning Side.'

This was a colossal sum, even if divided among numerous players.

To herald this new form of the game, on Shrove Tuesday a procession led by a veteran of the Battle of Waterloo, Matthew Burnett, bearing a Union flag, started out from the castle. Another man bore a gilded ball, similar in form to one featured at Duns (*see page 135*).

Music was provided by the Percy Artillery Band, with further accompaniment by the Piper to the Duchess, William Green.

Following this the festivities concluded 'in true rustic revelry' at the Town Hall, courtesy of a further five guinea donation by the Duke, a gesture that clearly did much to win public favour.

According to the *Alnwick Journal* of February 1861 Burnett kept his role for many years. But more interesting is a comment that the castle porter carried the footballs to the North Peth 'in his pocket-handkerchief.' This suggests that the balls were as small as those used in Scottish Border games.

The teams

Prior to 1828 there is no evidence for the existence of formal teams or goals. The game was »

▶ Preceding the **Alnwick** game is a procession from the Castle to the playing field. Members of the game's committee, which numbers around 50 individuals, each sporting red, white and blue ribbons, assemble with the players and supporters beneath the Castle barbican at 2.00pm. Committee members carry the Union Jack and the red and yellow flag of the Duke. Also present is the Town Waite, Adrian Ions.

The ball is then thrown down from the top of the tower by the Duke or his representative.

Before 1828 this throw-off would signal the start of the street game; that is, the ball would be contested by the players. The current tradition of a ceremonial throw off dates from 1933, after a *Gazette* report of the previous year noted how the committee regretted the loss of the tradition and hoped that 'another source' (meaning the Duke) would see fit to revive it.

This he did, the following year, the ball being simply caught, uncontested, by the scorer of the previous year's winning hale.

At this point the assembled crowd form a procession, led by the Duchess's Northumbrian piper (Since 1931, Shrove Tuesday has been the piper's only official duty.)

From the castle the procession continues down the Peth (*centre right*) and across the **Lion Bridge**, as seen below right in the 1920s.

A right turn then leads from the road onto Alnwick Pastures, on the far side of the river.

Another Alnwick tradition is that mint-flavoured Black Bullet sweets, a North-East regional speciality, are handed out to all and sundry.

A stone's throw from Lion Bridge is Malcolm's Cross, marking the place where King Malcolm of Scotland was killed in 1093.

» instead a free-for-all battle for possession, with the ball as the prize at the end (as was also the case at Chester-le-Street, and remains the case at Atherstone today).

Once Alnwick's game was confined to the Pastures, however, the Freeman divided into teams for the first phase (the 'regular match'), married v. unmarried.

This division was then common at other Northumberland games such as Wooler and Rothbury. (Rothbury males aged over eight who refused to play were fined a shilling, a fine many refused to pay. The game ceased in 1867 after complaints about damage.)

Alnwick's Freemen – their status either inherited or earned after seven years' service – were drawn from eleven companies incorporated in the town, these being cordwainers, skinners, glovers, merchants, tanners, weavers, blacksmiths, butchers, joiners, tailors and coopers.

The Third Duke, Hugh, died five days before Shrove Tuesday 1847, and so for the next few years the game did not take place. But when it did restart in the 1850s, under the new duke, Algernon, it did so with two further teams made up of townsmen representing two parishes, St Michael's and St Paul's. (The latter's church, to the south of the Castle, had been built in 1846.)

Alnwick from the south. Up to 1966 the pastures at the top were used for the game, whereas now the area closest to the river Aln is preferred. Lion Bridge, part of the procession route, can be seen top left. On the right is Alnwick Garden, opened in 2002 by Jane, the Duchess of Northumberland, and now one of the most popular attractions in the North East.

As late as 1886, according to the *Alnwick and County Gazette*, one ball was still contested by the married and unmarried Freemen, but clearly this old rivalry was dying out, and from then on it would be the parish teams who formed the main opposition, as they do to this day.

Under this division, the town is split by a line starting at Clayport Street, running east along the south side of the Market Place, and continuing in a southeasterly direction down Bondgate and Alnmouth Road.

In fact since 1982 St Paul's has served the town's Roman Catholic congregation, but that is irrelevant as far as Shrove Tuesday football is concerned.

One of the game's three written rules states categorically that players must play for the parish in which they live.

Alnwick Pastures
Accounts of the Alnwick game as played during the latter part of the 19th century suggest that, as now, it shared several characteristics with football as played at the time when the game split into the two codes of Association football and rugby during the 1860s.

Two sets of wooden goalposts were erected at either end of the field, albeit at a strength-sapping distance of over 700 yards apart.

Although no specific references exist to the form of goals used at Alnwick in the 19th century, photographs from the Edwardian period show them to have the unusual, gate-shaped design still in use today (*see page 96*).

It is also known that soccer teams were invited to Alnwick to demonstrate their 'new' game on Shrove Tuesdays during the 1880s, so clearly there was some

cross-fertilisation. For example, during the 1886 game the *Alnwick and County Gazette* noted that certain players, described as 'the aristocracy of football' – that is, 'those who love the honours without the work' – were to be seen 'dodging near the hales and endeavouring to finish with the ball.' In modern football slang they would be described as 'goal-hanging' or 'baby-lining'.

But as was commented half a century later by one former player, John Whinham, the game was also clearly influenced by rugby. 'In those days if you got out of a scrimmage without a broken head or a black eye you were the luckiest man in the world.'

Despite inches of snow on the ground, some 500 players were reported to have played in that 1886 encounter, while the Duke's piper, Thomas Green, had to walk

ten miles from Rothbury through the drifts in order to perform his duties. (The harsh winter of 1886 contributed to the demise of the original Duns game.)

Estimated crowds of 5,000 turned out in this period, some no doubt lured by additional cash prizes for wrestling, foot races and even snowball fights.

Subsequent reports of games often mention the participation of players otherwise known on the local soccer or rugby scene.

In 1921 Stanley Anderson, a rugby international and county cricketer, turned out for St Paul's. At one point, reported the *Alnwick and County Gazette* he 'stumbled over the ball, and the parish of St Michael's, acting according to the law, had a "heap lie on" scrimmage over him, all in splendid good humour.'

By this time the goals were only 440 yards apart. But there were still 150 per side.

Another source of reference for Alnwick football between the wars are cinema newsreels held in the collection of British Pathé Limited. The first of these was advertised in the *Alnwick and County Gazette* of March 11 1922, when the King's Hall Cinema announced on the front page, 'Instantaneous Hit of Shrove Tuesday's Football. You must see it. Don't wait till to-morrow. Come to-night.'

The 1922 footage appears not to have survived, but the Pathé News website (*see Links*) has nine other clips dating between 1924–38, all highly recommended viewing. (According to a *Gazette* report of the 1936 game, played in particularly muddy conditions, Pathé's camera narrowly escaped destruction in one mêlée, leaving 'the bewildered photographer' to pick himself up, 'a sadder and wiser man'.) »

▲ As seen here in 2006, **Alnwick** is one of the few festival games in which women, mostly students based in the Castle, play regularly.

According to the rules, the ball must be kicked, not handled, and when the bugler blows his bugle, the ball must be handed to an umpire to restart the game.

Otherwise the game is very much a long ball, stamina-testing affair on an uneven and often waterlogged pitch.

>> As it happened, Pathé's newsreels could have provided us with the last ever moving images of the game, for in the aftermath of the Second World War the game was not played, and might easily have disappeared had it not been for the Duke. In 1952 he encouraged former committee members to reconvene, and so the game restarted, albeit with steadily reducing numbers and a smaller playing area.

Since then the main change has been a move, in 1967, to a field closer to the river. Otherwise the game has been played on Shrove Tuesday since 1952, other than in 2001, owing to an outbreak of foot and mouth.

The game today

From 700 yards in 1886, to 440 yards in 1921, the Alnwick pitch today measures 200 yards in length and approximately 200 yards in width, although there are no touchlines. That is roughly three and a half times the size of a soccer pitch, but only a quarter of the area used in the 19th century.

After the procession has arrived at the field, the Union Jack is planted half way between the goals. One goal is at the Lion Bridge end, the other at the Denwick end.

Each parish, St Michael's and St Paul's, provides two umpires, who between them toss a coin to decide which way the teams will play. If present, His Grace the Duke kicks off; if not, then the committee chairman, having tried to catch the ball when it was thrown off the barbican, boots it up in the air. A standard soccer ball is now used.

Although there are no touchlines, the river to the south and rising ground to the north act as natural boundaries. Committee

▲ St Michael's hale in their 2-1 victory over St Paul's on **Shrove Tuesday, February 1937**. Note from this somewhat crudely retouched newspaper image how most players are garbed in street clothes. Indeed Pathé newsreels from the period confirm that many turned out in collar and tie.

Perhaps the most interesting aspect of the Alnwick set up is the design of the **hales**, or goals.

As seen right, in 2006, the current goals do not have extended uprights as in 1937, but the dimensions are the same, with the posts set four feet apart, and with a distance of 12 feet from the ground to the top of the arch.

In *The Sports and Pastimes of the People of England*, published in 1801, Joseph Strutt described the goals in football as 'usually made with two sticks driven into the ground, two to three feet apart.' This compares with 24 feet, as specified in the first rules of the Football Association, in 1863. It is therefore likely that Alnwick's have not changed substantially since the move to the Pastures in 1828.

As to the pointed arch, this might have been to echo the shape of a lychgate, or it may simply have been a one-off design dreamt up by the Duke's estate workers. Certainly no evidence of similar goals has ever been found.

Also of note are the decorative sprigs of conifer. Again, these might have been symbolic of spring, but equally their purpose could have been to make the hales more visible (which would have certainly helped when they were 700 yards apart, as in the 19th century).

members are stationed around the perimeter to return the ball and to take note of who is playing well.

The game is effectively the best of three hales. The first period lasts a maximum of 30 minutes, but ends immediately if a hale is scored. If, in the second 30 minute period the same team hales again, the game is over. If the other team equalises, a third period of up to a maximum of 45 minutes is played. Thus there are only three possible winning scores, 1-0, 2-0 or 2-1.

If no goal is scored in the final period the game will finish 1-1.

(An earlier unwritten rule, no longer necessary, gave the umpires freedom to disallow a goal if they could not identify the haler, as was easily possible when there were hundreds of players involved.)

After each hale – greeted by a blast from the bugler – the teams change ends.

As specified in one of the game's three rules, no handling is allowed, and there are therefore no goalkeepers. The bugler also blows, as directed by the umpires, when the ball goes out of bounds.

After the match is settled, the final part of the proceedings commences.

This is the contest to see who will gain the most important prize of all, the ball (*see opposite*).

Nowadays, instead of the much coveted half crowns of old, token prizes of £2 are awarded for good play, along with a commemorative certificate. £10 is given to each of the first two halers, and £20 to the third, if there is one.

These prizes are provided by the committee, which also lays on post-match refreshments (currently served in the John Bull pub), with the Duchess's Piper providing further musical accompaniment.

The future

In one sense the survival of Alnwick's Shrove Tuesday football was secured when it moved from the streets to the fields in 1828. Had it not, it might well have fallen victim to the Highways Act of 1835 (*see page 30*), as did Chester-le-Street in 1932.

The patronage of successive Dukes of Northumberland has always been crucial.

But the game has undoubtedly diminished since its restart after the war in 1952.

The town's dedicated band of organisers manages to rustle up 30-40 players once a year. These include a number of visiting students, many of them female, from St Cloud State University in Minnesota, which runs a Center for British Studies in Alnwick Castle. In most surviving festival games the average age of players is 25–40. At Alnwick it is younger.

This means there is a wide age gap between the players and members of the committee.

No doubt the American students see Shrove Tuesday football as another crazy cultural experience.

But it is surely the wider public in Alnwick and beyond that needs to be instilled with a stronger sense of the game's celebratory nature and of its historic importance in regional culture (if only as the last survivor of a once great Northumbrian tradition).

Increasing the prize money might be one solution. But better by far would be to restore Shrove Tuesday as a public holiday in the town, as it was before the Second World War, so that, as in Ashbourne, local schoolchildren would be free to join in or watch, and thereby form the next generation, not only of players but of organisers too.

▲ Drenched but triumphant, 22 year old coalminer John McKinley claims the ball to conclude the **1953 Alnwick** game, watched by a large crowd on the bank opposite. For this he was rewarded with £1.

This final stage of the afternoon starts with the ball being kicked up in the air. Whoever gains possession then has to convey the ball to the opposite bank of the Aln, by taking the long route, via either of two bridges, or, more directly and with less chance of being apprehended, by swimming across the ice cold waters of the Aln.

As stated earlier, the game is often played by female students. But only one, Allison Gray, has ever claimed the ball, after she braved the waters in 1967.

Immersion has long been part of local tradition. According to Robert Southey's *Common-Place Book* of 1851, 'At Alnwick, every burgess who takes up his freedom goes in procession to a large pond at some distance from the town, dressed with ribbons, makes a jump into it, and gets through as he can.

'A party generally perform at the same time, and then gallop back to the town, the foremost in the race being pronounced winner of the boundaries…'

Staged on St Mark's Day (April 25), this ceremony was said to have been instituted after a complaint from King John, who became stuck in a bog outside the town as he was passing by in the early 13th century.

Shrovetide

10. Scottish Border Games

A typical Scottish Borders handba' made from stuffed leather and decorated with ribbons, at Jedburgh in 2007. This uniformity of design is one of many shared customs throughout the region. In Scotland Shrove Tuesday is known as Fastern's E'en, or Fasteneven (meaning eve of the fast), as in the oft quoted couplet by John Hogg of Lilliesleaf: 'Of holidays throughout the year, there's nane that raises sic a steer, as Fasteneven'.

The two areas in which Shrove Tuesday football games were most common in 19th century Britain were Surrey, on the southern fringe of London, and the Scottish Borders.

Both, it will be noted, are now hotbeds of rugby union.

Of the former, none of the Shrovetide games remains extant. But there are five in the Borders, where Shrove Tuesday is known as Fastern's E'en, and where the name given to these games is ba', or more accurately, handba'.

These are at Hobkirk, Jedburgh, Ancrum and Denholm, all within a few miles of each other in Roxburghshire, and at Duns, in neighbouring Berwickshire. Each game is studied separately in the case studies that follow.

But before then, it is instructive to assess the Border tradition as a whole, and to examine how a sporting sub-culture developed in this particular region, with a shared sense of history and a common style of play.

As historians such as John Burnett have amply demonstrated (*see* Links), sporting activity is intimately woven into the wider culture of Lowland Scotland, with handba' being only one of many games played in the region since the medieval period. These included curling, caich (another form of handball played by individuals against a wall), bowls, archery, and of course golf.

Moreover, annual gatherings of the St Ronan's Society at Innerleithen in the 1820s and 1830s can be seen as the seeds of later Victorian Highland Games and athletics meetings. The Scots were not only keen sportsmen. They were great innovators and codifiers.

But in earlier centuries they were also warriors, and had to be in an area blighted by bloody incursions from across the border. In that context, festival football served to celebrate young men's strength and guile, and to relive previous victories. Several towns claim that their games originated with the heads of slain Englishmen being used as footballs.

Football could also provide a smokescreen. As Sir Robert Carey recalled in his memoirs, published in 1625, a great meeting of Scotch riders at Kelso, held ostensibly for the purpose of 'playing at football', was in reality a chance to plan raids against the English.

But while in later, peaceable years more rational forms of recreation were enjoyed by the aristocracy and gentry – and by the mid 19th century by the burgeoning professional classes – for the average working man, his spare time limited and his holidays few, festival football provided a rare outlet, and one which evolved its own, quite distinct sub-culture.

One of the factors that led to this shared set of characteristics is that, unlike in the rest of Britain, it has long been the practice in the Borders for ba' men to play in other towns and villages. Even in winter, the distances involved were short enough to make this a common practice.

This interaction had two main consequences.

Firstly, it led to agreement on the scheduling of games, so that now, ironically, there is no full game on the traditional day of Fastern's E'en.

Even the coffee shops take a break for handba', as here in Jedburgh.

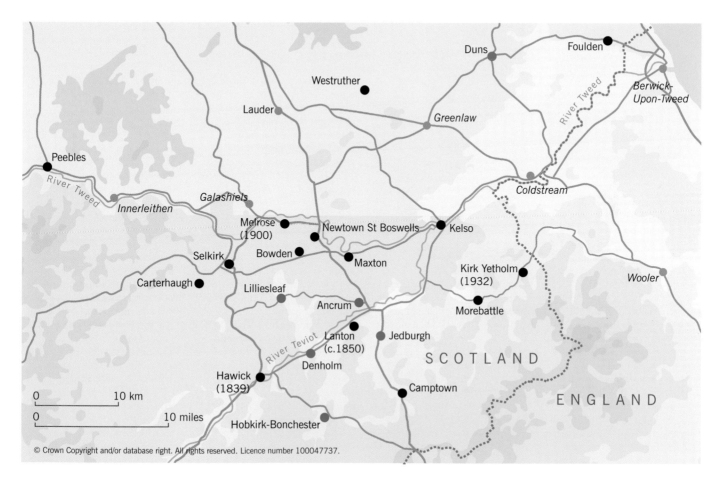

© Crown Copyright and/or database right. All rights reserved. Licence number 100047737.

Secondly, although no rules were ever written down, the gradual merging of ideas led to the same process of standardisation that occured in English football strongholds such as London and Sheffield in the mid 19th century.

One element of that process was a shift from football to handball. As the *Hawick Advertiser* noted in March 1856, 'Hobkirk ba' was anciently a foot one, the contest was held on Mackside Moor, but about the middle of the 17th century a hand ba' was adopted, and the play was transferred to the haughs of the Rule.'

(The haughs of the Rule were the low lying lands in the valley of the River Rule, or Rule Water as it is known locally.)

One explanation for this change is that handball caused less damage than football, and was therefore adopted as a means of appeasing local businesses and property owners. In Hawick these interests combined to ban the ba' game outright in 1780.

However this shift did not occur overnight, but at different times in different places, spread over several decades, either side of 1800. Moreover, some games

remained as football until their final demise.

Nor did the change rule out kicking altogether, though as will be seen, it plays very little part in those games that survive.

Cock-fights and bonfires
As discussed in Chapter Three, ball games were only one element of the nation's annual Shrovetide festive rituals.

Following the Restoration in 1660 the English custom of staging cock fights on the morning of ball games also took root in the Borders. »

Shown in green are those locations where games of handba' are still played annually in the region. Those in black are where now-defunct games have been recorded at one time or another, although no doubt there were several more for which no records survive. Where known, the date of the last game played is added in brackets. The special place of Carterhaugh in Scottish football history is explained on page 104. Locations marked in brown are other towns with strong sporting links.

▲ This ball from **Hobkirk** is a typical Border ba', crudely stitched, but extremely tough and durable.

Saddler **William Rae** (*right*) showed how such ba's are made in his **Denholm** workshop in 1983.

Each ball has a case made from four panels, often of saddle leather, stitched together with an opening at the top. Through this hole Rae inserted a stuffing made from sphagnum moss, collected locally and compacted tightly before the final stitches were added.

Only occasionally do such balls split, or, as sometimes occurs, they might be deliberately cut.

For example in 1857 the *Hawick Advertiser* reported on a match played at St. Boswell's on March 12, between local residents and the men of Maxton, against those of Ancrum, Bowden and Newtown.

With the score at 3-3 and darkness having set in before the seventh and final ba' could be hailed, the ball was instead sliced in two so that the prize money could be shared.

At **Jedburgh** there were agreed places for the cutting of ba's, close to the hailing points. These were the Goose Pool at the Townfoot Bridge for the Doonies (where witches were once drowned) and a stretch of river beyond the Abbey Cauld for the Uppies. A cut ba' was worth half a hailed ba'.

» Writing in 1824 in his history of Hawick, Robert Wilson noted that during the previous century this 'savage amusement' had been particularly popular on Candlemas Day amongst schoolboys, who were encouraged by their masters to supply the requisite cocks.

Cock-fighting was similarly part of Fastern's E'en festivities at the grammar school in Selkirk. As described by T Craig-Brown in *The History of Selkirkshire*, published in 1886, the boy whose bird had triumphed in the morning's cock-fight would be proclaimed 'king'.

This king would then have to supply a ball (perhaps from his winnings) and station himself at the town's Haining Gate, while other boys assembled at the West Port. On hearing a signal, the king would then hare off towards Howden Haugh, a mile or so off, in an attempt to hurl the ball over a burn and into the Haugh before his pursuers could catch up.

If he failed 'the royal honours obtained at cock-fighting were considerably dimmed'.

At Westruther the 'king' of the cock fight was similarly expected to supply the ball for the afternoon's sport.

By the end of the 18th century the link between cock fighting and ball games appears to have died out, while cock fighting itself was banned in 1849.

But the tradition whereby a 'king' provided a ball for play amongst his fellow pupils carried on in a quite different form in the 19th century. At both Jedburgh and Kelso the king was the boy who provided the most liberal offering to the Rector on Candlemas. This dubious practice of literally selling the honour was halted at Jedburgh in 1884.

In Hawick, another ritual which pitted rival groups of boys against each other involved the construction of bonfires, apparently in memory of how the town had been torched by the English in the 16th century.

Each side, consisting of boys and apprentices from the east and west sides of Hawick, formed themselves into regiments, with drums, standards and halberds, and even took up swords, clubs and stones to protect their accumulated stacks.

'These periodical quarrels,' wrote Robert Wilson, 'wherein one half of the inhabitants were mustered in predatory and fighting order against the other, had the most mischievous consequences, and made a complete separation of the people into two hostile tribes.'

(Similar battles were enacted on the Orkney Islands, where in Kirkwall rival factions of Uppies and Doonies contested a pole, set in the middle of a bonfire, while Stromness boys fought over a tree trunk, *see page 31*.)

Eventually, in around 1800, the Hawick magistrates prevailed, as they had done in suppressing the ball game two decades earlier, and the battle of the bonfires was halted, according to Wilson, 'without a murmur'.

Partly, he surmised, this was owing to 'the steady operation of education, or intellectual culture.'

Deprived of both their ba' game and their bonfires, Hawick's ball men travelled to other games in the region, especially to Hobkirk and Denholm. Thus, over time, the various Border practices melded.

The teams

Each of the four surviving ba' games in Roxburghshire is contested between teams calling themselves Uppies and Doonies. »

▶ A key feature of Scottish border handba' is **smuggling**.

Far from being frowned upon, it is considered a great skill.

In Kirkwall, the ball is itself the prize. In Sedgefield, people touch it for luck. At St. Columb it is thought to have magical properties. But in the Borders, the ball is never more potent an object than when it is invisible; when only one man knows where it actually is, and all the others are left guessing, their hands and fingers probing into the depths of the scrum with increased frustration and desperation.

There are two stages to this dark art. First the player must secrete the ball somewhere on his person, which explains why so many ba' players wear such bulky coats or jackets (though the cold weather is, of course, also a factor). Some players have even been known to sew flaps into their coats to provide yet more discrete hiding places.

To hide the ba' most effectively in the confines of a tightly packed scrum, a player must swap it from one hand to the other, leaving one hand in place, as if grasping it still, while subtly withdrawing the other so that the ba' may be transferred to its hiding place.

Often players act alone. Others depend on teamwork within the scrum, making it harder for the opposition to locate the ball. Because of this it is common for experienced rugby players, of whom there are many in the region, to be stalwarts of handba'. In modern terms one might say they possess transferable skills.

But it can take years to find out whom to trust. Best of all is the man who makes a promise, and keeps it, to share the prize should a hailing result from the smuggle.

The second stage of a smuggle is also largely dependent on deception, for somehow the player must extract himself from the scrum without arousing suspicion. No easy feat, for inevitably a man in possession of a hidden ball acts differently. His heart beats faster. Like Frodo in *The Lord of the Rings*, he senses this precious object glowing on his person, attracting unwelcome attention.

Experienced hands can detect this nervousness in others, like poker players picking up a tell.

One common ploy is to withdraw casually from play for an apparently mundane reason. To smoke a cigarette, for example, or to take a drink or a toilet break. The more often a player does this the less likely others will be to notice, or react, on the one occasion when he really does have the ball.

Of course the more players involved, the easier it is for smugglers to prosper. Where there are fewer bodies in the scrum, and fewer spectators (who may equally be players taking time out), immense guile is required to carry off the manoeuvre without inviting a challenge.

If successful, a smuggle may lead to an almost instant hail, either by the smuggler himself, or by a swift pass to a faster runner, usually a younger man.

But equally, as it often takes those left on the ground some time to realise that the ball has disappeared, the smuggler might bide his time, wait until the coast is clear, and all the while enjoy the spectacle of watching others battle for that which is his; doing nothing, and yet being the most important player in the game.

Or the smuggler might hide the ball, behind a wall or in a hedge perhaps, and retrieve it later, sometimes hours later, to hail it unopposed and unseen.

Every so often a man will stand up from the pile of bodies and others, sensing danger, will frisk him like a police suspect (as above at **Hobkirk**). Sometimes a mass frisking takes place, and the frisker himself is then frisked. If the ball is found, the man caught in possession must restart play by throwing the ball up in the air, above his head, for all to contest.

▲ On a wintry field in **Lilliesleaf** in 1991, an age old Borders custom is observed, as the boy who hailed the ball returns it to the ball's donor, Margaret Wilson, who hands over a £5 prize for his success.

The sums may vary between a symbolic few pence, up to perhaps £20. Or the hailer might receive beer tokens instead. For his part, the hailer is expected to buy a round or share the cash amongst those who helped him score.

Donors may be local businesses or organisations, or couples celebrating a recent wedding or an anniversary. Also common are donations from Scots or their descendants living overseas. In 1910 one Walter Graham sent a ba' from Chicago to Hawick with a generous gift of 15s. More usual at this time were prizes of 5s or 10s.

Another tradition is for the donor to hang their decorated ball in their front window in the days before the game. Shown on the right is another ball from the Lilliesleaf game in 1991. Its ribbon and small rosettes indicate that the donors wed during the preceding year.

For the 1856 game in Hawick each ball was named in honour of a hero of the Crimean War. The 'Sir Colin Campbell' ball was described as 'surrounded with a large quantity of ribbons of the usual colour, and suspended from a ring of artificial flowers wrought in the form of a crown, which was encircled by a wreath of evergreens, dotted with oranges'.

» The fifth game, in Duns, has the married men of the town playing against the bachelors.

This division – once common in Northumberland (in Alnwick, for example) and, indeed, in games all over Britain (*see page 24*) – was also seen at Morebattle and at Kirk Yetholm, where before games the ball was taken door to door so that women and children could gave it a kick for luck in return for a small donation. (In both these villages football remained the main form of game until their demise, which in Kirk Yetholm occured in 1932.)

In other locations local players were simply pitted against visitors. For example at Lanton the locals played against men from Jedburgh until about 1850, and thereafter against visiting players from Jedburgh, Camptown, Newtown St Boswell's and Melrose.

At Hawick and Melrose the teams varied, sometimes being divided by geography into East and West (as were the rival bonfire factions), sometimes splitting into married v. unmarried.

When Hawick's game was revived in 1842 it was as handba'. At Melrose it remained as football, and in 1879 was played between members of the newly formed rugby club versus the rest. The town council finally banned the game in 1900 under pressure from local tradesmen. Those who turned out the following year were arrested and fined.

However occasional ball games have been played in Melrose since, in keeping with another Borders tradition whereby in addition to Shrovetide, an extra ba' might also be played for after a wedding, regardless of the time of year.

In the past this tradition was strongest in Melrose and in the nearby town of Newtown St Boswell's. A more recent example was after the marriage of the Melrose and Scotland rugby player, Craig Chalmers, in 1989.

Another Scottish custom pertaining to marriage is recorded in the late 18th century, in which a horse race would be run to the happy couple's new home, with the winner receiving a prize, such as a bottle of whisky, from the groom's mother. Such races were called brooses.

Even today there remains a strong Borders tradition whereby married couples or those celebrating anniversaries will donate balls (*see left*).

Hawick Ba'

Of all the extinct games in the Scottish Borders, we know most about Hawick, mainly from the highly detailed newspaper reports that faithfully appeared every year.

Known best for its knitwear and hosiery makers, Hawick is the region's largest town, located on the banks of the River Teviot.

As previously mentioned, the town's Fastern's E'en game was suppressed in 1780 and revived in 1842, when it was moved to the Monday after Fastern's E'en. In later years it was switched to the previous Monday. A second game, for the youth of the town – known locally as the callants – was played on the preceding Saturday.

As had been the case during the 18th century, when the battle of the bonfires raged in the town, the players were divided between those who lived on the west and east sides of the Slitrig Water, which flows into the River Teviot in the centre of the town.

Certainly water played a significant role at Hawick, as shown opposite, in common with so many other festival games.   »

▲ Water play in **Hawick**, at one of the last games staged, during the 1930s. One man (*in the centre*) appears to have stripped down to his underclothes in the mêlée.

A report from the *Hawick Monthly Advertiser* of April 1 1854 provides a flavour of the wanton abandon that seemed to attend the Hawick ba':

'There swashed about most furiously, like a shoal of insane alligators, the ablution apparently – in some instances at least – not altogether unnecessary.

'Yet it appeared afterwards that the purifying effect of this wholesale baptism was only external, for the afternoon's sport was speedily followed by a night's drinking and riot – quite an ordinary finish to such work.'

Reporting on the callants' game in 1882, the *Hawick Express* noted, 'The banks of the river were crowded with onlookers, who, notwithstanding the drenching rain, seemed to enjoy the sport immensely. Indeed the drenching on land was so complete, that many, feeling that they would be no worse, entered the water and took part in the game.'

Twenty years later no-one entered the water. But that was because the Teviot had frozen over, requiring most of the play to take place on the ice.

Remarkably, given this accent on water play and the time of year, there seem to have been few accidents, and, according to one report in 1902, 'only one or two cases of drowning', despite many narrow escapes. The same report stated that West Enders hailed in what was called Coble Pool, while the East Enders hailed under the railway bridge.

The West Enders had a favourite taunt for their rivals, who, they claimed, had a tendency to over-indulge at the festive table.

Wassla waiter wuns the day
Eassla waiter canna play
For eatin' sodden dumplin's

'Sodden' in this context meant doughy. 'Waiter' meant water.

The report on the right is reproduced from the *Hawick Express* of March 1 1934.

*Then strip lads and to it, though sharp
  be the weather,
And if, by mischance, you should
  happen to fall,
There are worse things in life than a
  tumble on heather,
And life is itself but a game at foot-ball.*

from *Lifting the Banner of the House of
Buccleuch, at the great Foot-Ball match
on Carterhaugh*
Sir Walter Scott, 1815

▲ The notion that English public schools pioneered the staging of football matches between representative teams is now largely discredited. This etching, by James Stephanoff, depicts a grand gathering of some 2,000 spectators and players at **Carterhaugh**, just west of Selkirk, on December 4 1815, staged in honour of the victory at Waterloo.

Although not exactly a game of Uppies and Doonies as played in the streets and fields, it shared several characteristics.

The Duke of Buccleuch threw up the ball to start the game, while the two teams, representing Town and Country, were backed by the Earl of Home and the writer Walter Scott (whose 14 year old son is seen carrying the Duke's banner).

Home's players – shepherds and estate workers from the hills and valleys of the Yarrow, Ettrick, Teviot and Tweed – wore sprigs of heather.

Scott's team consisted of men from Selkirk, Hawick and Gala, each of whom wore a sprig of fir. The goals, one of which was Ettrick Water, were around a mile apart.

Hawick men were prominent in the early action, which lasted some ninety minutes and ended with the first hail, it is thought, by a Selkirk mason called Robert Hall.

For the next ba' the Gala men switched sides. There was (and remains) some friction between Hawick and Selkirk on one side, and Gala on the other. Perhaps the latter could not face the prospect of glory going to their rivals.

In any case, after a three hour struggle Yarrow men hailed next. But by then the light had faded, rivals had started throwing stones at each other and many a man had been ducked in the water. Rather than play a third ba', the match was therefore declared a draw.

Scott's love of football is still commemorated today, at a festival staged in Selkirk (see *opposite*).

>> There appears to be no one single reason why Hawick handba' did not reappear after the Second World War. Unlike in Chester-le-Street – that other major game which ceased in 1932 – there was no official ban, and nor, despite the predominance of play in the river, were there any drownings, at least not in the final years.

Rather, as reported in the *Hawick Express* in 1934, there seemed to be 'a marked lack of enthusiasm' during a period when, as locals put it, 'times is a bit severe'.

Nevertheless, its passing was a blow to the handba' community, which now turned to Jedburgh as its main point of focus.

Lilliesleaf and Selkirk
For all that the Scottish Borders handba' tradition derives from Fastern's E'en, the small village of Lilliesleaf, seven miles north of Hawick, on the Ale Water, is the only location where handba' now takes place on the day itself.

However, this is not a full game as described in the following chapters, but a re-enactment staged amongst pupils at the local primary school.

Until around the First World War the Lilliesleaf game was much like all the others in the region. It was contested between local men and visiting millworkers from Selkirk. Legend has it that, such was the rivalry between these two factions, the game was referred to as 'the Battle of Waterloo'.

But since the 1920s play has been confined largely to school children, split into the Easties and Westies (as in Hawick) and carefully supervised by adults.

Only when they get older may they try out the real thing, starting with the callants' game at Jedburgh.

Child's play at Lilliesleaf between the wars. Play then extended over a mile, where once it was nearer two. Today, three fields are used, with hedgelines around 250 yards apart serving as hailing points. Villagers celebrating anniversaries, teachers and the minister put up balls, with £5 as a prize. At Bog Park in Selkirk (*left*) children played with a handba' when the Scott festival began in 2000, but now use a rugby ball. The goals at each end are painted barrels.

In December a similar re-enactment is staged as part of the annual 'Scott's Selkirk' festival, inaugurated in 2000.

During this weekend many in town revert to early 19th century costumes, with actors chosen to play both Sir Walter Scott (once sheriff there) and his friend James Hogg, both of whom figured prominently in the great game at Carterhaugh in 1815 (*see opposite*).

Two games were staged in the Selkirk festival's early years. But the adult version soon fizzled out when the rugby and football clubs refused to release players in the middle of the season. It has therefore since been left to junior members of the rugby club to re-enact the game on the Sunday morning (*as seen above*).

Shrovetide

11. Hobkirk, Roxburghshire

Uppies and Doonies on a quiet country lane in the hamlet of Hobkirk. Play lasts around three hours, but these days seldom involves more than 30 players. In its heyday during the 19th century, when the field numbered hundreds, the game could extend over a considerable expanse of open country, with various hailing points, or goals, located in the estates of local lairds.

Hobkirk, originally Hopekirk, is a rural parish eight miles from Hawick. The parish runs north to south along the valley of Rulewater and is eleven miles long but only one and a half miles wide at its narrowest point.

In terms of population, other than Ancrum (*see page 120*) Hobkirk is the smallest community left in Britain still staging a game of *Uppies and Downies*.

Handba' is of course the game in question, contested between the two main settlements in the parish. Uppie territory is south of the church in Hobkirk. A mile north up the valley – Doon in handba' terms – lies Bonchester Bridge, once a small cluster of homes that in the past half century has outgrown Hobkirk.

For this reason Hobkirk's handba' is also known locally as the Bonchester game.

The game starts on a stretch of road by the Hobkirk parish church, but ends up in the evening with drinks at the Horse and Hounds in Bonchester Bridge.

Until the mid 17th century, it is thought, when the game was still essentially footba', it was played on Mackside Moor, to the east of the river, between workers from the two estates of Abbotrule and Wolfelee, which lay on either side of the Moor.

Thereafter the game moved to the haughs of the Rule, that is the low lying grounds in the river valley, where the first parish church was built in the 1690s.

One unusual characteristic of the Hobkirk game was the sheer number of goals – six were cited in a commentary published in 1922 (*see page 108*) – spread across an area measuring as large as nine square miles of open country. Only the Cornish hurling game at St Columb surpassed this in scale.

With their intimate knowledge of the terrain, local shepherds thus enjoyed a real advantage over their counterparts down in the village.

But why such a large expanse of play?

One thought is that local landowners each decided to offer prizes to the worker who hailed at a point within his own estate.

As there were several such patrons so there were several hailing points; as many as three for the Uppies and four for the Doonies. (The role of pubs in the Haxey Hood game is similar.)

Among the landowners offering these incentives were the Elliots and the Turnbulls. Another prominent patron was Walter Scott who, as a young man, turned out to cheer on the Uppies from his grey horse in the late 1700s. (Scott's love of Border traditions and of football in particular is evidenced on page 104.)

Hobkirk's game was played during these years not on Fastern's E'en itself (Shrove Tuesday) but on the preceding Monday.

Apparently the custom at this time was for a 'certain lithe dalesman' to climb up onto the church roof in the early hours of the morning and tug the bell rope in order to alert villagers of the impending sport. The same custom was also noted at Jedburgh in 1704.

Hobkirk's game would start at noon with a ball thrown over the church roof – then a lower, more modest one, thatched in heather – into the churchyard beyond.

Despite the parish's relatively small population, recorded as 760 in 1801, Hobkirk ba' was a much grander occasion than it is today, partly as a result of the suppression of nearby Hawick's own ba' game in 1780.

Consequently, on June 9 1803 the Hobkirk heritors, or landowners, gathered to consider 'the pernicious effects of a vast number of people assembling from this and other parishes for the idle purpose of playing at Ball'.

They resolved upon two courses of action. Firstly, the schoolmaster was ordered 'to lay an absolute prohibition upon his scholars from producing any Balls to be played on that day and from going up on the church and ringing the bell, and to inform their parents that they shall be prosecuted at law for their children offending...'

Secondly, the Heritors pledged themselves 'to prevent their own servants from coming to Hobkirk... for the purpose of playing at Ball.'

But their resolve did not last, perhaps because in the same year many men volunteered for military service to counter the mounting threat of an invasion by Napoleon. In such circumstances how could they deny their menfolk such simple and robust pleasures?

The authorities were tested again in 1823 when heavy snow prevented the arrival at the Ba' of many of the local shepherds, who played for the Uppies. The shepherds claimed the game should have been postponed and turned up at the church to play the following Monday. For this impertinence they were each fined by the Justice of the Peace, James Elliot of Woollee (Wolfelee).

In 1842 Hawick's own game was revived, to be played on the Monday following Fastern E'en. This allowed Hawick boys to continue their participation in Hobkirk's game, traditionally held seven days earlier.

Around 1850, the Hobkirk game achieved its highest renown when four brothers from Hawthornside, playing for the Doonies – James, Robert, John and William Stewart – became so dominant with their speed and stamina that two further Doonie goals were added, at Drythropple and Abbotrule, to make the contest less predictable.

A report of the Hobkirk game of 1856, published in the *Hawick Advertiser* of March 1 that year, captures some of the atmosphere of this period. 'On Monday se'ennight... there was a large muster of our stalwart borderers – the Taylors, the Turnbulls, the Olivers, the Wallaces, the Douglasses, the Smiths, and a host of other septs (clans), who displayed their ancient courage, strength and intrepidity.'

The hails, it was reported, were at Hobsburn Foot and Harriet (later Harwood) Mill.

'As the day was fine there was a splendid turn out of the fair sex, who animated the contending parties by their shouts of applause and anxious smiling faces.'

On that occasion the Doonies were assisted by the Callants, or youths from Hawick, 'led by the indoubtable Ormiston'.

But they would not return, for the date of the Hawick game was subsequently moved to the same day as the Hobkirk ba' (that is, the Monday before Fastern's E'en). Instead, those Hawick lads who wished to find a game on the Monday after Fastern E'en had to travel to Denholm, whose own players, meanwhile, turned out for the Doonies at Hobkirk. »

▲ Between five and ten balls are usually played at **Hobkirk**, some, such as these two offered in 2006, wrapped in ribbons to mark a wedding or the anniversary of a couple in the parish.

Delightful tradition though it is, however, players soon find these ribbons a hindrance, and it may be only a matter of minutes before they stop to tear them off.

After a ball is hailed it is returned so that the scorer can claim his prize, typically £20. The ball can then be re-used in following years, and patched up if necessary.

Few balls are ever lost. But if there is a shortage on the day, alternatives, such as a cricket ball, might be pressed into service.

As is the Borders tradition, the balls consist of four panels of leather, roughly sewn, and filled with a stuffing of moss.

▶ Reports of the Hobkirk ba' are rare, but at least **seven hailing points** are known to have been used. Six of these, as described by George Watson in 1922 (*see Links*) were houses. Local memory has it that in order to hail, the ba' had to be touched against the back of the kitchen hearth.

The **Uppie** goals were as follows:

Harwoodmill, on an estate bought by the Elliots in 1637.

Highend Farm, on the hill to the west of the church. In the first half of the 18th century, Robert Douglas ran a public house there.

Wolfelee, home of various branches of the Elliot family until 1912, in the foot of the valley. The original house featured in Sir Walter Scott's 1818 novel *The Heart of Midlothian*, as Wolfcrag Castle. A later house, built in 1825, was destroyed by fire in 1977, but its stable block survived and has within its walls a stone reckoned to be the hailing point. This bears the inscription 'Teak Tent A Time, Ere Time Be Tent', loosely meaning 'time waits for no man'.

The **Doonie** goals were at:

Hobsburn Foot in Bonchester Bridge, where the stream runs into Rulewater, behind the Horse and Hounds.

Hawthornside (pronounced Hathernside), on the Hawick road. This estate was sold to John Elliot in 1562. Several generations of Turnbulls later lived there.

Drythropple, recently restored but originally built in 1815 by George Cleghorn, who refused to let his stonemasons drink any alcohol. Thus they nicknamed the house Drythropple, meaning 'dry throat'.

Abbotrule, a parish in its own right until 1777, with a church and mansion. Only the stable block survives, now housing kennels for the local hunt.

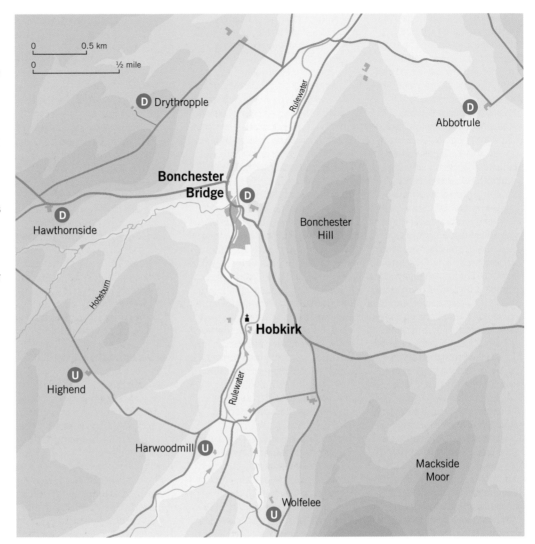

>> This was quite some network – a real community of sportsmen.

Although not stated overtly, the lack of the Hawick contingent appears to have had a positive effect on the atmosphere at Hobkirk. As a report of the 1857 game in the *Hawick Advertiser* noted, 'there was an absence of the usual quarrelling and swearing which too frequently prevail on these occasions, owing, it is presumed, to the non-attendance of whisky-dealers – there not being a single tent on the ground.'

Moving into the early 20th century, Hobkirk continued to attract around a hundred players. In the 1930s these numbers were bolstered by millworkers employed at the North British Rayon Company in Jedburgh, at least until its closure in 1956.

There was also at this time in Hobkirk a separate callants', or boys' ba', held in the morning.

One death has been attributed to the Hobkirk ba'. In 1783 William Telfer, a shepherd known for his strength as a player, went into Rulewater after a ball and later succumbed to hypothermia.

The game today

As explained on page 112, the scheduling of handba' games in the Scottish Borders is a complex matter. But Hobkirk and Bonchester always provide the opening game of the eight day season. Usually this takes place on the day before Shrove Tuesday, or Fastern's E'en. But it can also be the Monday following. Any intending participant or spectator is therefore advised to check the up-to-date calendar available on the *Played in Britain* website.

There is no precise start time, but usually around 4.00pm people start to appear as if from nowhere,

like gunfighters in a Western, only wearing fluorescent jackets instead of long coats.

Once there are enough players (double figures will suffice), the first ba' is thrown up from the wall of the churchyard into the middle of the road, where in an instant the first scrum will form.

In the past, when numbers were greater and the goals were spread across a wider expanse of country, play would often extend beyond the road. In those days participants were as much orienteers as ball players, requiring a thorough knowledge of the terrain, and plenty of stamina, especially as the valley slopes steeply upwards on both sides.

Nowadays, however, most of the action takes place along a >>

◀ No need for boarding up windows or stopping the traffic at **Hobkirk** once the ba' game begins.

As can be seen from this action in 2006, rugged outdoor gear and winter wear is the favoured mode of dress, partly to stave off the cold, partly to withstand the stresses and strains of scrimmaging on a tarmac surface, but also to make it easier to smuggle the ball.

Flourescent clothing is a further bonus for the final hour or so of play, which is invariably conducted in darkness.

Fortunately the main road between Bonchester Bridge and Hawick is away to the west, so traffic is extremely light on this stretch of road.

But as can be imagined, for any passer-by unfamiliar with local customs, the sight of a handful of grown men lying in a scrum on this quiet country lane can be just cause for bewilderment. Has there been an accident? Or has someone lost a contact lens?

But when the play gets caught up in a narrower part of the lane, the players have no choice but to break off and let a vehicle pass. The man in possession must then, by convention, throw the ball up in the air above his head, and hope to regain possession for the next passage of play. Some, as a result, have become adept at barely letting it leave their grasp.

>> 200 yard stretch of the road, by the church (the churchyard itself being deemed out of bounds).

But once the ball is 'away' – having been thrown, passed or smuggled out to a runner and sent clear, either towards Bonchester Bridge, or southwards in the direction of Forkins – it is considered to have been hailed, and the next ba' is thrown up.

In effect, therefore, there are no longer any specific hailing points, but points on the road beyond which no-one challenges the player in possession.

Were there more players to mark effectively, the play could extend further to the old goals. But most players among the usual turnout of around 30 individuals seem to prefer the warmth of the ruck to the cold of the open road, and are content to allow younger legs to sprint into the distance.

Occasionally a pursuit is successful, resulting in a smaller ruck away from the church. A ball may go into the fields or down to the river, to be contested by a breakaway group, who will later return and join in with the next, or a later ba'.

As in all Scottish Border games, smuggling is a key feature at Hobkirk, particularly as darkness descends and it becomes increasingly difficult to spot someone hiding the ball in their clothing. The last balls of the day are therefore usually hailed more quickly than the first.

Finally, around 7.00pm it is time to walk back to the Horse and Hounds in Bonchester Bridge, to share out the prizes, drink health all round and warm up after the afternoon's wintry exertions.

There are, after all, three more games still to look forward to in the Border handba' season.

The future

Hobkirk's game has little to threaten it directly, being played away from any major settlements and on a relatively quiet road. Only a few cottages in the immediate vicinity of the church are ever vulnerable to damage, and then it is mainly their fences that suffer.

Of far greater concern is the paucity of new players entering the fray, and the absence of a boys' game to help nurture the next generation. However, as long as its band of brothers wishes to dedicate one afternoon a year to the sociable traditions of Fastern's E'en handba', this most rural of games surely has a future.

Before the Industrial Revolution, such scenes as the one above, in February 2006, would have been commonplace all over the British countryside. Games were closely tied to a way of life that has now disappeared, with agricultural estates and the patronage of squires and aristocrats at the centre. The parish of Hobkirk provides us with an important reminder of this past, its ba' game earthy, charming and at times extremely bracing.

Shrovetide

12. Jedburgh, Roxburghshire

'Nobody runs the ba'. It's a labour of love – a real enjoyment,' Jedburgh veteran Billy Gillies told the *Southern Reporter* in March 2007. 'There's no organisation. If you organise it, it becomes something different. It's the old men that keep the ba' alive because it's them that pass on the tradition each year to the young folk. Every year they say it's better than the last, and this year it was really brilliant.'

Following Hobkirk, the second game to take place on the calendar of Scottish Borders' handba' occurs at Jedburgh, or 'Jethart' as it is known locally.

Since the cessation of the Hawick ba' in 1939, Jedburgh is, with a population of around 4,000, the largest Border town where a festival game survives.

Straddling Jed Water, ten miles north east of Hawick, it is also an ideal setting to enjoy the classic Uppies and Doonies experience.

Two games are played, one for boys, another for all-comers, amid a streetscape dotted by many a fine historic building.

The two goals are only a few hundred yards apart, plus there are several narrow closes into which players may sneak away. Just as importantly, Jedburgh has plenty of establishments where followers of the game may seek refreshment.

Traditionally the Callants' Ba' – the boys' game – was played on Candlemas Day, February 2, while the adults played on Fastern's E'en itself (Shrove Tuesday). In 1971, however, both were switched to the Thursday after Fastern's

E'en, to coincide with the town's half-day closing. Not only did this allow more people to join in, it also saved local shops and businesses the expense of having to board up their windows twice.

But confusingly, even to many locals, the match day can be put back to the following Thursday; that is, nine days after Fastern's E'en. The reason for this rescheduling is a traditional verse:

First comes Candlemas
Then the new moon;
And the first Tuesday after
Is Fastern's E'en.

There are years when Fastern's E'en is especially early, so that the

first new moon after Candlemas is later than Fastern's E'en. Also, there may be a new moon on Fastern's E'en itself. So, in order to comply with the verse that means putting back the matches to the Thursday after.

(Would-be spectators without access to a lunar calendar are therefore advised to check the updated calendar of games available on the *Played in Britain* website beforehand.)

Strictly, in those years when the game is put back to the following week it cannot be considered a Shrovetide festivity, as it falls within Lent. As the Reverend Rupert King wrote in the *Jedburgh Gazette* in 1948, 'It is not that

Action from the Market Place in Jedburgh c. 1910, with a view down Canongate and the boarded up windows of WM Henderson's Abbey Temperance Hotel and Hood's ironmongers' shop behind.

we think it wrong to indulge in athletic pursuits or a moderate amount of innocent entertainment in Lent. What we do feel is that, in view of the widespread observance of Lent all over the world, we should not call a celebration held in Lent a Fastern's E'en celebration.'

Reverend King blamed this situation on 'diehard lovers of the misguided rhyme'. But if there is one aspect of the Jedburgh ba' which characterises it most of all, it is the sheer persistence of those 'diehard lovers' of tradition.

For some 300 years the game has weathered every single challenge to its survival.

One of the legends surrounding the Jedburgh game concerns its origins. As told in William Hone's *Every-Day Book*, published in 1826, the story goes that in 1548 (cited as 1549 in other accounts) a party of Scots (some say assisted by the French) recaptured Ferniehirst Castle – the family seat of Sir John Kerr, a mile south of Jedburgh – during the occupation of the area by the Earl of Hertford's army.

During the battle one of the Scots recognised an English officer who had raped his daughter, and promptly decapitated him. The officer's head was then used as a ball in a celebratory kickabout. »

▲ Provost Young and Town Clerk Thomas Colledge-Halliburton (holding the ball) prepare to get the **Callants' Ba'** under way on Candlemas Day, 1916. Most organised sport was suspended during the First World War, but not the Callants' Ba'.

As a boy, in 1884, Colledge-Halliburton had been the last boy to be crowned Candlemas King of the Grammar School, an honour blatantly sold by the Rector to whoever made the largest Candlemas offering. His sister was appointed Queen.

One of the King's duties was to throw up the ball to start the

Callants' Ba', a role Colledge-Halliburton carried on for 57 years until his death in 1941.

In 1933 Colledge-Halliburton was a founder member of the Callants' Club, which has organised the handba', unofficially, ever since. Since 1947 Jedburgh has also staged an annual Callants' Festival, at the end of June, to commemorate the bravery of local axe-wielding youths in their battles against the English, and particularly the celebrated Redeswire Raid of 1575. Two weeks of ceremonial horse rides to key locations in the area, including Ferniehirst Castle, culminate with a Callants' Ball.

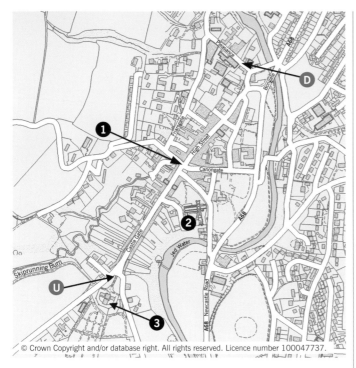

▲ Ba' games in **Jedburgh** take place within a relatively small area of the town centre, an area dotted with historic buildings, such as the bastel (fortified) house where Mary Queen of Scots lived in 1566, and the ruins of Jedburgh Abbey. There are also narrow closes and yards in which play can get bottled up, such as Atholl Court, by the library.

But most of the play takes place along the town's relatively straight thoroughfare, with only a sharp turn into the Pleasance, location of the Doonie goal. As a result most balls are hailed after an escape up Castlegate or down the High Street. A player will smuggle the ball out of the ruck before sprinting away or throwing the ball to a swifter colleague.

The Uppies have the distinct disadvantage of playing against a slope which rises from the town to their goal. Castlegate, the shortest route, is particularly steep.

A short dash down Canongate from the start in the Market Place can bring the Jed Water into play. For the canny smuggler a riverside path offers a secluded means of progress, plus numerous places for 'planking' (or hiding) a ball until later. A stone wall next to the path is perfect for this.

Play in the river itself is, however, no longer the regular feature it used to be. But there was a time when both teams had an agreed piece of water where they could shred the ball with a knife in order to cut the game short.

U   Uppies goal
D   Doonies goal
1   Market Place
2   Jedburgh Abbey
3   Castle Jail

The legend – which mirrors similar tales in footballing history, such as the use of a Danish warrior's skull as a ball on the Roodee at Chester – goes further by suggesting that the streamers traditionally attached to Border balls represent the slain Englishman's flowing mane.

One of the earliest references known to any of the surviving games of *Uppies and Downies* is found in Jedburgh, from 1704.

That year, the Town Council 'having duly considered that the tossing and throwing up of the football at Fasternse'en within the streets of the burgh has many times tended to the great prejudice of the inhabitants, calls now at once for a discharge thereof, there having been sometymes both old and young near lost their lives thereby. Therefore, they, with all unanimous advice and consent, do discharge the gayme now and in all time coming.'

Of course this had no effect, and two years later the Fleshers' Corporation had to fine some of its members who had been found 'guiltie at the rastling at the football'. The word 'rastling' implies a tight struggle.

The transition from kicking to handling, a common feature of Border games, is reckoned to have occurred in Jedburgh around 1800, a direct result of the town's development and the resultant increase in damage to property.

In 1849, as cholera swept through the town, the authorities tried once again to impose a ban. The game, so they argued, was 'detrimental to the peace, order and good government of the Burgh... Every kind of business is thereby interrupted, and the shopkeepers find it necessary to shutter their shops for protection.'

A ban was duly proclaimed in the streets, but once again ignored. As a result, several players the following year were arrested and fined 10 shillings by the Burgh Court.

But still the 'diehard lovers of tradition' refused to capitulate and took their case to the High Court in Edinburgh. At the subsequent hearing on June 2 1849, the Jedburgh magistrates confidently stated that 'as the game sought to be prohibited was eminently dangerous in the time of pestilence, and was moreover an obstruction to the business of the town, they had power to prevent the same by giving due warning, and to punish a violation of their order.'

Remarkably, the Lord Justice Clerk did not agree. Instead, he reminded the magistrates that they did not have the power to act as Commissioners of Police, by prosecuting players under a law which had never been adopted in the burgh.

Thus on a legal technicality the ban was overturned. But more than that, the judge concluded by declaring, 'I, for one, should hesitate to encourage the abolition of an old and customary game, which from time immemorial has been enjoyed by the community.'

The history of mass football is littered with condemnations from figures in authority. Yet here in Edinburgh was a respected judge showing his support for the people's game.

It was a rare and wonderful moment, and one celebrated in Jedburgh that same evening by an impromptu procession through the town, headed by a ribbon-bedecked handball borne high at the top of a pole and accompanied by drums and pipes. »

▲ February 2007 and Craig Smail, with Billy Gillies, prepares to throw up the ba'. As custom demands they stand on the site of the old **Mercat Cross** in **Market Place**, marked by a metal plaque since the cross was moved to make way for road improvements.

Two hundred yards to the north, on the Pleasance, another slab of steel on the road marks the vicinity of the Doonie goal, albeit unintentionally. The standard issue inspection cover (*above right*), leads down to **Skiprunning Burn** now hidden below in a culvert. The original Doonie goal was the bridge here, on the old Edinburgh road. The hailing point ran all the way to the confluence with Jed Water, a few yards to the north. The ball is rolled across the road for a hail.

Water goals also feature at Kirkwall, Workington and Ashbourne, but none are as compromised by modernity as this.

In contrast, the Uppie goal is formed by the railings outside the **Castle Jail** at the top of the town. Set on the site of a 12th century castle, the prison was built in 1820 on the reforming principles of John Howard, and is now a museum.

▲ 'To many of us,' remembered Provost Ella Blair in 1942, 'the morning of **the second of February** was the most exciting and the merriest of our school years.

'I can still see the clothes' basket running over with oranges, and the bakers' boards heaped with glistening cookies; and I can also picture the handing over of the ball to the 'Queen', to whom, with her maids of honour, was given the privilege of arranging for the decoration of the ball with ribbons.

'The ball was then presented to the 'king', who was carried shoulder-high by his school-mates up the High Street to the Mercat Cross, where he performed his high office of throwing up the ball.'

Although the Callants' Ba' (as seen above in 1975) now takes place later in the month, the right of young Jedburghers to play ba' on Candlemas Day is still asserted, in a ceremony in which the head boy of the grammar school throws up a token ball at noon on February 2.

Alas oranges and cookies are no longer handed out, and nor do callants receive the weak toddy that was customarily served up in the 19th century.

》 A great bonfire finished off the memorable night of rejoicing.

Since 1849, whenever there has been any threat to the games, the Edinburgh judge's words have always been aired, almost word for word, by friends of the ba'.

And to some effect. Neither of the two World Wars, nor the heavy snowfalls of 1947 and 1963 – when balls were hidden deep in the drifts – have stopped the game from taking place.

Even in 2001, when the police barricaded the High Street during the height of a foot and mouth outbreak – the same contagion that put a halt to the Ashbourne game – two token ba's were played following a full and frank exchange (in which the judgement of 1849 was of course once again freely quoted).

In fact only once has the game not been played at all in Jedburgh, and that was in 1901, when the day of the game coincided with the funeral of Queen Victoria. But even on that occasion a ba', painted black and decked with black ribbons, was ceremonially thrown up in the Market Place by a gathering of local dignitaries, as a way of showing respect, yet continuing the tradition.

The two sides

In Jedburgh allegiance to either side is traditionally decided, not by residence but by place of birth.

Those born south of the site of the Market Cross are Uppies (also known in the 19th century as Toonheiders). Those born to the north are Doonies (or formerly Toonfitters).

Nowadays, of course, home births are rare, with the majority of Jedburghers being delivered at the Borders General Hospital in Melrose, some ten miles north. 》

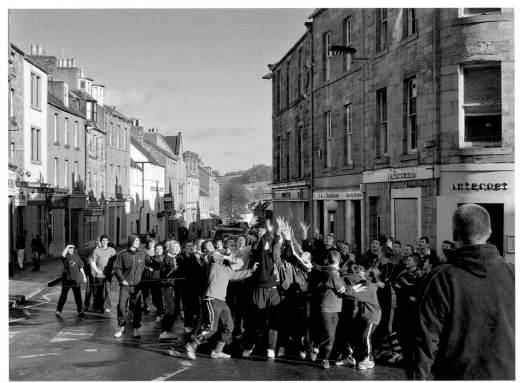

Action from the Callants' Ba' in 2005 and 2007. Some 50-60 boys currently participate, always under the watchful eye of a senior, who might at any time haul a lad out from the scrum to be reminded to 'play the ba' and not the man'. Compared with the senior game, running and tackling play a much greater part than smuggling.

Jedburgh balls are made from leather, stuffed with moss or hay, in true Border style. Once in play, honour attaches to the removal of the ribbons, which may on occasion be presented to a girl in the crowd (of whom there are many in attendance). After being hailed, the ba' is handed back to the donor in return for prize money or beer tokens. A ball may thus be used several times, even in games elsewhere in the region.

>> As the most direct route back from the hospital to Jedburgh enters Doonie territory first, it is not unknown for Uppie families to skirt the town so that they enter via the Castle Jail instead.

The game

Handba' in Jedburgh conforms to all the usual characteristics of games in the Scottish Borders, but with an impressive number of ba's being played courtesy of local businesses, organisations and individuals celebrating marriages or anniversaries.

Donors or their representatives throw up their balls from the site of the Mercat Cross, starting with the first callants' ba' at noon.

Occasionally the boys might still be playing by the time the men's first ba' is thrown up at 2.00pm, which can add extra amusement should the two scrums find themselves in close proximity.

Once the boys have finished, the braver amongst them will muck in with the men, to be joined, as the afternoon wears on, by those who have just finished work or who have arrived from elsewhere. Bonchester men, for example, always play Up at Jedburgh.

The direction of a throw-up is dependent on where the previous ba' was hailed. If Up, players stand on the Castle side of the starting point and the ba' is thrown in that direction. If Doon, the positions are reversed. This is the only Borders game where this happens.

Smuggling is very much a feature of the Jedburgh game. With a fair number of players and spectators, it is much easier to slip out of the ruck unnoticed than at, for example, Hobkirk.

Such is the level of support for handba' in Jedburgh that play can continue for several hours.

Despite the protective boarding, this window of a Jedburgh florist's was cracked not by a ball but a ruck of players during the Callants' Ba' of 2007. Such breakages are rare in games of Uppies and Downies, and are usually covered either by insurance or by funds raised by players and supporters. Meanwhile action from adults' game in 2007 *(left)* shows Uppies and Doonies challenging for the ba' from the throwing-up point in the Market Place. As several balls a day are usually contested players get plenty of opportunities to hone their skills.

The future

The decision to move both boys' and men's games to Thursdays, when the shops close early – and thereby save the expense of boarding up properties twice a year – shows how pragmatism can be the saviour of tradition.

Most of all, the careful nurturing of Jedburgh's youth players looks likely to maintain an unbroken sequence that goes back to at least 1704, whereas the games in Hawick, Melrose and Selkirk are now but distant memories.

This continuity is not only commendable. It is vital for the welfare of the region's other games. There is many a Jethart Callant who will one day end up in a ruck in Hobkirk, Denholm, or our next port of call, Ancrum.

Shrovetide

13. Ancrum, Roxburghshire

Holding out against the tide – Ancrum resident Iain Heard plays his part in February 2006. Without his efforts there would be no ba' in the village any more.

That handba' at Ancrum – a small village four miles north of Jedburgh – has, within living memory, been resurrected after years of laying dormant, should serve as an inspiration to members of those many other Border communities where this once common tradition has died out.

After over 150 years of recorded play, and probably much longer in practice, the Ancrum game appeared to have finally expired in 1974 through lack of support.

But one young Ancrum resident, Iain Heard, was a great enthusiast for handba' and resolved not to let the old custom fade.

Thus in February 1975, on the traditional Ancrum matchday – the Wednesday after Fastern's E'en – Heard carried a ball from the ancient Market Cross on the village green to both the Uppie and Doonie hailing points, determined that the continuity of tradition should not be broken.

With extraordinary doggedness, Heard repeated this symbolic gesture every year for the next 22 years. Sometimes other villagers would accompany him on his poignant trail. Often he performed the ritual alone. But never once did he let go of the hope that one day Ancrum handba' might be revived.

Finally, in February 1997 Heard made the breakthrough for which he had longed. By moving the day of the game from the Wednesday to the Saturday – so that it fell between the nearby games held in Jedburgh and Denholm – he was, that year, able to muster enough individuals from the village, from Jedburgh and other Borders communities, to form two teams of Uppies and Doonies.

At last, after nearly a quarter of a century's gap, handba' was back.

Not only that, but again, thanks to Heard's dedication, Ancrum was in subsequent years able to revive its boys' game too, putting the village well and truly back on the local calendar.

Of Ancrum handba' prior to 1974, as might be expected of such a small village, little is known.

As at Jedburgh, local legend has it that the game originated with 16th century Scottish warriors using the severed heads of English soldiers as footballs, a tale which relates to the most momentous event in local history, the battle of Ancrum Moor, fought just north of the present village on February 12 1545.

In the weeks before the battle the English, led by the ruthless Sir Ralph Evers and Sir Bryan Layton, had laid waste to the two original settlements in the area, Over Ancrum (which lay north of the Ale Water) and Nether Ancrum (where the modern village lies).

But in a bloody battle in which both Evers and Layton, and some 800 others were slain, the Scots wreaked their revenge.

One of the dominant families in the locality, incidentally, was the Kerrs. Robert Kerr, brother of Sir John – liberator of Ferniehirst Castle in 1549 (*see page 113*) – built the original Ancrum House in 1558 (since rebuilt in 1874 and demolished in 1970). The family also owned much of Hobkirk parish, with a seat there at Abbotrule. Thus there are three locations closely linked with this illustrious Borders family where surviving Uppies and Doonies' games take place.

Pit up the ba', pit up the ba', they're waitin' in the square
They're braw lads and bonnie lasses, half o' Ancrums there.
There's twa three Jethart lads aboot but no saw many ava,
Sure they'll be landin' here in droves come on pit up the ba'.

A 1934 poem on the popularity of the Ancrum ba' game amongst men from neighbouring Jedburgh (or Jethart)

These links were mirrored by the movement of players between the various Border games.

Writing of his Ancrum parish in 1837 in *The New Statistical Account of Scotland* (published in 1845) the Rev John Pator noted, 'There is no species of amusement to which the parishioners are especially attached, with the exception of the game of "ball", which is played only on one particular day of the year, in the month of February, the young men of one district being pitched against those of another.

'Similar games are also held annually, and about the same season, in some of the neighbouring parishes, and seem to create a considerable interest amongst the young men of the district.'

Indeed it was 'young men of the district' and especially from Jedburgh who helped to ensure the survival of the Ancrum game from that era until 1974. As that great chronicler of Scottish handba', George Watson (*see Links*) wrote in *The Border Magazine* in February 1925, 'the opponents of the (Ancrum) villagers are the Jedburghers, who, despite their exertions on the previous day, walk over to wage battle with them.'

The 1934 poem reproduced opposite makes the same point.

But on which side would these outsiders play?

The sides

Strictly speaking, amongst the Ancrum-based players, the issue of who plays Up or Doon should be determined by one's place of birth or residency, either north or south of the Market Cross.

But in practice, prior to 1974 Ancrum people tended to combine to play Up, while those from Jedburgh played Doon.

Since the Ancrum revival in 1997, compromise and pragmatism on the day have been required to create two roughly equal camps.

As a result, unlike in Kirkwall or Workington, where there is a fierce loyalty to one's roots as either an Uppie or a Downie, in Ancrum local men who should be Doonies may find themselves playing Up with players from Jedburgh, against a Doonie team composed entirely of men from Hobkirk and Denholm. Equally, there may be amongst those Hobkirk men playing Doon at Ancrum a few who, in their own villages, are lifelong Uppies.

To add to the mix, individuals who were opponents at Hobkirk on the previous Monday, or at Jedburgh on the preceding Thursday, may well be allies at Ancrum on the following Saturday.

With no-one quite sure which way each individual is playing, unpredictability is therefore increased and the Ancrum game zips merrily along.

The game today

Ancrum handba' now takes place on the first Saturday after the first Monday after the New Moon following Candlemas. Simple really.

As mentioned earlier, that means it falls on the Saturday between the Hobkirk and Denholm games (both of which are staged on Mondays).

The boys' games start at around 11.00am, with the men's beginning in the early afternoon.

Balls are thrown up from the steps of the Market Cross, and the last one is usually away by late afternoon. The day normally finishes around 7.00pm, with food and drink at the Cross Keys pub or

at the headquarters of the Ancrum Bowling Club.

The future

Iain Heard's efforts and the sensitive manner in which the boys' games are conducted offer a lesson to every local community.

Lost games can be revived, and the younger generation can be coaxed back, for the benefit of both the community and the individuals involved.

But there can never be any room for complacency. Having lost their ba' game once, the people of Ancrum will have to rally round for many years to come before the future is assured.

A box full of ba's at Ancrum in February 2007. Tradition requires that all couples married in the parish during the previous twelve months should provide a ball for the annual game. But the village is hardly large, with a population of only around 390 people, so nowadays local businesses or those celebrating special events or anniversaries chip in with their own cash and other prizes (often beer) to keep up the number of ba's. The ball designs, it may be seen, are typical for the Scottish Borders area; that is, a simple leather case tightly stitched around a stuffing of moss or rags, and bedecked in ribbons.

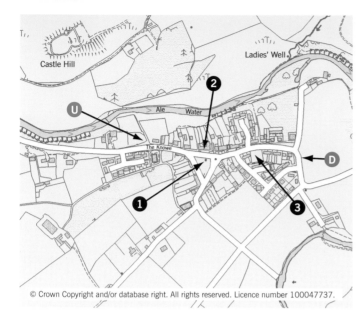

▲ The name **Ancrum** derives from Alne, an early name for Ale Water, and 'crumb' meaning a crook or bend. Part of this bend can be seen above, enclosing the village to the north and east, before the Ale Water meets up with the Teviot, half a mile south of the village.

Most of the play today takes place on or close to The Knowe, the main street running along the north side of the triangular green.

In a corner of the green is the surviving stump of a 13th century market cross, from which the balls are thrown up.

Occasionally balls are taken via fields to the south or via Ale Water. But water plays much less of a role than in the past. In 1909, for example, after the the home team (playing Up) had won 5-0, the *Hawick News* lamented that 'it is many years indeed since there was so much play in the river.'

U **Uppies goal** (*see below right*)
D **Doonies goal** (*see above right*)

1 **Market Cross**
2 **Cross Keys pub**
3 **Ancrum Bowling Club**

▲ Young Doonies demonstrate the **two methods of hailing** allowed in the Ancrum game, touching or throwing. This latter, highly unusual method, which was also permitted at the now extinct handba' game at nearby St Boswell's, echoes the method of scoring used in the Roman game harpastum, when players propelled the ball over a base line at the back of the court.

(Dere Street, a Roman road, runs to the north east of the village.)

The **Doonies** goal (*above*) is a length of dry-stone wall at the bottom of the village. The road splits into a track, to the left, and continues on southwards to the right. Balls can be hailed on both sides of the junction.

The **Uppies** goal is a corner of the wall of the Manse, around an ivy covered door which has a lintel commemorating the residency of the dissenting minister John Livingston, from 1648 until his banishment in 1662 by the Privy Council, for refusing to swear allegiance to the newly restored King Charles II. The present Manse was built in 1751 and extended in 1833.

▲ Iain Heard, in the fluorescent jacket (*top left*) prepares the young Uppies and Doonies of Ancrum for the ba' game in March 2006.

Since the revival of the Ancrum ba' in 1997 the **boys' games**, with girls joining in on occasions, have, uniquely, been divided into specific age groups, in order to give every player as much feel for the game as possible.

The under 8s play a ball or two, the under 12s and under 16s perhaps three or four each.

At this age the players go to ground far less than the men, and are encouraged to play the ball, not the man. Smuggling is not encouraged.

But the children appear just as dogged as their elders – several of whom will be family members

– and will fight over a ball right to the point at which it is hailed.

Clearly this focus on juvenile participation and enjoyment is a deliberate response to the 23 year gap when no games took place, losing a whole generation in the process, and placing an even greater onus on the adults of today, both from Ancrum and elsewhere, to lead by example.

Terrain and tactics

As these photographs from the 2006 game show, the terrain around Ancrum offers a variety of conditions, from open fields, the village green, the churchyard and woodland, to the hard tarmac of The Knowe and the gravel paths of the village's housing estate.

Only the bowling green and all private gardens are considered out of bounds.

The steep banks of Ale Water behind the Cross Keys pub offer an alternative route to goal, but are perhaps too challenging to be taken by anyone without detailed local knowledge.

Ancrum blends two of the three characteristic features of the Border ball games to perfect effect. Periods of grappling for possession on the ground are ended by a swift break, when the ball is often thrown.

Skilled interpassing over just a few yards also occurs.

With sufficient players, say 15-20 a side, the Ancrum game can readily achieve equilibrium.

Enough men lie off to mark any breaks and, after a solid tackle on the escaper, build a new pile of bodies on the ground.

This way it can take as long as an hour to hail one ball, although the next might easily be away in a matter of seconds, if the first man in possession can throw it out to a speedy associate.

Unusually for a Borders game, smuggling is rather frowned upon in Ancrum. But, as illustrated right, from outside the Cross Keys pub, dummy runs can still happen.

The player in blue appears to hold something in his hand as he breaks from the pack, but once clear – perhaps after a team-mate has broken in another direction – he literally 'shows his hand'.

Shrovetide

14. Denholm, Roxburghshire

Denholm resident Beattie Watson prepares to throw up the first of seven ba's hailed at the 2007 game. As may be discerned from the choice of ribbons, the ball was donated by a couple, Jim and Rae Oliver, who had recently celebrated their golden wedding anniversary. (Indeed Beattie was Jim's best man.) The Olivers offered a prize of £25 for the hailer of their ba'.

Lying midway between Hawick and Jedburgh, Denholm stages the fourth and final game of the Scottish Borders' eight day handba' season, on the Monday following Ancrum.

Denholm is a village of some 500 inhabitants, built around an extensive Green. The River Teviot runs along the northern edge of the village. The busy A698 road, linking Hawick and Jedburgh, runs through the centre.

Both hailing points are along this road, although as shall become apparent, the action can extend to the fields rising up on the south side of the village.

As with Hobkirk and Ancrum, few early records of the Denholm game exist, other than references to the usual Border legend; that is, that the game originated with the use of an English invader's head as a football.

But we do know that Denholm has been an integral part of the Border handba' network since at least the mid 19th century, when reports mention men from Hawick arriving in the village to play. A report from the *Hawick Advertiser* in

February 1869 also adds that that year men from Denholm played at Hobkirk, for the Doonies.

Unusually for such a small village, three games have been played at Denholm in the past (although exact dates are unclear).

A boys' game was played on the first Friday after Fastern's E'en, followed by two on the following Monday. The first of these, starting at 9.00am, was an apprentices' ba' (a direct throwback to the widespread medieval custom of apprentices playing football on Shrove Tuesday). This was followed by the men's game in the afternoon.

Thus every age group could play a part, including, in 1886, even senior citizens. According to the *Hawick News*, one ball at Denholm that year was hailed by Mr R Amos, a joiner, 'who, having passed the

allotted three score and ten, 'twas quite proud of his feat'.

Reading the report, however, his age may not have been such a handicap since 'unlike the play at Hawick, taking to the water at Denholm is the exception'.

Today only the men's game is played, with most of the action taking place on or around the large central Green.

Although village greens of this ilk are common south of the border, Denholm's is significant in that, when first laid out in the 17th century it formed the centrepiece of what was effectively a new village, the previous hamlet having been destroyed by the English during the 1530s.

In this sense Denholm differs from the unplanned villages that are more characteristic of Roxburghshire (such as Ancrum).

The process began in 1664, when the laird, Sir Archibald Douglas, leased over eight acres of land around what would become the Green, to smallholders, for them to build cottages with small plots attached. But rather than keep the Green clear, the villagers turned it over to agricultural use, apparently resulting in a noisome agglomeration of pigsties, dung hills, peat stacks, henhouses, heaps of firewood, sawpits and muddy holes frequented by geese.

Hence in the 18th century the village gained a reputation as 'Dirty Denholm'.

In time the villagers grew more prosperous, not from their smallholdings but from cottage-based work as stocking weavers, supplying the hosiery manufacturers of Hawick.

Thus began moves to clear the Green, starting in 1835 when the laird at that time, James Douglas, allotted more land behind the houses to enable smallholders to relocate their animals, followed in 1862 by the granting of further land for husbandry at the Crofts and on the haughs by the Teviot.

Around the same time a Feuars Committee – that is, people paying the laird a feu (similar to a leasehold) for their properties – was set up to improve the Green.

A low wall was built on three sides, with railings erected to the south, while the north east corner was sectioned off as the Under Green (now called the Wee Green).

Other than in deep midwinter, the turf expanses of the larger Green were mainly let for grazing. At other times they hosted a regular calendar of twice-yearly fairs, bonfires in November (not for Guy Fawkes but according to a pagan tradition known as Bough of the Haughs), markets, »

▲ Measuring some 2.5 acres, **Denholm Green** is large enough for handba' players to roam freely without ever troubling the locals.

As can be seen in this view from 2006, the Green is dominated by a memorial, erected in 1861, to the scholar Dr John Leyden, who was born in a cottage (still extant) on the north side of the Green in 1775, and who worked closely with Walter Scott, collecting ballads from the Scottish Borders. Leyden died in Java at the age of just 36, after travels in India and Singapore.

Next to his monument lies a small stone ring, the base of Denholm's old Mercat Cross, where in previous centuries the ba' game would have started.

Balls are now thrown up a few yards from this point.

During the 19th century the Green was enclosed on one side by railings. According to the memoirs of a local resident, John Ramsay (born in 1885), during one game a player called Best, believed to have been an outsider, was fatally impaled on these railings.

They were eventually removed, not for reasons of safety, but to assist with the war effort in 1939.

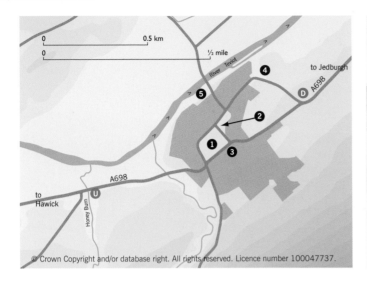

U Uppie goal (Honeyburn Bridge)
D Doonie goal ('the Gang')

1 Denholm Green
2 Wee Green
3 Fox and Hounds
4 Cemetery
5 The Quoiting Haugh

The quoiting haugh is a small stretch of the riverbank, previously used to stage wrestling bouts, and where quoits was played until the 1920s. It is now a public garden, but the old name has stuck. Information on the ancient game of quoits will appear in a future Played in Britain study, *Played at the Pub* (see *Links*).

▲ **Denholm** conforms with the pattern for many games of *Uppies and Downies* in that one goal is linked with water, and the other is on dry land. Thus the **Uppies'** hailing point is Honeyburn Bridge (*below right*), about half a mile from the Green. This is where the main A698, leading to Hawick, crosses the Honey Burn, close to where it joins the Teviot.

Unlike Ashbourne or Kirkwall, however, the Uppies need not enter the burn itself. Instead, they merely have to touch the ball against the side of the bridge.

Not so obvious is the exact location of the **Doonies'** goal, a matter on which not even regular players of the game appear to concur. What is agreed is that the hailing point is located somewhere on a stretch of the A698 known as 'the Gang', meaning 'the going' – as this is the point at which, just beyond a left turn off towards the cemetery, the road takes its leave of Denholm en route to Jedburgh, five miles to the east.

But which part of the Gang? Some say it is the line of a hedge that runs from the Gang down to the river. Others are not so sure, suggesting that there might have been other points used in the past.

Ironically, in order to reach the Doonie goal players have to run the last few yards uphill (*as above in 2005*), while the Uppie goal at Honeyburn Bridge is actually downhill from the village. This is because, although water play does not feature at Denholm, the flow of the Teviot, running west to east, dictates that Doonies play down river, as is the custom wherever *Uppies and Downies* play.

>> livestock sales, gatherings of the local fox hunt – there is a Fox and Hounds pub overlooking the Green – and of course, Shrovetide games of ba'.

But as the income from grazing fell, in 1920 the feuars were invited to buy out their leases and exert more control over the Green. As a result, in 1946 the village council determined that it should be set aside purely for recreation.

There have been only cosmetic changes since; the lowering of the boundary walls, the laying out of a playground and a pitch for cricket, football and rugby, and briefly, the provision of a putting green.

Fortunately, another proposal, to build a road across the Green in 1959 came to nothing, and in 1971 the Green's status was formally recognised when the historic centre of the village was designated as a Conservation Area.

The teams

Denholm tradition required that married men played Doon, while the unmarried ones, perhaps appropriately, played Up.

Reports from the 1920s suggest that each side usually numbered around 50 players, fewer than at Jedburgh, Ancrum or Hobkirk.

Yet today teams of around 10-20 each are more common.

Currently Men from Denholm play Up, while the Doonies, who have in the past consisted largely of players from Bonchester, are now supplemented by men from Jedburgh and Ancrum.

As can be imagined, this has not made it easy for the Uppies and so players will often change sides to even things up.

The game

Denholm games start from a point on the Green, just to the east of the Leyden monument. But because play takes place on a Monday, a working day, the first ball is not thrown up until 4.00pm.

This means that play continues until after dusk, and also that, because the A698 forms the most direct route to both goals, the players have to contend with a regular stream of homeward-bound traffic.

Remarkably, considering there are two sharp bends in the road on either side of the Green, this hardly seems to dampen the action, although (*as shown below right*), constant vigilance is vital.

But most of the scrimmaging – the key element in all Border games – takes place on the Green, until, sooner or later, a runner will emerge and get away and onto the road.

With the onset of darkness, the players' smuggling prowess offers more likelihood of the last couple of balls being hailed promptly, so that it usually takes around three to four hours to hail six or seven ba's, before the game concludes around 7.30pm.

This being the final match of the year, the players – several of whom might well have played in all four Border games – then retire to one of the village pubs to soothe their aching limbs and swap stories of smuggles and hails.

And so as darkness descends on Denholm Green, the handba' season in Roxburghshire ends.

The future

Some of the keenest exponents of the dark arts of handba' come from Denholm. But as there is no boys' game to supply the next generation, the future prospects seem as fraught as in Hobkirk.

Both villages have stayed true to their history by maintaining their traditional Monday schedule. Yet this makes it harder to attract a quorum of players until after normal work hours.

It is therefore to Ancrum, with its various youth games, and to Jedburgh, where the Callants receive every encouragement, that the veterans of Denholm must now look to ensure a steady supply of bodies on their own home turf.

A break from Denholm Green in 2004 (*top*) sends the players scuttling off to Main Street, where the action appears not to threaten the butcher's windows. Boarding up is not a feature in the village, but bunching up on the pavement, as shown above in 2006, is all too necessary to make way for the regular stream of traffic passing through.

▲ With its wide open expanse and its soft, pliant turf, **Denholm Green** provides one of the least injurious places for a novice to enter a mass football fray, certainly after the hard roads of Jedburgh and Ancrum.

In the distance is the Free Church, built in 1844, with the Wee Green just visible to its left.

Seen here in 2006 is a rare example of where, as a result of a double bluff, two scrums have formed. Arms push through narrow cracks into the centre of both piles, where fingers feel for the ball.

This questing for possession, the very essence of handba', offers little excitement for spectators, but is often accompanied by lively banter. Indeed for older, heavier players, who are unlikely to get away with a ba', it is the best part of the game.

Standing watchfully on the far right is Ronnie Notman, well known for his uncanny ability to grasp the ball unseen and, just as importantly, act is if he has not got it at all. His much-repaired coat is famous among the handba' fraternity. It is entirely possible that he or any one of the men standing outside the scrum has the ball, and is simply playing it cool.

▲ As daylight fades over **Denholm**, an Uppie from Hobkirk (*right*) sets off in pursuit of a distant Doonie, in a lonely game of cat and mouse.

For all that games of *Uppies and Downies* depend on mass participation, occasionally, as here in 2006, they end up in a private head-to-head duel.

But this was no simple chase.

After some feinting and doubling back, the player in possession ran right up the far hill and headed to the left, overshooting the Doonie goal by several hundred yards.

On reaching the cover of a wood, he then hid the ball in a tree.

Undeterred, his tracker kept up the pursuit and, guessing that the ball had been secreted, spent several fruitless minutes hunting for it.

Meanwhile, the Doonie returned to Denholm Green, where another ball had already been thrown up, biding his time until he could safely return, retrieve the ball and proceed to the hailing point.

So the pursuer can never be sure. Does the other man really have the ba'? Has it already been hidden? Stamina is one thing. But guile is a ba' man's greatest gift.

Shrovetide

15. Duns, Berwickshire

Their colours are the same – the red and black of Duns Rugby Football Club – but when it comes to the ba' game they play on rival sides; one player is married, the other a bachelor. The game as played today is a more compact version of the town's ancient handba', last played in 1886 and brought back to life in 1949.

Once the county town of Berwickshire, Duns lies only 25 miles to the north east of Jedburgh, yet its own version of *Uppies and Downies* differs in three key respects from all other Scottish Border games so far profiled.

Firstly, Duns – where the town motto, 'Duns Dings A' (Duns beats all) is thought to recall how local men scared off English soldiers in 1372 with rattles made of wood and dried skins – is the only location in Britain in which the centuries old tradition of dividing players into married and unmarried teams still persists.

Secondly, at Duns they play with a form of ball that is quite unique, resembling a small flat cushion.

Thirdly, since 1949 the Duns game has been staged not on its traditional date of Fastern's E'en, but during the town's summer Reivers' Week festival, on the Friday evening of the first full week in July. Again this makes it unique; the only British festival game to have shifted from the usual seasons associated with *Uppies and Downies*, namely Christmas, Shrovetide and Easter.

In every other respect, however, this is an archetypal Fastern's E'en game, and was played as such for at least 200 years.

Indeed two of the earliest references to festival football appear in the town's annals.

The first appeared in 1686, when one John Bayne complained, apparently unsuccessfully, to the bailie (or chief magistrate) of Duns, then to the sheriff, and finally to the Privy Council, of being roughly treated during that year's Shrovetide football match.

That the Duns bailie proved unsympathetic to Bayne appears ironic in view of a subsequent document dating from 1724, in which the incumbent bailie, John Gray, himself complains, this time to the Lord Justice General in Edinburgh, of being ill-treated by a shoemaker called William Home, and others, whom Gray accused of causing 'riots and tumults' on the occasion of the ba' game.

The complaint, which is held in the documents collection at Duns Castle and is reproduced on page 22, describes how, in an attempt to stop the game taking place,

Gray confiscated the drum that was traditionally used to muster ba' players. Angered by this, a mob stood outside his house, 'threatning and swearing revenge and mischief against him'. After completing their game, against Gray's orders, they returned to his house, some 2-300 strong, to try to seize the drum by force. Stones were thrown at his door and windows were smashed as the crowd swore that unless he gave up the drum they would destroy Gray and his family.

Not a pleasant affair, and far from the spirit of communal celebration that Shrovetide games were supposed to engender.

Depending how one interprets the text, either Home and his cohorts were an idle and malevolent mob, or they were simply acting as staunch defenders of an ancient but unwritten right to play football in the streets on Fastern's E'en.

Either way, the document leaves us in no doubt as to the frictions which football created between the forces of law and order and the perceived rights of the townsfolk.

*An' then the ba' men wi' their friens
Adjourn tae some ane o' the inns,
Where langsyne yarns the landlord spins
O' what he's dune an' seen;
An' when the noise and din has ceased
Then pork an' dumplins crown the feast
Washed doon wi' toddy o' the best
To wind up Fastern's E'en.*

Robert McLean Calder (1841–95)

The document also confirms that the game in question was indeed football, whereas by the mid 19th century handball appears to have taken its place.

No doubt, as at Jedburgh and other towns in Scotland, this was a response to growing urban development within Duns and the consequent need to reduce the level of damage caused by the kicking game.

A hint of this transition from football to handball appeared in the *Berwickshire News* in 1885, when a certain J McC recalled the game as it was staged in the 1830s. 'I remember my father being carried shoulder high round the Market Place, for kicking the "Ba".'

Did he mean that by then kicking was regarded as a rarity, or that his act was seen as a deliberate gesture of defiance against the authorities?

Whichever, it is clear that by the 1880s support for the ba' game was in decline, culminating in the last ever Fastern's E'en match played in Duns on March 16 1886. In fact this was a week after Shrove Tuesday, almost certainly because the town had been beset by an appalling winter, 'the most trying ever known' according to *The Berwickshire News*.

Snowbound for almost three months, the town, which had little industry and was still dependent on farming, had fallen deeply into debt, having borrowed £5,000 from the Caledonian Insurance Company and the Public Works Loan Commissioners. In such straitened circumstances, the loss of the ba' game was no doubt the least of the town's worries.

No game was staged in 1887, nor the year after, nor again until the modern era. Duns, it appeared, had joined the ranks of all the other Scottish towns where Shrovetide handba' had become a dim and distant memory.

The modern revival

As mentioned before, after a 62 year hiatus, handba' was revived in Duns, not on Fastern's E'en, but as part of a newly organised July festival called Reivers' Week.

Instituted by the Burgh Council, the festival mirrors those of several other Border towns (such as Jedburgh's Callants' Festival) in commemorating the area's long running battles against the English and sundry border raiders and cattle rustlers.

Various ceremonies take place, including the Riding of the Parish Bounds, to show that the area has remained free of encroachment. The week also sees the election of two local youths as Reiver (which literally means raider, or robber) and Reiver's Lass, and the crowning of a young girl, elected from local primary schools, as the 'Wynsome Mayde o' Dunse' (Dunse being a former spelling of the town's name).

The ba' game takes place on the Friday of the festival, and is an amalgam of ancient and modern practices, tied in with the rites of the festival.

Although it is regrettable that the game has thus been detached from its Shrovetide origins, there are advantages to the new schedule. Not least, the weather is likely to be more favourable in July and the town is already en fête.

Also, as the first ball is not thrown up in the Market Square until 6.00pm (compared with 1.00 or 2.00pm in the 19th century), more local residents, not to mention holidaymakers in this most scenic of destinations, are able to enjoy the spectacle.

▲ Prior to the game's demise in the 1880s, hailing in Duns was known as either **kirking** or **milling**.

Married players had to take the ball right into the parish kirk, which was kept open for that very purpose, and touch it against the pulpit, whereupon the bells were rung in celebration.

Seen above is the fourth structure to have served the parish, although as it was completed only in 1880 it is unlikely to have seen much action before the final game took place in 1886.

As the kirk stood only a hundred yards or so from the Market Square, where balls were thrown up, this gave the married men a distinct advantage.

Their unmarried opponents had much further to travel, their aim being one of several mills dotted around the town. Of these the nearest was the Clock Mill (called Cloack miln in John Gray's 1724 document), half a mile west from the Square. Because this was the most obvious target, however, the married men were able to defend it in numbers, placing the bachelors at a further disadvantage.

Otherwise they had to go further, to mills such as Langton, Putton and Manderston, all at least a mile distant from the Market Square.

Once arrived at any of these mills the unmarried players had to touch the ball against the hopper, at which point the miller would dust the scorer's hat and coat with flour. As Thomas Brown wrote in the journal of the *Berwickshire Naturalists Club* in 1834, 'Like the laurel wreaths of other regions, this marked them out for the gaze of their fellow townsmen.'

The miller would then provide the scorer and his colleagues with a traditional Shrovetide dish of pork and dumplings.

(Note that mills also act as goals at the Ashbourne game in Derbyshire, *see page 75*.)

▶ The Duns ba' has long benefitted from the patronage of the Hay family, resident at Duns Castle since 1696. This is a **subscription sheet** issued by William James Hay for the last ba' game to be played before its long hibernation, on March 16 1886 (the year it was delayed owing to adverse weather).

The money subscribed, totalling £2 19s 6d, was used to pay for the balls, prize money, and hospitality after the game.

But the fund raising did not stop there. Remember the drum in the story of John Gray in 1724?

On the Wednesday before Fastern's E'en, three men were chosen as 'Ba' Men' at a ceremony known as 'the shaping of the ba'.

It was their duty to solicit further donations around the town and its surrounds, accompanied by the drum and a fiddler (similar to the rounds still made by the boggins of the Haxey Hood, *see page 60*.)

In his letter to the *Berwickshire News* in February 1885, 'J McC' recalled, 'Many a time I have crossed over fields with the "Ba-men", as they did not keep by the roads on their way to the big houses.' Among them was old James Dewar, repeatedly playing a chant which went 'Never let the gree (prize) gang doon, for the gude o' oor toon.'

'The poor man was blind but the boys led and helped him over the dykes.'

To add further to the coffers, until around 1800 the honour of throwing up the first ball was auctioned in the churchyard on Fastern's E'en morning.

Men from various trades clubbed together to bid. According to Thomas Brown in the journal of *The Berwickshire Naturalists' Club* in 1834, the carters once paid the handsome sum of 15 shillings.

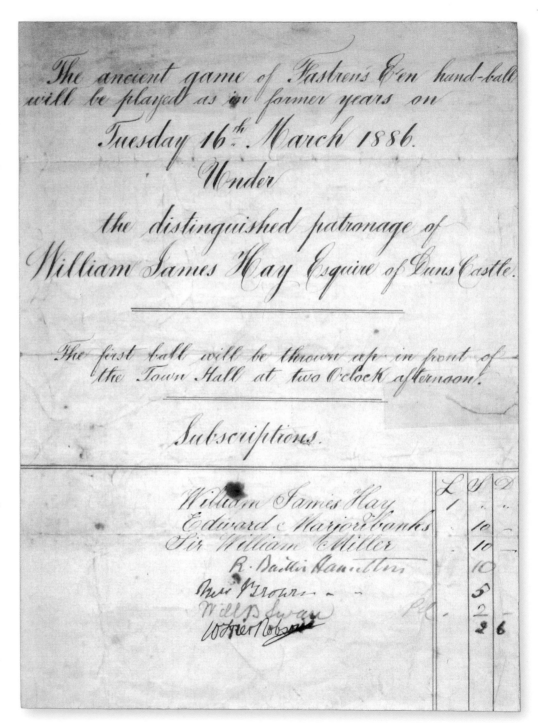

◄ Held at the museum office above Duns Library, these decorated ba's date from 1878, 1881, 1884 and 1885. Each bears the goat's head crest of the Hay family and the family motto, 'Spare Nought'.

Note that the balls are slightly flatter on two sides, like cheeses, and in common with those used in Roxburghshire, each measures approximately three inches in diameter (8cms) and appears to be stuffed with moss, hay or sawdust.

Each year four balls of this design were prepared, three for play, one spare. The first was painted **gold** and, by the mid 19th century, carried a reward for its hailer of 1s 6d (7.5p). The second, painted **silver**, was worth 1s (5p), and the third, painted **red and black**, sometimes with spots, was valued at 6d (2.5p). The fourth ball, according to some accounts, was presented to the subscriber whose post-match hospitality had been the most lavish, which invariably meant the Hay family.

The modern ba's (*left, not shown to scale*) are supplied by a Kelso saddler. Eight inches in diameter and about three inches deep, they are made from stitched leather with a loosely stuffed, white wool flock filling. But their colour coding is the same, and each carries only a symbolic value to their hailers of 15p, 10p and 5p (double the 19th century rate).

Reiver's Lass Lisa Fortune (*right*) displays the silver ball in July 2006, before throwing it up in the Market Square (*opposite top*). Each year's festival has a different colour scheme for the ribbons attached to the silver ball, and for shields displayed around the Market Square. The other balls carry red and black ribbons. After being hailed the ball is handed back to the thrower, to keep as a memento. Seen below is one of Lisa's predecessors in action, Hilda Nairn in July 1951. The first, golden ball is thrown up by the head of the Hay family, currently Alexander Hay, or his representative, while the third, red and black ball is delivered by the Wynsome Mayde.

Teams and terrain

With a population of 2,500, and without the network of visiting players that characterises the Roxburghshire scene, the Duns game is shorter in duration, and more compact than any other in Britain. The two teams, married and unmarried, usually consist of no more than 5-10 players each, while play is confined solely to the Market Square, with the two goals no more than 100 yards apart.

When the game was revived in 1949 barrels placed in two corners of the Square acted as the goals. Now, rather disappointingly, litter bins are used. As local wits put it, 'dumpers for goalposts'.

The married team aims for the bin outside the Post Office, near a passage leading to the kirk (*opposite, below centre*). The single men aim for the one standing by the corner of the White Swan pub (*opposite, below right*).

Also in the Square is the Mercat Cross (*opposite, below left*), the traditional starting point for so many games of *Uppies and Downies*. First erected on the north side of the square in 1792, it was removed in 1816, then relocated to Duns Park in 1897. Following a redesign of the Square in 1994 it was then returned, and now stands on the south side.

The game

In such a tight area and with so few players competing for each of the three ba's, the Duns game proceeds at a rapid pace, with none of the lengthy scrimmaging seen elsewhere in the Borders. In some respects it is similar to the handball played at the Olympics.

The ball is thrown from player to player with precision and frequently off-loaded in the tackle. A goal minder may be kept in the rear, but this leaves a small team lighter in numbers in the middle.

Order is kept by a referee (*seen opposite in a blue and green shirt*), and if a ball gets lodged somewhere or a window seems likely to break under pressure he can sound his whistle to signal a break.

But even with short breaks the game rarely lasts more than half an hour. If the third goal arrives too soon, one ball may be thrown up again to prolong the action.

After the match the evening concludes with the Reivers Ball.

The future

Although lacking the spectacle and broad canvas of some surviving games, the modern version of Duns ba' serves as an

intriguing model of how a mass street game may be adapted to modern circumstances. Rather than brute force, familiar concepts in modern sport, such as agility, speed, finding space and 'pass and move' play a much greater part.

The game's confinement to a small area, combined with its scheduling, also make it more manageable to stage, even if visitors from other *Uppies and Downies* games might well deem it to be a sanitised and emasculated shadow of the real thing.

For sure more could be done to restore some of that vitality; by encouraging greater numbers to participate, or by expanding the playing area and adopting further hailing points. Even if they no longer produce flour, all the former mills still exist, after all, where it could well be possible to revive the custom of dusting scorers in one form or another.

And yet surely the modern Duns game is better than no game at all,

As the saying goes in Duns: 'Never let the gree gang doon, For the gude o' oor toon.'

Civic pride and the ba' go hand in hand.

Shrovetide

16. Cornish hurling

On the edge of Bodmin Moor near the village of Minions are three Bronze Age stone circles known as the Hurlers. Writing in 1610, William Camden explained: 'the neighbouring inhabitants terme them Hurlers, as being by devout and godly error persuaded that they had been men sometime transformed into stones, for profaning the Lord's Day with hurling the ball.' In a similar vein the Merry Maidens, south of Penzance, were turned to stone for dancing on the Sabbath.

Among the many characteristics that make Cornwall so culturally distinct from the rest of England is the county's unique form of *Uppies and Downies*.

The name hurling is most commonly associated with the Gaelic game, played mainly in Ireland, in which teams of 15 a side play on a large pitch with two rugby-style goals, and a small ball, or *sliotar*, propelled by a stick called a *camán*.

Cornish hurling, however, although patently part of the wider Celtic tradition, is played without sticks and is more similar to the form of handba' found in the Scottish Borders (*see page 98*).

It also, uniquely, uses a small wooden ball, encased in silver.

Two forms of the Cornish game have co-existed and blended together: 'hurling to goals' and 'hurling to country'. In the former, the playing area and numbers are limited. The latter is a more expansive version. In both cases, the goals may be specific points or a boundary line.

Given that Cornish hurling is primarily a handling and throwing game, its connection with mass football might seem tenuous. Yet as shall become apparent, there are several important links. Not least, in common with several of its festival counterparts, Cornish hurling is strongly associated with Shrove Tuesday.

Today, only two games survive, at St Columb Major (*see page 142*) and St Ives (*page 150*). But before turning to them, in this chapter we focus on Cornish hurling's history, a history that has been well documented for many years.

Richard Carew's *Survey of Cornwall*, for example, published in 1602 (*see opposite*), reveals a complex game whose rules predate certain basic conventions now applicable to modern football codes, such as, a set number of players and two goals; no forward passing (as in rugby) and the use of goalkeepers (as in soccer).

Further elements are common to the Welsh game of Cnapan (such as players on horseback – *see page 24*) and to the Scottish form of handba' (the playing of games on wedding days and the use of gentlemen's houses as goals).

Carew's account is therefore of immense value to historians, not only of Cornish customs but of ball games generally.

To Carew's description we can also add that of John Norden.

In his *Speculi Britanniae pars* (completed by 1610), Norden describes two native Cornish sports, wrestling and hurling.

'The Cornish-men they are stronge, hardye and nymble, so are their exercises violent, two especially, Wrastling and Hurling, sharpe and seuere actiuities; and in neither of theis doth any Countrye exceede or equall them.

'The first is violent, but the seconde is daungerous: The firste is acted in two sortes, by Holdster (as they called it) and by the Coller; the seconde likewise two ways, as Hurling to goales, and Hurling to the Countrye.'

A further reference appears in the *Moderate Intelligencer* of May 4 1654. This reports a May Day hurling match having been staged in Hyde Park, London, for the enjoyment of Oliver Cromwell, Privy Councillors and 'divers eminent gentlemen.' »

This wonderfully detailed description of hurling, extracted from Richard Carew's *Survey of Cornwall,* published in 1602, is a seminal text for sporting historians, full of clues as to the origins of many of the rules applied in modern day football and rugby. In the final paragraph the word Crowner translates as Coroner.

Hurling taketh his denomination from throwing of the ball, and is of two sorts, in the East parts of Cornwall, to goales, and in the West, to the countrey.

For hurling to goales, there are 15. 20. or 30. players more or lesse, chosen out on each side, who strip themselues into their slightest apparell, and then ioyne hands in ranke one against another. Out of these ranks they match themselues by payres, one embracing another, & so passe away: euery of which couple, are specially to watch one another during the play.

After this, they pitch two bushes in the ground, some eight or ten foote asunder; and directly against them, ten or twelue score off, other twayne in like distance, which they terme their Goales. One of these is appoynted by lots, to the one side, and the other to his aduerse party. There is assigned for their gard, a couple of their best stopping Hurlers; the residue draw into the midst betweene both goales, where some indifferent person throweth vp a ball, the which whosoeuer can catch, and cary through his aduersaries goale, hath wonne the game. But therein consisteth one of Hercules his labours: for he that is once possessed of the ball, hath his contrary mate waiting at inches, and assaying to lay hold vpon him. The other thrusteth him in the breast, with his closed fist, to keepe him off; which they call Butting, and place in weldoing the same, no small poynt of manhood.

If hee escape the first, another taketh him in hand, and so a third, neyther is hee left, vntill hauing met (as the Frenchman sayes) Chausseura son pied, hee eyther touch the ground with some part of his bodie, in wrastling, or cry, Hold; which is the word of yeelding. Then must he cast the ball (named Dealing) to some one of his fellowes, who catching the same in his hand, maketh away withall as before; and if his hap or agility bee so good, as to shake off

or outrunne his counter-wayters, at the goale, hee findeth one or two fresh men, readie to receiue and keepe him off.

It is therefore a very disaduantageable match, or extraordinary accident, that leeseth many goales: howbeit, that side carryeth away best reputation, which giueth most falles in the hurling, keepeth the ball longest, and presseth his contrary neerest to their owne goale.

Sometimes one chosen person on eche party dealeth the ball.

The Hurlers are bound to the obseruation of many lawes, as, that they must hurle man to man, and not two set vpon one man at once: that the Hurler against the ball, must not but, nor hand-fast vnder girdle: that hee who hath the ball, must but onely in the others brest: that he must deale no Fore-ball, viz. he may not throw it to any of his mates, standing neerer the goale, then himselfe.

Lastly, in dealing the ball, if any of the other part can catch it flying between, or e're the other haue it fast, he thereby winneth the same to his side, which straightway of defendant becommeth assailant, as the other, of assailant falls to be defendant. The least breach of these lawes, the Hurlers take for a iust cause of going together by the eares, but with their fists onely; neither doth any among them seek reuenge for such wrongs or hurts, but at the like play againe. These hurling matches are mostly vsed at weddings, where commonly the ghests vndertake to encounter all commers.

The hurling to the Countrey, is more diffuse and confuse, as bound to few of these orders: Some two or more Gentlemen doe commonly make this match, appointing that on such a holyday, they will bring to such an indifferent place, two, three, or more parishes of the East or South quarter, to hurle against so many other, of the West or North. Their goales are either those

Gentlemens houses, or some townes or villages, three or foure miles asunder, of which either side maketh choice after the neernesse to their dwellings. When they meet, there is neyther comparing of numbers, nor matching of men: but a siluer ball is cast vp, and that company, which can catch, and cary it by force, or sleight, to their place assigned, gaineth the ball and victory. Whosoeuer getteth seizure of this ball, findeth himselfe generally pursued by the aduerse party; neither will they leaue, till (without all respects) he be layd flat on Gods dear earth: which fall once receiued, disableth him from any longer detayning the ball: hee therefore throwet the same (with like hazard of intercepting, as in the other hurling) to some one of his fellowes, fardest before him, who maketh away withall in like maner. Such as see where the ball is played, giue notice thereof to their mates, crying, Ware East, Ware West, &c. as the same is carried.

The Hurlers take their next way ouer hilles, dales, hedges, ditches; yea, and thorow bushes, briers, mires, plashes and riuers whatsoeuer; so as you shall sometimes see 20. or 30. lie tugging together in the water, scrambling and scratching for the ball.

A play (verily) both rude & rough, and yet such, as is not destitute of policies, in some sort resembling the feats of warre: for you shall haue companies layd out before, on the one side, to encounter them that come with the ball, and of the other party to succor them, in maner of a fore-ward. Againe, other troups lye houering on the sides, like wings, to helpe or stop their escape: and where the ball it selfe goeth, it resembleth the ioyning of the two mayne battels: the slowest footed who come lagge, supply the showe of a rere-ward: yea, there are horsemen placed also on either party (as it were in ambush) and ready to ride away with the ball, if they can catch it at aduantage. But they may not

so steale the palme: for gallop any one of them neuer so fast, yet he shall be surely met at some hedge corner, crosse-lane, bridge, or deep water, which (by casting the Countrie) they know he must needs touch at: and if his good fortune gard him not the better, hee is like to pay the price of his theft, with his owne and his horses ouerthrowe to the ground.

Sometimes, the whole company runneth with the ball, seuen or eight miles out of the direct way, which they should keepe. Sometimes a foote-man getting it by stealth, the better to scape vnespied, will carry the same quite backwards, and so, at last, get to the goale by a windlace: which once knowne to be wonne, all that side flocke thither with great iolity: and if the same bee a Gentlemans house, they giue him the ball for a Trophee, and the drinking out of his Beere to boote.

The ball in this play may bee compared to an infernall spirit: for whosoeuer catcheth it, fareth straightwayes like a madde man, struling and fighting with those that goe about to holde him: and no sooner is the ball gone from him, but hee resigneth this fury to the next recyuer, and himselfe becommeth peaceable as before.

I cannot well resolue, whether I should more commend this game for the manhood and exercise, or condemne it for the boysterousnes and harmes which it begetteth: for as on the one side it makes their bodies strong, hard, and nimble, and puts a courage into their hearts, to meet an enemie in the face: so on the other part, it is accompanied with many dangers, some of which do euer fall to the players share. For proofe whereof, when the hurling is ended, you shall see them retyring home, as from a pitched battaile, with bloody pates, bones broken, and out of ioynt, and such bruses as serue to shorten their daies; yet al is good play, & neuer Attourney nor Crowner troubled for the matter.

▲ Held at the **Penlee House Gallery and Museum, Penzance,** this magnificently battered silver hurling ball dates from 1704 and is one of two that was shown to the Natural History and Antiquarian Society of Penzance by Richard Edmonds in 1846. Both had been donated to Edmonds by Richard Pearce, whose ancestors from Kerris (just south of Penzance) had won them 'above a century ago' in the adjoining parish of Paul.

The ball measures 7cm in diameter and has the now barely discernible Cornish inscription: *Paul tux whek Gware Tek heb ate bux Henwis. 1704.* This meant 'Paul men – fair play is good play'.

The latter phrase was inscribed on most balls of the period. But why the silver case?

Originally, it is believed, hurling balls were made from plain wood, onto which silver coins were nailed to symbolise good luck and prosperity at Shrovetide.

Boys would collect the coins from local households and take them to the blacksmith to be hammered into shape. The fact that silver was, until the late 19th century, commonly extracted from Cornwall's many lead and tin mines, was therefore largely coincidental.

Clearly by the time this ball was made in 1704 the craftsmanship had advanced so that the wooden core was neatly encased in two silver hemispheres, riveted at the seams. Applewood was chosen because it rarely splits.

A ball such as this one would probably have been used on many different occasions, hence its battered appearance. However it is also known that to save money for more routine hurling matches, stones or even turnips were often used instead.

Today's silver balls (*see page 146*) are made from exactly the same materials.

≫ Two teams of Cornishmen competed, 50 per side, one set wearing red caps, the other white.

'The ball they played withal was silver, and designed for that party which did win the goal.'

(Cromwell, it should be noted, had been a keen footballer in his youth, albeit not with a silver ball.)

A similar exhibition match was played in London after the Restoration.

Back in Cornwall, games were staged both as annual showpieces and routinely throughout the year. So, for example, we learn from a churchwarden's notes that one William Trevarthen, buried at Camborne on August 13 1705, had three days earlier been 'disstroid to a hurling with Redruth men at the high dounes'.

But although hurling was indeed a dangerous game – in his *Tour Through the Whole Island of Great Britain* in the 1720s Daniel Defoe described it as being played by 'boors... brutish and furious' – Trevarthen appears to have been a rare fatality.

That said, by the mid 19th century the game appears to have been on the wane for some time.

In a paper entitled *On Some Ancient Customs in the Western extremity of Cornwall*, presented to the Natural History and Antiquarian Society of Penzance in 1846, Richard Edmonds, wrote that on the occasion of saints days 'the common athletic amusements... were formerly quoits, wrestling and hurling'.

Note his use of the word 'formerly'.

Regarding hurling, Edmonds added, 'about a century ago, two or more parishes contended against certain other parishes, each party having its own goal, which was either the mansion house of one of the leading gentlemen of the party, a parish church, or some other well known place. A ball about the size of a cricket ball, formed of cork or light wood and covered with silver, was hurled into the air midway between the goals. Both parties immediately rushed towards it, each striving to seize it and carry it to its own goal .

'In this contest, when any individual having possession of the ball, found himself overpowered or outrun by his opponents, he hurled it to one of his own side, if near enough; or, if not, into some pool, ditch, furze-brake, garden, house or other place of concealment, to prevent his adversaries from getting hold of it before his own company could arrive...'

Edmonds indicated that apart from the usual forms of hurling – that is, hurling to goals and hurling to country – the games as played at St Columb, St Ives and Helston belonged to 'another species'. From his description of this 'species', however (explained more fully in the following two chapters), it seems to have been more a hybrid of the two usual forms.

He then continued, 'A fourth description of hurling... is played annually at the parish feast of Germoe, seven miles from Penzance. There the hurlers, instead of forming two parties, act independently, every individual striving to catch the ball for himself, and whoever succeeds in lodging it thrice at the goal wins the game and obtains a prize.'

Apart from St Columb, St Ives and Helston, Edmonds concluded that hurling had otherwise died out throughout Cornwall.

Writing nearly two decades later in 1865, in his first collection of *Popular Romances of the West of England*, Robert Hunt reported that 'from the many accidents that usually attended (hurling), it is now scarcely ever practised,' whereas 'until a recent period' it had been played on Sunday afternoons in various parishes to the west of Penzance, 'sometimes between Burian and Sancreed, or against St Leven and Sennen, or the higher side of the parish played against the lower side.'

At Boloeit 'all the gentry from the surrounding parishes would meet... to see the ball brought in.'

As to the division of teams, there appear to have been two main distinctions; geographic (east v. west, or one set of streets against another) and, as recorded in Truro, the once common *Uppies and Downies* delineation of married v. unmarried, as seen now only at Duns (*see page 136*).

Apart from St Ives and St Columb, only a few physical reminders of Cornwall's hurling heritage remain.

We know from Richard Edmonds that in Helston the door of the Guildhall, built in 1839 and still extant, formed the goal.

Helston's game, which pitched residents of two streets against the rest, was held in May, on Ascension Eve, and formed part of the annual 'beating of the bounds' ceremony which, according to

Robert Hunt, was a favourite day for Cornish hurling. The big day in Helston now is May 8, when the Furry or Flora Dance takes place.

In the east of the county, hurling still takes place once every five years at Bodmin, again as part of the beating of the bounds.

On the most recent occasion this took place, in May 2005, the walk around the parish perimeter ended at the Salting Pool, where the Mayor threw a silver ball into the water. As at Alnwick, a battle for possession then ensued, after which the winner returned the silver ball to the town's Turret Clock to claim a prize of £10.

A repeat is next scheduled for May 2010.

Finally, one port of call for anyone wishing to revisit Cornwall's hurling past is the Grade I listed parish church of St Mawgan-in-Pydar (*right*), just north of Newquay Airport.

In the past St Mawgan would have hurled against St Columb, four miles away, the ball having been thrown up in the country between. For St Mawgan their goal, just inside the lychgate, was a stone trough (*below right*).

One of several important treasures in this delightful churchyard, this simple piece of granite is identical to the two surviving goals on the outskirts of St Columb (*see page 144*).

On Bodmin Moor the hurlers were turned to stone for playing on the Sabbath. At St Mawgan the goal was actually a trough in the churchyard, surrounded by Christian memorials, one of which is a Grade II* lantern cross. The trough, its date unknown, lies a few yards up the path, past a lychgate (*top*) designed by William Butterfield in the 1850s.

Shrovetide

17. St Columb Major, Cornwall

Wherever you are in the Cornish town of St. Columb Major, you are never far from a banner or badge bearing the motto of the town's hurlers, 'Town and Country do your best, For in this parish I must rest.' The words are also inscribed on the ball, and recited before each game starts. Town and Country are the names of the two competing teams.

The small Cornish town of St Columb Major – just east of Newquay and not to be confused with either St Columb Minor or St Columb Road – has two claims to distinction.

Firstly, since records began in the 19th century, and possibly for much longer, its annual Shrove Tuesday game of hurling has been played every year without a break, not even during two world wars. Only once was it postponed, by a month, owing to an outbreak of foot and mouth disease in 2001.

Secondly, the area of play covers the entire parish of St Columb, covering some 25 square miles (*see map on page 145*). This makes it not only the largest expanse of any of our featured games of *Uppies and Downies*, but also the largest *de facto* sports ground in the world, as verified by the *Guinness Book of Records*. (The parish's extent was even greater until boundary changes in the 20th century.)

Long-time resident and player, Ivan Rabey, has done most to piece together the story of St Columb hurling in his excellent book *The Silver Ball* (*see Links*).

From a collection held by the Newquay Old Cornwall Society, Major Murray, captain of the East team, calls up the ball on Towan Beach, Newquay, during the period 1896–1914, when St Columb Major played summer matches against other parishes on the Newquay sands. The goals were marked by crosses, and crowds of up to 400 were reported.

The earliest references Rabey has found to hurling appear in parish accounts from the reign of Elizabeth I. In 1594 it is noted:

John Menheere owith for a silvr ball dd to Tobye at his instance and upon his word Xs

That is, John Menheere owes Toby ten shillings for a silver ball. A year later a second entry, apparently resolving the issue, reads:

Receaved of Toby Bennet for the silvr ball for wch Jo. Menheere withn is charged and thus dyscharged Xs

Ten shillings then was the equivalent of around £70 today, whereas the price of a silver ball today is estimated at nearer £300.

As previously noted (*see page 140*), in his 1846 report to the Natural History and Antiquarian Society of Penzance, Richard Edmonds described the St Columb game as 'another species' from the usual forms of 'hurling to goals' or 'hurling to country'.

At St Columb, he noted, the game was generally played either as Town v. Country, by one part of the town or parish against another, or by married v. single men.

A gentleman who had often played in the game described it to Edmonds as follows:

'In the afternoons of Shrove Tuesday and the Saturday-week following, the shops being closed and business suspended, many hundreds of persons of all ranks from the town and country are assembled in the streets waiting for the hurling of the ball, the townsmen forming one party and the countrymen the other, each having its own goal – a low granite post with a concavity in the top to receive the ball.

'The goals are about one mile and a half apart, having the town midway between them. The party

which wins the game by lodging the ball at its own goal, keeps it as a trophy until the following year.'

No place, Edmonds added, was 'privileged' during the game, so that hurlers frequently entered private shrubberies, gardens, and houses. And yet the game did bring members of the community together. 'St. Columb is the only place where gentlemen now unite with the rest of the inhabitants in this diversion.'

Edmonds' description is remarkably consistent with the game as it is still played today, but with one important distinction.

In addition to the two goals mentioned, at St Columb the rival teams can also score by carrying the silver ball to the parish boundary, much further from the town than the goals.

In other words, the game combines both 'hurling to goals' and 'hurling to country'.

Either Edmonds omitted to mention this in 1846, or this practice is a later development.

It is also worth noting that although, as Edmonds stated, two games were played at St Columb – on Shrove Tuesday and on the Saturday of the following week (as is still the case today) – during the 19th century other games took place throughout the year.

For example the Newquay Regatta of July 1858 saw the hosts play three 20-a-side games on the beach, v. St Columb Major, St Columb Minor and the County.

The two St Columbs, Major and Minor, also regularly played each other, with men from Newquay often hurling for the Minor parish, in which the northern part of Newquay lay.

On one such occasion, on the sands at Newquay, on September 30 1896, a fine day was marred by

controversy. As reported in the *Newquay Visitors Notes & Directory,* 'The respective goals were the cavern on Town beach at the one end & the cavern under the old quarry at the other... The game was developing into a well fought contest... when two boys from Newquay, forgetting that off the beach was "out of bounds" took the ball to sea and lost it...'

George Hicks, who had given the ball, then threw up a tin ball as a replacement, 'but the majority of the St. Columb Major men, on the advice of their leaders, would not recognize it & so the real game came to a sudden end.'

The return match, staged on 27 November at Parkyn's, a smithy on the boundary between the two parishes, drew over 500 people.

This time, according to the newspaper, St Columb Major got their revenge when, within minutes, Harold Jones 'made a dash down the field into Nanswhyden Wood, where he was caught & delivered the ball to Sam Stephens of Gluvian, a well known wrestler, who proceeded through the wood to St. Columb Major where he arrived just before 3 o'clock and "Called Up" the ball in the Market Strand.'

To achieve this victory, the two St Columbans had caused 'great indignation' by 'shuffling' the ball (that is, smuggling, or hiding it in their clothing). And all because Newquay boys had themselves not abided by the spirit of the game.

Sadly this local derby fell into abeyance after the First World War.

Before the Second World War the St Columb hurl was preceded by a procession featuring the Queen of the Hurling on a wagonette. As shown here in 1925 children would sell ribbons to the crowd: blue for the town, red for the Country and white for the neutral. Winners at this time received a medal as well as a sovereign.

▶ To passing motorists and ramblers, if noticed at all, they appear to be small stone troughs embedded in the turf by the side of minor road junctions. But to the hurlers of St Columb these unmarked and undated slabs of granite are the goals.

On the right, barely visible in front of an ancient milestone, is the moss-covered **Country goal**, a mile to the north east of St Columb, at a T junction known as the Tregamere Turn. As seen on the map opposite, in order to reach this spot hurlers have to proceed under the busy A39 St Columb bypass.

The rain-filled **Town Goal** (*below right*) is more visible, located at a junction called Cross Putty, where the old Newquay road meets the new one (A3059), a mile to the south west of St Columb's centre.

In addition to these two granite troughs, only one other hurling goal of this design is known to have survived, in the churchyard of St Mawgan-in-Pydar, a few miles to the north west (*see page 141*).

Confusingly however, as explained on the right, St Columb hurlers can also score without going anywhere near to the two goals. Such is the blending of 'hurling to goals' with 'hurling to country'.

In either case, spectators are unlikely to witness a ball being goaled unless they keep up very closely with the action.

▶ The largest sports ground in the world, according to the *Guinness Book of Records*, otherwise known as the **parish of St Columb**, extends to some 25 square miles, with the town itself on a plateau in the Vale of Mawgan. The ground rises to the south of the town, but falls away sharply on the other three sides.

In fast-moving traffic on the A39, St Columb Major is easy to miss. Yet the construction of this bypass in 1978 has had an effect on the hurling game, taking traffic away from the town centre, where the streets are barely wide enough for two cars to pass, never mind avoid a pack of men chasing a ball.

As explained on the left, there are two goals. However, as these fixed points and their approaches are more easily defended, the game also allows hurlers to score by carrying the silver ball to the parish boundary. Although those boundaries have contracted a little to the south, that still leaves a lot of open country to cover.

The flow of the game is therefore radial from the town centre, with a variety of routes to choose from, along roads or across country.

Any spot along the boundary will suffice, but in practice hurlers tend to head for an obvious crossing point, such as Whitewater. Those to the east, some of which are marked opposite, are now less popular owing to the bypass.

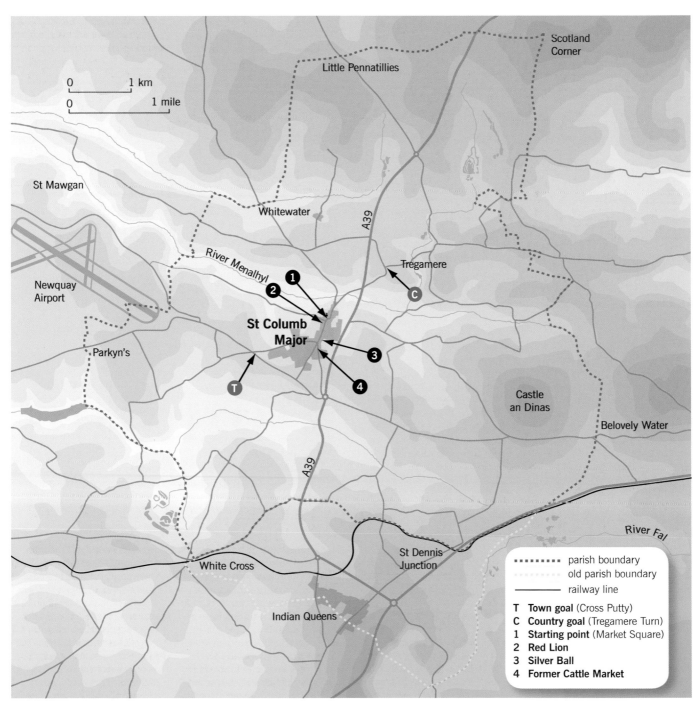

Scotland Corner

Little Pennatillies

St Mawgan

Whitewater

A39

River Menalhyl

Tregamere

1

2

C

Newquay Airport

St Columb Major

3

Parkyn's

T

4

Castle an Dinas

Belovely Water

A39

White Cross

St Dennis Junction

River Fal

Indian Queens

.... parish boundary
.... old parish boundary
———— railway line

T Town goal (Cross Putty)
C Country goal (Tregamere Turn)
1 Starting point (Market Square)
2 Red Lion
3 Silver Ball
4 Former Cattle Market

0   1 km
0   1 mile

▲ Bearing both the date and the traditional St Columb inscription 'Town and Country do your best', the modern **hurling ball** measures 84mm in diameter and weighs approximately 567g. That is slightly larger than a cricket ball, yet three and a half times heavier.

Encased in silver 2mm thick, as was the method used in the 18th century (see page 140), its core is still made from locally supplied apple wood, which does not split readily when pierced. (In the 1970s a plastic core was tried, but was not popular with players.)

As can be seen, nowadays the seam is protected by a raised central band, attached to the wood by silver rivets.

Since 1990 the St Columb balls have been crafted by Colin Rescorla, a local silversmith who is also an undertaker. Each ball takes 20 hours to make, and although its cost is a few hundred pounds – the exact amount is confidential – its silver value is relatively low.

Hence only one has ever gone missing, in 1963, and that was later returned, apparently from an address in the Midlands.

In the past balls were used repeatedly. Rescorla knows of one ball from the 1940s that lasted for 23 games. Today's winners prefer to keep them however, even though this obliges them to pay for a replacement for the following year.

Images of the ball abound in St Columb, most famously at the Silver Ball pub, on Fair Street.

Before 1960 it was called the Railway and Commercial Hotel.

The teams

For both St Columb games, on Shrove Tuesday and the Saturday of the following week, the two teams are known as Town and Country, a division also found at Sedgefield.

(A further link between the two towns is that in both the ball is seen as a symbol of good luck and is therefore frequently passed between players and spectators, young and old, for all to touch.)

A report in *The West Briton and Cornwall Advertiser* of March 3 1854 distinguished the two teams in terms that some might consider apposite today.

'The country, with their stalwart limbs, fortified with corduroys and hobnail dew-beaters, and by their occupation inured to fatigue, would seem to have a vast superiority over their towns brethren, whose slender frames and more sedentary habits one would fancy badly fitted them for such heavy work, but their unflagging activity fully compensated for the deficiency in physical force...'

Country players at this time were also distinguished by their white smocks, known as dickeys.

Unusually in the world of *Uppies and Downies*, it is possible to swap sides at St. Columb, for example if a players moves from the town to the countryside or vice versa.

One noted player, Rundle Lawrey, even managed to score for both teams, goaling for the Town in 1950 after ten previous successes for the Country.

However, this flexibility does have ramifications, because as the number of agricultural workers has declined over the years, so too has the Country team reduced in size. Their ranks can be bolstered by players from further afield, particularly neighbouring parishes. But true outsiders are not deemed eligible for participation in either decisive breaks or for scoring.

Currently there are around 50 players competing overall on Shrove Tuesday, with more usually turning out on the Saturday game, which is also better attended by spectators.

The game

As can readily be imagined, a small, dense metallic ball thrown around in narrow streets can be a fearsome missile. Before both matchdays therefore local businesses and householders in the centre of the town take special care to protect their windows with shutters, boards, chicken wire or even just cardboard.

The procedure for both matches is the same.

From 4.15pm onwards crowds gather in front of the town's war memorial in the Market Square, where the individual chosen to throw up the ball shows it to all and sundry and names it as either 'Town' or 'Country', depending on which side won the previous encounter.

The ball is then thrown up at 4.30pm.

Thereafter the hurl tends to follow a pattern. At the throw-up, a knot of men forms around the ball, very much as seen in the Scottish Borders. But the first man to break free is not trying to escape. He soon passes it on.

To cries of 'heads!', the ball is then thrown between the players as they run up and down Fore Street and Fair Street, between the starting point and the old Cattle Market, just past the Silver Ball.

During this first phase of the game neither side is attempting to

◀ Showing the **silver ball** before it is thrown up in February 1982, with musical accompaniment provided by the town crier.

The individual who starts the game – usually a local politician or personality, nominated by the previous year's winner – calls out the traditional phrase, 'Town and Country do your best, for in this parish I must rest.'

Nowadays this duty is carried out from the top of a step-ladder, a somewhat less onerous task than the previous custom, ended in 1931, in which the starter was required to climb up a lamp-post.

As at Sedgefield, the ball is widely regarded as a lucky charm, so that during the early stages of the game, as in March 2007 (*above*) it will be passed around for all and sundry to touch.

This part of the day is highly sociable and has the added benefit of giving younger players a tantalising feel for the ball before the adults get down to business.

Women are free to take part in the later stages, though to date none has won. The game's youngest ever winner was 11 year old Scott Bennett, for the Town, in the Saturday game of 2002.

score. Rather, they are bound by convention to keep the ball within the town centre for the first hour.

If they can manage this, the winner will receive an extra £10.

This is no easy task, however, for not only is the prize no longer the incentive it used to be when a gold sovereign was the reward, but the younger, faster hurlers find it hard to contain their natural urge

to head off, either to the goals or the distant parish boundaries.

With no-one quite sure when this might happen during the first hour, it is hard for older players to contain an escape. Players and spectators may therefore be disappointed when the play leaves town before the hour is up (in which case the £10 is donated to charity). »

▲ High spirits outside the **Red Lion** on Fore Street (*top*), in February 2007. One former landlord of the pub, James Polkinghorne, was a champion Cornish wrestler. In 1826 he came out of retirement to fight the Devonshire champion, Abraham Cann, for £200. The bout was drawn. But no doubt Polkinghorne would have agreed with Robert Hunt's description in the 1860s of the ideal hurler as one who had 'a nimble hand, a quick eye, a swift foot, and skill in wrestling; as well as strength, good wind, and lungs.'

Little has changed, although the first hour of the game (*above*) mainly offers everyone a chance to cavort around the streets, celebrating the silver ball's power to create good cheer and bring luck.

Tactics

As the minutes pass there builds the growing sense that one of the hurlers might 'do a runner' before the hour is up. This is particularly likely on Shrove Tuesday when numbers are lower.

So, in the second half hour, the Town team will try to move the ball south towards the junction at the Cattle Market; the Countrymen countering in the opposite direction. Any sudden move provokes the familiar cry heard in almost every game of *Uppies and Downies*: 'has it gone?'

Following the usual false alarm or two, the chances are that after around 45 minutes of manoeuvring around the streets, a decisive break will occur. Around a hundred players and keener spectators will then give chase in the hope of catching up.

If the opposition can keep up, a tackle, or 'stand', will lead to a scrum being formed. It is at this point that hurling, Cornish-style, is at its most exciting. Friends and team-mates will work together to gain possession and utilise decoy runs, called 'splitting', to confuse their opponents.

Although rarely condoned, underhand tactics can play a part at St Columb, as has certainly been the case since 1602, when Richard Carew mentioned progress to goal being either 'by force, or sleight' (*see page 139*).

So the ball may be taken inside a house, or perhaps even pressed into soft ground or hidden in the undergrowth, a tactic aptly known as 'planting'. On one occasion a hurler 'planted' the ball in his own child's pram, until his wife thrust it nonchalantly aside.

Once the play has left the confines of the town, it is almost impossible for spectators to follow the action. In practice, a runner can, if quick enough, often go on to score with impunity.

Should a player head off across country, much depends on their familiarity with the terrain and whether the route has been anticipated by any rivals.

If it has, once they approach the parish boundary – which can be as far as three miles from the town – it is theoretically possible for them to be dispossessed and for their opponent then to carry the ball over the last few yards and claim the goal himself (since both sides may score in this way at any point along the boundary).

This might seem unfair, at least to an outsider. But it is a rare occurence, since neither side can possibly patrol the entire parish border.

If a breakaway is not thwarted within the first mile, therefore, the game is usually as good as up, not least because an experienced player will vary his route to avoid detection.

The victor

Victory goes to the last person to be holding the ball as it is either placed in one of the stone troughs, or carried across the boundary.

The scorer may then be borne on the shoulders of his team-mates to loud cheers in the Market Square. This is usually within two hours of the start, but it is not quite the end of the match.

Instead, tradition dictates that the scorer must wait until 8.00pm to declare the ball as 'Town' or 'Country' in the Market Square before the game is officially over.

The honours board in the Town Hall reveals the multiple successes of certain families, like the Bennallicks, the Lawreys and the Weldhens. Michael Weldhen is the most prolific individual, with 17 wins for the Countrymen between 1953 and 1982.

If no-one manages to score before 8.00pm, the ball is thrown up once more on its return to the Market Place. Whoever catches it this time is declared the winner. However this has not happened since 1929.

Once declared, the winner and his team-mates proceed on a tour of the town's pubs, where gallon jugs of beer await.

In order to spread the luck that victory is supposed to bring, the ball is dunked in the jug so that all may partake of what is called thereafter the 'silver beer'.

The future

As the venue for the sole surviving adult game of hurling in Cornwall – a county once famous for the sport – St Columb Major fulfils an exceptionally important role in Cornish culture.

Certainly the hurl here is truer to the tradition of fierce competition than at St Ives, even if the customary hour of play within the town centre is proving harder to maintain then ever. Perhaps the incentive should be raised to more than £10. Or should the hurlers of St Columb be confined to the town until the church clock strikes 5.30pm, or a klaxon is sounded?

Therein lies the problem for a game with no rules and no organising committee. In such circumstances, changing habits is not easily achieved.

Yet the play through the streets remains immensely enjoyable, and the silver ball still seems to be as eagerly touched as ever. And given the distances involved, surely any man whose legs and lungs carry him to the distant parish boundary well deserves his silver beer.

The 1949 Shrove Tuesday winner Cyril Lawrey returns triumphantly to the Market Place after securing victory for the Country. As he is carried shoulder high his supporters sing the hurling song, with lyrics to match their victory: 'For we roll, we roll the Country ball along'. In the evening the ball is taken to all the pubs in town to be dipped into a jug of beer, as captured (*left*) in 1972 by that great chronicler of British customs, Homer Sykes. Nowadays winners usually opt to keep their ball, but must then fund a replacement for the following year.

Shrovetide

18. St Ives, Cornwall

Displayed in the Guildhall at St Ives, this silver ball – dating from 1976 – is virtually identical in design and construction to the one used at St Columb. But as well as having to survive the rigours of town and country, the St Ives ball has to cope with dunkings in both well water and seawater. As at St. Columb in the past, the inscription 'fair play is good play' is inscribed in Cornish. Since the St Ives game is now restricted to children the ball is returned after each game.

Our final stop on the Shrovetide trail is at St Ives, in west Cornwall, where the county's second surviving game of hurling is now played only by children.

Strictly speaking it is not a Shrovetide game at all, being just one element of the town's annual Feast Day celebrations. However, as these take place on the first Monday after February 3 – the date of the parish church's consecration in 1434 – it often falls close to Shrove Tuesday and so for convenience is included here.

The Feast Day in question is in celebration of St Ia (also written as Eia or Hya, and anglicised as St Ive), a fifth century Irish missionary who, according to legend, missed the boat that was to carry her and her fellow Christians across to Cornwall, but managed instead to make the journey by floating on a magical ivy leaf.

Hurling on saints' days was once common in Cornwall. Robert Hunt's *Popular Romances of the West of England* (1865) relates that St Ives played initially against two villages to the south; Lelant, two miles away, and Ludgvan, five

miles away. Lelant's patron saint, Uny, was Ia's brother, and as all three communities celebrated their feast days at the same time of year, the hurling matches formed a short season in February.

Given the distances involved, the games were almost certainly the variety known as 'hurling to country' rather than 'hurling to goals'. In his description of 1602, Richard Carew (*see page 139*) adds to this supposition, reporting that hurling to country was preferred in west Cornwall.

Detailed information is sparse, but it appears that as the years passed Ludgvan ceased to participate, leaving only one saint's day match between St Ives and Lelant, with the church porches in both places serving as the goals. The starting point, midway between the two, was a stone at Chyangweal, now part of Carbis Bay.

But as St Ives grew larger, reaching a peak population of over 9,000 by 1871, and as Lelant shrank, literally – as the result of encroachment by sand dunes – the contest became increasingly unequal and was discontinued.

By the time that Richard Edmonds made his report to the Natural History and Antiquarian Society of Penzance in 1846 (*see page 140*), the men of St Ives were competing amongst themselves, in two teams, with a pole on the beach acting as the single goal. 'The aim of each party,' Edmonds noted, 'is to touch the goal with the ball, and to prevent the adverse party from doing so.'

Edmonds also explained the unusual method used to divide the teams at this time. Instead of splitting, as one might expect, into teams representing the upper and lower parts of St Ives, they divided according to their names.

Action at St Ives in the 1930s, when a goal was set up on the beach, as in the 19th century. But there are drawbacks. In 1930 the silver ball was thrown into the sea, forcing the players to wait several hours until the tide turned and the precious orb could be retrieved. At least, being silver, it could not rust.

'All the "Toms", "Wills" and "Johns" are on one side, while those having other christian names range themselves on the opposite.'

Hence there arose a saying:

'Toms, Wills and Jans,
Take off all's on the san's' (sands)

It was as good a way of dividing the townsmen as any. Indeed the same method was used in some early soccer and rugby clubs.

According to *Kelly's Directory* for 1856, there were 72 traders called John, Thomas or William, compared with 82 otherwise named. In other words, a fair split in numbers.

How long this division of teams applied is not known, but later in the century a more obvious division was adopted, pitting Upalongs against Downalongs, or, as local people pronounced the words, Uplongs and Downlongs.

Tinners (or miners) living higher up the hill were Uplongs, while fishermen living near the harbour were Downlongs. (A similar division between the mining and fishing communities also identified Uppies from Downies at Workington.)

These terms were not invented for hurling but were used more widely – and still are – to describe which part of town people came from. The curved-fronted Market House, dating from 1490 in the centre of the town, marked the boundary between the two areas.

Now, instead of a single goal on the beach, two goals were agreed; on Porthminster beach for the Uplongs and at the harbour for the Downlongs.

Around this period the economy and character of St Ives changed markedly. Firstly a steep decline in the pilchard fishing industry led to a reduction in the population by the 1890s. Meanwhile the arrival of the railway in 1877 led to a growth in the number of tourists.

These were accommodated in a burgeoning network of hotels and guest houses in Uplong territory (as patently the town could only expand uphill). At the same time the network of narrow lanes that formed the Downlong area became depopulated.

Then in the 20th century St Ives famously became a favourite haunt of artists, such as Ben Nicholson and Barbara Hepworth.

Hurling survived these changes, and although it lapsed during the First World War, and was replaced on the Feast Monday of 1919 by a rugby match (St Ives v. RAF Mullion), it restarted in 1920.

In 1921 the ball was thrown up on the Malakoff, a viewpoint above the railway station (named after a stone tower stormed during the Crimean War).

The *Western Echo* reported, 'The Old Cornwall Society recently offered the town a silver ball, that by it the good old custom may be kept up and the youths of the town always play at hurling on Feast Day.'

In 1923 'two capital sides' were selected to play on Porthminster Beach. By now the teams were also being distinguished by their clothing. Whites played Reds.

A further drift towards the conventions normally associated with rugby and soccer occurred in 1932, when each side was limited to twelve players, and there was even a break for half-time.

The Uplong team won 4-1, with each of their players receiving 2s 6d from the Mayor, Mr. Hollow, and the losers collecting a shilling per man.

After the Second World War, the St Ives hurl fell into a steady decline and might well have died out altogether had it not been for the intervention of the Mayor, Keith Slocombe, in 1972.

That year the 19th century practice of putting up goals on the beach was revived, using basketball nets. A prize was also offered for whichever player returned the ball at noon. Once again, the Downlongs wore white and the Uplongs red.

But the basketball nets were used only briefly, and since then the game has changed again, played only by children and integrated within other elements of the Feast Monday ceremonials.

A wonderful occasion it is too. But only a shadow, it has to be said, of what once was a much more robust and competitive Cornish tradition.

St Ives from the south, with Porthminster Beach in the foreground and Porthmeor Beach and the Tate Gallery on the far shore. Hurling today starts on the small beach next to the harbour (*centre*). Nearby, just behind the short New Pier, is the Market House. Below this and to the east is the part of town called Downalong. Above it is Upalong. Such divisions are the basis of most mass ball games in Britain.

▲ Feast Monday in St Ives begins at 9.30am with a procession from the Guildhall to the **sacred well of St Ia**, also known as Venton Ia, behind Porthmeor Beach.

The Mayor carries the silver ball in a basket decorated with ivy (in memory of Ia's voyage), followed by a band of musicians repeating the same tune, over and over. But still it is a rousing one, entitled *Bodmin Riding*. Children, let off school for the morning, dance in their wake.

Once at the well (*above right*) the vicar dips the ball in the well, scatters water over those assembled, and after prayers and a hymn, gives his blessing. Until 1843 this same well provided the main water supply for the Downalong part of the town.

Finally, oranges are thrown to the children (a typical Shrovetide custom) before the procession returns to the churchyard, which overlooks a path known as **Lambeth Walk**. Then at 10.30 the Mayor throws the ball out over the beach (*right*), where older children, aged 11–15, prepare to hurl.

The game

Hurling in St Ives is quite different from its counterpart in St Columb. Here adults watch while children compete, and there are no teams.

After the ball is thrown up, the initial skirmishes take place on the beach. Often small groups of pals act in unison. Some even bring along dummy balls or silver baubles to throw around, so as to distract their rivals.

But the excitement does not last for long, because as soon as one of the older boys manages to grab hold of the ball, off he will sprint into a neighbouring bay, thence to disappear up one of the town's many steep lanes, having previously agreed a rendezvous, usually someone's house.

From then on there is nothing more anyone can do than play aimlessly on the beach or wait around until noon (although another distraction is a gathering of the Western Hunt in Royal Square at 11.00am).

Then, as the appointed hour approaches, younger children gather in front of the Guildhall, where pennies are handed out, until at midday, an individual nominated by the group which managed to keep hold of the ball – sometimes a friend or relative – is presented with a silver crown, worth around £5, by the Mayor.

The Mayor and his party then climb the stairs of the Guildhall and reappear on the balcony to throw hundreds more pennies down to the older children below.

Like kittiwake chicks on a cliff, they make a noise quite out of proportion to the morsels offered.

Thus ends the main event of Saint Monday, to be followed in the evening by the annual rugby match between St Ives and a Cornwall XV.

The future

Although the St Ives hurl offers a valuable lesson in history, as a competitive game and a spectacle it is disappointingly brief.

Fully supported by the town's officialdom as it is, here surely is a festival game with plenty of scope for a more meaningful revival.

Perhaps the old system of having goals on the beach would improve matters, both for the children and spectators, as would the restoration of teams.

Its survival is to be applauded. But now it needs to become even more involving. St Ives, after all, is a town highly geared for tourism. Hurling could therefore offer a genuine attraction at an otherwise quiet time of the year.

Action on the beach in 1972, as seen from Lambeth Walk. On the left, Mayor Bill Fry receives the ball from the 2007 winners, outside the Guildhall. The boys, all of whom play junior rugby for St Ives, nominated the young son of rugby legend Joff Rowe to receive the silver crown from the Mayor.

Easter

19. Hallaton, Leicestershire

HAVE YOU GOT
THE BOTTLE?

If you have, just be aware that the Hallaton Hare Pie Scramble and Bottle Kicking – to give it its full title – is a gruelling cross country contest in which the 'bottles' are actually three small wooden barrels. So no real bottles and, in truth, very little kicking, especially as two of the barrels are filled with ale. In 1807 John Britton described the scramble as 'a singular and ridiculous ancient annual custom'. Some might say it has barely changed.

After forty days of Lent and all the various rites and rituals of Easter Week, with not a ball kicked, thrown, hurled or hailed since Shrovetide, Easter Monday would seem to offer the perfect opportunity to indulge in a further bout of festival ball games.

But while it is true that Easter Monday has long been associated with japes and jollities, fairs and fun, mass football, it would seem, has seldom featured among the sports associated with the day, or indeed with Easter in general.

This is reflected in the fact that Easter games of *Uppies and Downies* take place in only two locations: Hallaton, in Leicestershire, and Workington in Cumbria (*see next chapter*), and that no extinct games from the Easter period have otherwise been identified.

That said, the Hallaton Hare Pie Scramble and Bottle Kicking game encompasses several rituals that are common to other Easter folk traditions.

Moreover, as noted left, although the bottles are actually small wooden barrels, and as such are hardly kicked at all, Hallaton's game is otherwise a typical *Uppies and Downies* encounter; that is, a rough and tough contest played across open country by two teams of unlimited size, with goals a mile or so apart.

For that reason we can describe it as a game. But before the mid to late 19th century the emphasis was on the scrambling rather than the kicking, and the aim was not to score but to grab as much food and drink as possible.

Which is where the hare pie comes in.

The hare is of course the original Easter bunny; a symbol of the pagan goddess of fertility, Eostre, from which the word Easter is thought to derive. Hares were associated with the coming of spring and were sacrificed to ensure a fertile year.

Thus in Leicester, 13 miles west of Hallaton, a hare was hunted on Easter Monday until the late 18th century, the mayor and aldermen leading the chase in their scarlet finery. At Coleshill, Warwickshire, as recorded by Thomas Blount in *Ancient Tenures of Land and Jocular Customs* (1784), anyone able to catch a hare before 10.00am on Easter Monday could claim a calf's head, 100 eggs and a groat.

Hares are similarly central to today's rituals at Hallaton, not in terms of the game as we now see it, but as part of the traditional build up to the bottle kicking.

One of the most detailed accounts of the game's history is by John Morison and Peter Daisley (*see Links*). In common with Haxey (*see page 56*), the story begins with a legend involving a lady, or in Hallaton's case, two.

Crossing a field one day, the women were suddenly chased by an angry bull. But just as it neared them, a hare popped up, distracted the bull, and the ladies were able to make their escape.

To show their gratitude they decided to donate the rent from a grazing pasture known as Hare Crop Leys to the village rector. In return, every Easter Monday, he was required to hold a special service and provide two hare pies, some ale, and two dozen penny loaves for the villagers to share.

In both Haxey and Hallaton it is possible that such legends evolved

as a palatable way of justifying pagan practices; the sacrifice of bullocks at Haxey, hares at Hallaton. Both involve innocent women and the gift of land.

But there is evidence in Hallaton (as there is also at Haxey) that the granting of land rights might well be bound up in the ritual's origins.

In Hallaton the evidence comes in 1771, when the village's 3,000 acres of common land were being enclosed. As this meant that the rector would lose his right to the rent from Hare Crop Leys, he was allocated another patch of land, later known as Parson's Leys.

Perhaps thinking that the loss of Hare Crop Leys freed him from his obligations, the rector in c. 1789, Reverend CJ Bewicke, decided to withdraw his support of the Easter Monday custom. The response?

'No pie, no parson and a job for the glazier' was daubed – in blood it is said – on the church door and throughout Hallaton.

Bewicke swiftly relented, and the pie has been produced annually ever since.

Around the same time two of the first accounts of the hare pie ritual appeared. In Volume IX of *The Beauties of England and Wales*, published in 1807, John Britton describes two large pies.

'These are divided into parts, and put into a sack; and about two gallons of ale, in two wooden bottles, without handles or strings, are also put into a sack: the penny loaves are cut into quarters, and placed in a basket.

'Thus prepared, the men, women and children form a procession from the rector's, and march to a place called Hare Pie Bank, about a quarter of a mile south of the town.

'In the course of this journey the pieces of bread are occasionally

thrown for scrambling; but the pies and ale are carried to the grand rustic theatre of contention and confusion.'

This 'theatre' Britton noted, was 'of old formation, and, though not upon so great a scale, or destined for such bloody feats, as the Roman amphitheatres, yet consists of a bank, with a small trench round it, and a circular bole (bowl) in the centre.'

Hare Pie Bank, it should be noted, is the point where the game still starts today, and has had this name since at least 1707, when John Wing surveyed the area.

One theory is that the site – which occupies a natural vantage point above Hallaton – was once a stow; that is, a sacred place during the iron age, the centre of which was this 'theatre... of old formation.' Could the pie and ale ritual therefore hark back to a pagan spring time offering?

After the Conquest the Normans built on or near this site a chapel dedicated to one of their favoured saints, St Morrell. So did the ritual relate to this?

And does any of this speculation link to another theory that the name Hallaton itself derives from 'Hallowed' or 'Holy' Town.

But returning to Hare Pie Bank. Into the circular bowl in the ground, Britton continued, 'the »

The rector of Hallaton cuts up the hare pie before the 1905 Easter scramble. Note the two retainers on hand to scoop portions of the pie into sacks, to be scattered amongst the crowds at Hare Pie Bank. Nowadays only a hare filling will do, but in 1807 the pie was described as being made with veal and bacon. During the Second World War Spam was used. Yet while eating the creatures is deemed acceptable, to satisfy modern sensibilities the hare that is now hoisted on a pole at the front of the procession is a bronze (see *opposite*), designed by Ken Ford in 1994. Prior to this, the corpse of a real hare was used.

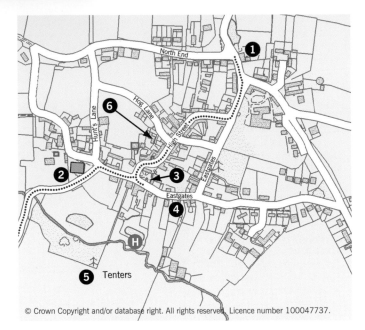

▲ The centre of Hallaton, showing (in red) the routes of the two **Easter Monday processions**, from the Fox Inn to the church, then back to the Buttercross, and finally out to Hare Pie Bank (see *map on page 159*).

H   Hallaton goal

1   Fox Inn
2   St Michael's Church
3   Buttercross
4   Bewicke Arms
5   St Morrell's Well
6   Museum

In order to score, the Hallaton players must convey the bottle to the north bank of the stream, across a field known as Tenters.

Hallaton is now a village of 500 residents with two pubs. But in earlier times on festival days, any private house was allowed to serve alcohol if an ale bough was hung outside (a tradition which dates back to the Romans).

Nowadays, however, ale boughs are displayed on Easter Mondays only at the Fox Inn and the **Bewicke Arms** (*below*).

» pies and ale are promiscuously thrown, and every frolicksome, foolish, and frantic rustic rushes forward to seize a bit, or bear away a bottle. Confusion ensues, and, what began in peurile (sic) sport, occasionally terminates in that common, but savage custom, a boxing-match.'

A similar account, written a few years earlier in 1796, by John Tailby of Slawston, was quoted in John Nichols' mammoth *History and Antiquities of the County of Leicester*.

After the sacks are emptied of their pies and ale, Tailby wrote, 'a scene of noise and confusion takes place, and bloody noses and bruised fingers are often the consequence: one will seize a piece of Pye, or a bottle of Ale; a second will trip up his heels, and fall upon him; and a third perhaps seize and keep possession of the prize, until a fourth serves him with the same; and so on, until four or five fellows agree to form a party, and assist each other in bearing away the wished-for bottle to a convenient place, and there divide the spoil.'

Thus from Britton and Tailby's accounts we can see that there were no identifiable teams and no goals in what was, in essence, an unseemly grab for food and drink.

Moreover, the scramble was only one of several contests on the day. Others noted by Tailby included the 'ringing of bells, fighting of cocks, quoits and such like exercises, by Hallaton and the neighbouring youth.'

Given Hallaton's importance as a market town, in which fairs were staged twice a year, clearly the day's activities drew participants from a wide area.

Inevitably visitor numbers increased further with the arrival of the railway at Hallaton in 1878. Indeed, after Irish navvies

working on the railway joined in with the game that year, perhaps not coincidentally there was a proposal to substitute gentler sports in the interests of progress.

Not only was this defeated at a parish meeting, but the event grew in popularity. From 1882 onwards special trains brought spectators from Market Harborough, Melton Mowbray and Leicester.

From a journal published by John and Thomas Spencer – *Leicestershire and Rutland, Notes and Queries and Antiquarian Gleaner* – we also know that villagers from Medbourne, two miles to the south, had become active participants by 1890. During the previous two years 'parties from Desborough' also joined in.

So it was that the scramble gradually evolved into a team game, with the securing of the 'bottles' becoming the principal objective.

Participants from Hallaton and nearby villages such as Slawston and Horninghold played for the 'home' team, while the rest rallied under the Medbourne banner, bolstered by players from other villages to the south, such as Cottingham and Wilbarston.

In this way the Easter Monday celebrations developed into a full blown festival, packing the streets with sightseers and providing a roaring trade for local pubs and orange sellers alike.

Accompanied by the Hallaton Brass Band, representatives from two local organisations led the procession, the Hallaton Friendly Society and the Loyal Farmers' Delight Lodge of Oddfellows.

Their members then went onto their Easter Monday feasts; the Friendly Society to the Fox Inn and the Oddfellows to the Royal Oak (no longer extant).

As in other locations, Hallaton's game suffered greatly during the First World War, and it was left to local women to contest the bottles in order to keep the tradition alive.

Then came the closure of the railway in 1953, followed in the 1960s and '70s by outbreaks of hooliganism – an echo of the violence that infected Association football during the same period. One of the organisers was even attacked in the street.

Fortunately matters improved once a Medbourne representative was invited onto the committee, and since then a great effort has been made to revive the day as a whole, restoring some of its pomp, music and costumery.

Quite a day it is too.

Pre-match build up

The Easter Monday attractions begin some six hours before the bottle kicking even starts.

First thing in the morning is the best time to visit the rival village of Medbourne, where a band plays to get locals into the spirit. Then it is over to Hallaton, where a children's procession leads from the Bewicke Arms to a church service at St Michael's at 11.00am.

This leaves plenty of time for refreshment, or to visit the small museum in Hog Lane – much of which is devoted to the Easter Monday celebration – until, as the number of spectators swells, the main procession leaves from the Fox Inn at around 1.45pm.

Its destination is the parish church of St Michael's, where the vicar awaits with the hare pie. Since 1962 responsibility for making the pie has been assumed by the game's organisers. But the vicar is still expected to bless the pie and distribute it, as required by the legend of old. »

▲ As seen in 2006, the Hallaton procession is led by the **warrener**, dressed in a splendid green robe and cap. In former times the warrener, or gamekeeper, would have provided the dead hare that was traditionally attached to the pole. A bronze substitute serves in these more delicate times.

Behind him girls carry the hare pie and sacks, while a woman in a red pinafore carries a basket of two dozen penny loaves. These used to be reserved for the needy but are now handed out, mainly to children.

Behind the leaders, strong-armed players hold aloft the three barrels that will be contested later. This is no easy task. Each one is 27cms tall and 20cm wide. Two are filled with nine pints of specially brewed Bottle Kicking Ale, and weigh around 5kg each. The third, painted red, white and blue, is a dummy and weighs 3.5kg.

They are called bottles because small barrels of this type were used for refreshment by farmworkers out in the fields.

Once at the church gates the vicar says a prayer before cutting up the hare pie into small portions. These are snapped up by those within easy reach and either eaten or scattered into the crowd (*right*).

Wasteful though this might seem it actually commemorates an older rural Easter custom in which food was scattered over crops in the hope of promoting abundance. In Monmouth a similar act was accompanied by the words 'a bit for God, a bit for man, and a bit for the fow's of the air'.

The remaining pieces of the pie are then placed inside the two sacks and the procession reforms and doubles back on itself to the Buttercross on the village green for the next stage in the proceedings.

» After the pie cutting and scattering at the church gates the procession returns to the Buttercross. This is an unusual, Grade II★ listed conical structure, built in local ironstone and thought to date back to the 16th or 17th centuries.

Here, the three barrels are decorated with red, white and blue ribbons (*as in 2006, left*), while the penny loaves are distributed. Note that a buttercross also features in the Haxey Hood game (*see page 63*).

Finally, as 2.45pm approaches, the barrels are marched back to the Fox Inn, where the last part of the procession starts again, back down the High Street, past the church, and up Bridge Hill towards Hare Pie Bank. By now the assembled crowd can number 2,000 spectators. A band joins the procession on this route, playing a traditional tune known as *Old Easter Monday*.

Once assembled at Hare Pie Bank, the remaining scraps of pie are sent skywards over the heads of onlookers, at which point, battle, or rather bottle kicking, can at last commence.

The game

As already noted, the number three features in several games of *Uppies and Downies*. At Hallaton three barrels are contested, with the dummy barrel always being the second to be thrown up. This duty is performed by the Master of the Stowe. He throws each barrel up three times (*as in 1983, left*), and only on the third drop can play start.

As shown on the map opposite, the aim of each team – whose numbers might be quite unequal – is to convey the barrel across the streams which serve as the respective goals.

Terrain

As indicated on the map, the Hallaton game is played entirely across open countryside, with steeply-sloping ground and a number of obstacles – hedges, fences and ponds – all making progress difficult.

From the start, Medbourne are faced with the task of crossing a field boundary at the back of Hare Pie Bank. Then there is a double hedge either side of Love Lane, which heads across the fields towards their goal. It is therefore vital for Medbourne to make early headway to stand any chance.

The Medbourne goal is a stream just across the Blaston Road, a mile south from Hare Pie Bank.

In contrast, Hallaton have less ground to cross, fewer barriers, and a severe slope down to the stream that is their goal.

The bottle must be thrown or carried onto the far bank, nearer the village, to score.

Even compared with other games of *Uppies and Downies*, bottle kicking is extremely rough, with men, and some women, launching themselves into the fray and often knocking those in the centre of the scrum to the ground.

Should a player fall to the ground, however, a cry of 'back up!' will be heard and the fallen will be helped to their feet. But woe betide anyone lying at the bottom of the pile with a bottle between their ribs and the ground.

Another hazard is the usually generous spread of dung littering the fields.

The game is decided as the best of three barrels, and so because the second dummy barrel is lighter than the other two, whichever team scores first has the added incentive of trying to dash home to victory by 2-0, rather than having

to compete for the third, heavier barrel, when legs are tired and the light is fading.

Bottle kicking can therefore be a real test of speed and endurance, as well as strength, particularly in wet and muddy conditions.

Indeed, as night falls, many people drift away from the action and retire to one of the pubs in Hallaton to await the outcome.

Eventually, the players stagger back for the post-match celebrations. These take place in Hallaton even if Medbourne wins.

There are no rewards, other than the winning side being able to shin up the Buttercross to enjoy the first swig of beer from one of the barrels – warm and frothy after a good shaking up, but tasting just fine to the victors.

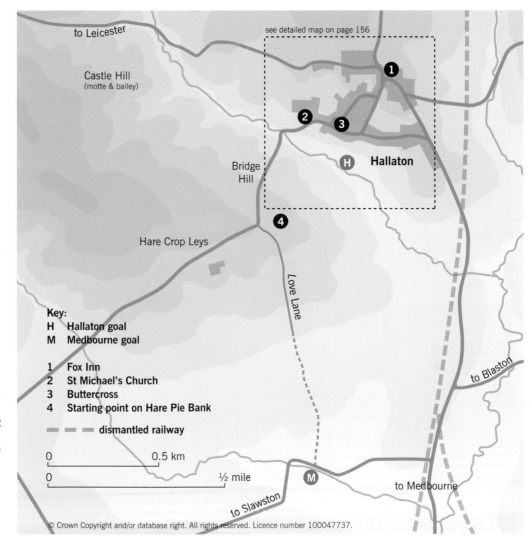

see detailed map on page 156

to Leicester

Castle Hill
(motte & bailey)

Bridge Hill

Hallaton

Hare Crop Leys

Love Lane

to Blaston

Key:
H Hallaton goal
M Medbourne goal

1 Fox Inn
2 St Michael's Church
3 Buttercross
4 Starting point on Hare Pie Bank

– – – dismantled railway

0 ——— 0.5 km

0 ——— ½ mile

to Slawston

to Medbourne

▲ An unusually sunny day greets Hallaton and Medbourne on Easter Monday 2006.

As shown here on **Hare Pie Bank**, for the most part the bottles are carried, rugby style, in frenetic bursts, interspersed with slow moving scrimmages. But the bottles can also be thrown, rolled and even kicked, at least by anyone wearing steel-capped boots.

Otherwise there are no rules, other than an understanding that the use of horses (as was tried in the past), and now motor vehicles, is contrary to the game's spirit.

As can be seen from the shirts, rugby players figure prominently. The red and green shirts (*right*) are those of the Leicester Tigers. Walter Gilby, a Leicester player from the Edwardian era, was apparently a keen bottle kicker.

However, one of the greatest bottle carriers was one 'Deerfoot' Butteriss, who played for Hallaton in the 19th century and was named after the native American long distance runner, Louis 'Deerfoot' Bennett, who thrilled crowds in England in the 1860s with his record breaking feats.

More typically muddy conditions in the early 1980s (*top left*) captured by veteran folklorist Doc Rowe, showing how tough bottle kicking can get. Apart from confronting their opponents, players must also work as a team to sneak under barbed-wire fences, through hedgerows and thorns. More experienced players, as above in 2006, help to co-ordinate the approach to these obstacles, sending runners ahead to catch the barrel on the other side of a hedge, a tactic also often seen at Ashbourne.

▶ Obviously unconcerned that they are balancing on the finial ball of an historic monument, players from the winning teams at Hallaton have for over a century posed on top of the village's **Buttercross** (which has been listed Grade II* since 1984).

And who would dare stop them in their hour of victory?

On the right, seen in 1900 with jug of ale and a barrel on his knee, is **Omar Neal**, a victor with the Hallaton team.

Opposite, in jaunty mood, the 1946 winner, his name unknown, celebrates again for Hallaton, as does a more recent Hallaton player after the 2000 game (*lower right*).

Hallaton have dominated the competition since well before 1890, when results were first recorded. Indeed with a shorter distance to carry the bottle and a steep, indefensible approach to their goal, they managed to prevent Medbourne from winning a single bottle until 1929.

Then at last, in 1936 Medbourne won their first game, albeit with Scottish reinforcements from the nearby steelworks at Corby.

They then lost only once between 1948–67, and remained undefeated from 1981–87.

Since then, however, Hallaton have regained their ascendancy, winning in every year from 1988 through to the end of the Millennium.

The future

No question, bottle kicking is an extreme sport, a human landslide fed by successive generations drunk with bravado. Perhaps for that reason it seems to go from strength to strength, bolstered by players for whom modern games have perhaps lost their edge.

But the Hallaton event has also been charmed back to life by the dedication of its supporters, who have restored to the day its sense of pageant, colour and passion.

The game's opponents argue that injuries are common, and that the East Midlands Ambulance Service should not have to bear the brunt. In response, the organisers say that no fatalities have ever been recorded – unlike either rugby or soccer – that it all takes place on private land, and that players are advised that they take part at their own risk. As no-one is employed in the game's organisation, so the weight of Health and Safety legislation is lessened.

Also in Hallaton's favour is the fact that, unlike in urban settings, broken windows, trampled gardens and blocked highways have never been factors here.

A 'singular and ridiculous ancient annual custom' it might well be, but as long as blood is red and there are hares in the fields, this is one Easter Monday fixture that seems secure for now.

Easter

20. Workington, Cumberland

'Curley' Hill holds up the ball after hailing for the Uppies on Easter Tuesday, 1903. Since reporting of Workington's *Uppies and Downies* began in 1775, the names or allegiances of the winner have not always been recorded. But as at Kirkwall, one team has tended to gain ascendancy for a period before the opposition rallies. In other words, both sides have their ups and their downs.

Workington is much the largest town where mass football survives.

Its *Uppies and Downies* also play more often than elsewhere; on Good Friday, Easter Tuesday and the following Saturday. This makes it possible to have an overall victor in each year's 'best of three' series.

Of the three, Easter Tuesday's encounter is considered the most prestigious, as this is the original match day, described by the *Cumberland Pacquet* in 1775 as 'long-contended'. Indeed the *Pacquet*'s account of the Easter Tuesday game of that year, played on April 20 1775, is one of the earliest reports of a football match ever to appear in a British newspaper.

The report describes a crowd of over 2,000 people. 'Sometimes 30 or 40 of them were all in the river Derwent together; the whole afforded great entertainment to the spectators.'

Workington's two other games followed in the mid 19th century and were initially contested by boys and apprentices. The Good Friday match was first staged in 1865. In 1878 it was reported that 'the preliminary play took place on the Cloffocks amongst the younger lovers of football'.

Of the third game, also introduced around this time, the *Whitehaven News* noted in 1885, 'Formerly the contest was indulged in on Saturday night by the apprentices alone, but of late years the game has become a repetition of the great match on Easter Tuesday.'

Workington's *Uppies and Downies* attracted considerable crowds during the 19th century, with stalls selling oranges and gingerbread being set up on the main vantage points, such as Brow Top (*see map on page 167*), and other sports, especially Cumberland and Westmorland wrestling, also being staged on match days.

Occasionally the sports would merge, as in 1915 when one participant was 'cross-buttocked' in the Beck.

Meanwhile trains were laid from other Cumbrian towns, including Whitehaven, Maryport and Cockermouth. In 1873 the crowd was estimated at 10,000. To put this into perspective, the first FA Cup Final, staged in London the year before, drew only 3,000.

The popularity of *Uppies and Downies* increased further after the First World War, when a reduction in hours at the local steelworks meant that two of three shifts were always free to play.

On Easter Tuesday 1930 the total attendance was estimated at an astonishing 20,000.

The numbers watching today are, by contrast, around 1,000.

Workington games have always been rough (*as described on page 166*), but no deaths have been recorded as having been caused by an aggressive act. As an editorial in the *Whitehaven News* of April 19 1928 noted, there were 'no rules, but amazing good humour and

Mudlarks in Mill Beck c.1900. These days players face not only mud and cold water but litter, including the inevitable supermarket shopping trolleys.

fairness, and little of the violence of association football.'

That said, there have been four deaths, all caused by drowning.

The most recent victim was Robert Storey, on Easter Tuesday 1983. George Young died in 1828, Christopher Smith in 1882 and John Johnstone in 1932.

Given the combination of fast water, deep mud, low temperatures and the fact that much of the action takes place after dusk, it is perhaps surprising that the number is not higher.

The two sides

Although variations of the words *Uppies and Downies* are commonly used to describe rival sides in festival football, Workington is the only place in England where those exact names are currently used.

Previous team names used in the town have included Upper and Lower Town (cited in 1777), Uppergate and Priestgate (1784), Up-Town and Down-Town (1849), and Uppey-gyates and Downey-gyates (1882).

The sides originally divided not just on geographical lines but according to the occupations and loyalties of the players.

Most Downies earned their living, directly or indirectly, from the sea, as sailors, dockers or carpenters. This meant that, as at Kirkwall, Downie numbers were often dependent on the number of ships docked in the harbour.

A report of the Easter Tuesday game in 1849 noted that only one vessel was in, but that 'the Shipwrights were well supported by a gallant brigade of the same class from Maryport.'

From the 1870s the Downies were joined by Northside ironworkers, after production of Bessemer steel began in the

town in 1872. (At one time a large proportion of the world's railway tracks were forged in Workington.)

For their part the Uppies were made up largely of colliers working in the mines owned by the Curwens of Workington Hall. By the end of the 18th century four pits operated, employing 400 men. (Workington's last remaining pit, Solway, closed in 1973.)

Workers on the Curwen estate also turned out for the Uppies.

The Curwens were typical Whigs. John Christian Curwen (1756–1828) set up a savings bank and various friendly societies, supported Parliamentary reform and promoted agricultural improvements.

In a letter to the *Pacquet* in 1831, Messrs Curwen, Falcon and others announced 'that if there was no fighting or disturbance during the contest, something handsome would be given for refreshment.'

Apparently they were able to make good on this promise.

Meanwhile the town docks were controlled by the Lowther family, who also owned the steelworks and much of Whitehaven.

That the Lowthers were firm Tories, while the Curwens were Whigs added further nuance to the *Uppies and Downies'* rivalry.

Nowadays the teams divide on two sides of an imaginary line drawn from the game's starting point on the Cloffocks, south through Vulcans Lane; Downies to the west and Uppies to the east.

Similarly, people from north of the Derwent, from Northside on to Seaton, tend to be Downies. Those to the south of Workington itself, in Mossbay and Salterbeck, are usually Uppies. Changing sides is not unknown, particularly if the numbers are noticeably uneven.

▲ An Uppie story has it that the first **Workington ball** was an overcooked pudding, too hard to eat and so kicked about by Curwen men. Today's balls consist of a leather case stuffed tight with flock and marked with the year and the name of both the match sponsor and the charity chosen to benefit from fundraising associated with the game.

Surprisingly, given that from the late 19th century until 1978 Workington's balls were all made either by John Ellwood or his son

Jimmy – saddlers on Wilson Street – the size and weights have varied widely, from over 4lbs in 1901 to less than 2lbs in 1930. The 1939 ball was unusually large at 7lbs, whereas the 'Victory Ball' of 1946 was half that.

Nowadays the balls weigh a more consistent 2lbs each and in size fall somewhere between the larger balls used in Kirkwall and the smaller ones of Scottish Border games. But of course there are no standard dimensions and the design may yet change again.

Anthony Daglish pictured in 1872, holding the balls he had hailed for Uppies that year and the year before. Daglishes have been throwing off the Tuesday ball for at least two hundred years. Robert performed the task in 2007. Anthony both threw off and hailed in 1872, a rare feat matched by his great nephew, Harry, in 1944. According to the *Whitehaven News* in 1931, the Daglish family once owned a three hundred year old ball won by an ancestor. On the Downie side the most well-known family is the Lawmans, who were responsible for throwing off the Saturday ball. Maurice Lawman hailed six times between 1964 and 1970.

▲ Fashions and hairstyles may have changed, but this action from **Workington** in 2005 would have been easily recognisable to one Sergeant Hall, writing in 1899.

'For grotesqueness and whimsicality, for fragrant odours and filthy defilement, football at Workington, as I saw it on Easter Tuesday just licks all creation...

'Something like seven or eight thousand people of all ages and conditions in life are seen trampling, and shoving, and squeezing to look at the players up to their knees in the horrible filth of a beck not more than a dozen feet wide, and the whole of them rammed, and jammed, and twisted into one inextricable knot...

'Look at the smoke and steam ascending to heaven from this living human cauldron. Look at them, panting, struggling, twisting, tumbling and striving.

'Too hoarse to shout, they can only eject their bare arms from that living mass, and wave them either to the east or the west to show in which direction they want the ball to go...

'One fellow has lost the biggest part of his trousers and the whole of his shirt with the exception of one sleeve...

'Not one out of twenty has a whole garment about him.'

Set against this, a report of the game in 1804 clearly regarded such games as ideal preparation for battle against the French. Noting the robust nature of the game, the writer extolled the virtues of 'British Valour, which is not to be subdued'.

A century later, in 1905, and the tone had changed again, this time complaining about the drunken behaviour of the players.

'For an exhibition of strenuosity, a sight to startle the Gods, and make the ordinary civilised individual weep for his fellow creatures, the Easter Saturday football play at Workington scooped the pool.

'The game is not particularly elevating at the best, but when the players are loaded up to the neck with beer, make fools of themselves,and behave as they did that night, it is time the "good old custom" was relegated to the limbo of the "once weres".'

It would seem that every generation interprets the game according to its own prejudices.

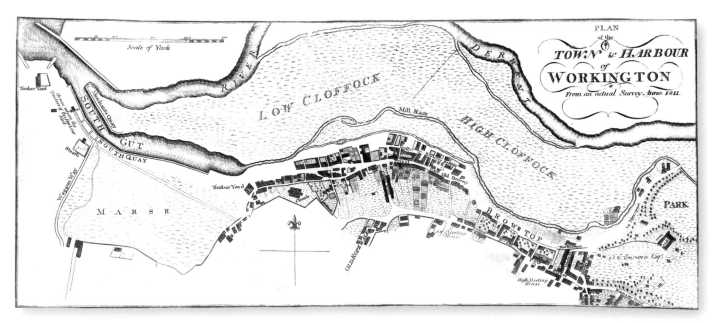

▲ As illustrated by this map of **1811**, reproduced from **Jollie's Cumberland Guide and Directory**, Workington developed around two separate hubs; to the east, Workington Hall, and to the west, the harbour, with the glebe land of St Michael's lying between.

Across Mill Beck, on the northern boundary, lies the **Cloffocks**, part of the natural flood plain of the River Derwent, contained to the south by a steep rise up to Brow Top, and extending west into the Marsh.

Although neither of the goals are located within the Cloffocks, the area is seen as the cradle of *Uppies and Downies*, without which the Workington game might well not have existed, let alone survived.

Contrary to popular belief the Cloffocks are not common land. Instead they were gifted to the town in parcels, by the Lowther Estate, from 1902, it is thought for recreational use only. Even so, over the years the *Uppies and Downies* have had to continually adjust

their tactics to take into account developments on the Cloffocks.

These started with the arrival of the railways in the 19th century; first the coastal line, then a local line to Cleator in 1880. The latter is now disused but the high embankment remains and features prominently in the Easter games.

In 1901 the decision to build a road bridge linking Northside and Workington gave rise to rumours that that year's Easter Tuesday game would be the last. Some 6,000 people turned out for what were thought to be the last rites.

Further development saw no fewer than three large sports grounds: Lonsdale Park (originally for rugby, then football, then greyhounds from 1927); Borough Park, home of Workington Football Club, in 1937, and Derwent Park, home of Workington Town Rugby League Club in 1956. But bowls was the first sport to colonise the area. A green is marked on the 1867 map but in the south west

corner of what is now the cricket field. This was lost to the railway in 1880 but the club returned to its present site in 1900. The cricket club soon became neighbours.

Such a dense cluster of sports venues is rare enough, but at least they were created for recreational use, and left plenty of space for the *Uppies and Downies* to play on.

More recently, however, the Cloffocks have been further threatened. Somehow the deeds for the land have been lost, leaving Allerdale District Council greater scope for development, free of any covenants. The Council started this process, building itself new offices, Allerdale House, in 1990, and a large car park near the Long Bridge.

Next came a supermarket, built between the football and rugby grounds and now operated by Tesco. That company has since been trying to gain permission for a larger store right on Laundry Field, where *Uppies and Downies* spend long periods contesting the ball.

Some councillors argue that selling the site would finance new sporting facilities for the town.

The scheme promises a new stadium, to be shared by the football and rugby clubs, on the site of the existing supermarket.

A concerted campaign to halt further development has gained considerable support (*see page 171*). But nothing can be taken for granted. If the Cloffocks contract further, there can be little doubt that the character of the *Uppies and Downies* game will change irrevocably.

▶ Billie Safill, granddaughter of the match sponsor Townsley Boyd, throws off the ball from Long Bridge to begin the **Good Friday** game in April 2007.

According to custom, with no preamble or call to arms she turns her back on the waiting teams and throws the ball over her head, high into the air.

Whoever performs this role – also known as 'scopping off' or 'wanging off' the ball – can then, if they so choose, join their team-mates in the ensuing fray.

Long Bridge itself, as shown below, is barely a bridge at all, more a concrete walkway linking both banks of the Beck, at its narrowest point between Allerdale House and Borough Park football ground. In the distance, on the far right, is the Tesco supermarket.

As the action shows, there are times during a Workington game when only a handful of players are actively involved, with hundreds more watching from the sidelines, many of them ready to join in at a moment's notice.

All those pictured are male. But

girls and women do occasionally play for short periods. Indeed in 2006 Catherine Malloy, a 29 year old from Salterbeck, became the first female ever to hail at Workington, after her boyfriend smuggled the ball out from the Cloffocks and asked some fellow Uppies, appropriately enough gathered on Ladies Walk, to spirit it to her at Workington Hall, where the Uppies goal is located.

The terrain

Workington has it all for the mass football enthusiast, fields and streets, a beck and a river; embankments and culverts, roads and railways.

In short, obstacles galore.

Games commence at Long Bridge on the Cloffocks. The bridge, originally wooden but now concrete, lies between the Council offices and the Borough Park football ground (*see below left*).

For the Uppies, the goal lies at Workington Hall (often referred to in early reports as Curwen Hall). For the Downies the goal is a promontory in the mouth of the River Derwent.

But although the distance between the goals is less than two miles, there is no straightforward route to either.

Because of this challenging terrain, and with games starting at 6.30pm, only one ball is played per match day. That is, the game ends once one side scores.

Water plays a major part in the proceedings. The Cloffocks are segmented by the meandering Beck – known locally as 'the stream of a thousand smells' – and bounded to the north by the Derwent, a major river whose currents flow quickly around Easter time, often fed by snow melt from the western fells of the Lake District.

It is therefore a primary tactic of the amphibious Downies to get the ball wet, or 'give her a drink' as soon as possible. Once in, they can make rapid progress to goal, and even, quite legitimately (much to the surprise of outsiders), make tactical use of boats.

While one or more of their number makes progress with the ball, often wading in the Derwent or the mouth of the Beck, others

will commandeer one of the many small craft tied up in that area before a rendezvous with their team-mates. The ball will then be smoothly ferried to the promontory on which a capstan once stood, where it can be hailed.

For the Uppies, a land-based approach is the only way. Usually the Uppies prefer to head across the Cloffocks, towards the town, giving them an easier route up towards their hailing point at Workington Hall.

But first comes a subtle but significant obstacle for the Uppies, the rise outside the Bingo Hall, which they call 'the biggest little hill in the world.' Once over this bump in the road, however, and through a tunnel, they are well on the way to victory.

Alternatively, they can carry on through the Cloffocks to the police station. Northside, on the far side of the river, is very much Downie territory (where Uppies fear to tread, according to the Downies).

As can be seen on the map opposite, the terrain is dotted by public and private buildings, roads and car parks; the football ground, the rugby league ground, the Council offices and the supermarket.

On the east side of Borough Park lies the site of Lonsdale Park, the oval of its former dog track still visible. This sports ground housed the soccer club until 1937, and also hosted speedway, cycling and athletics.

Eastwards towards Workington Hall lie the bowls and cricket clubs, thus completing one of densest concentrations of sports' sites in the whole country. In addition, there are patches of land given over to allotments.

But the game is by no means confined to the Cloffocks.

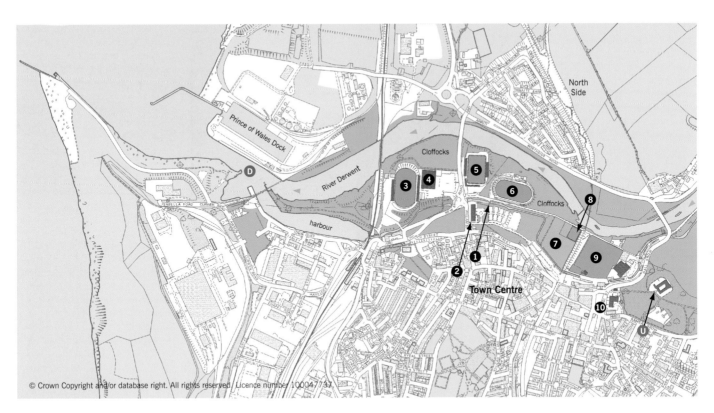

Although they provide a wide pathway to the goals, much as the fields on either side of the River Henmore used to do at Ashbourne, the Uppies often seek recourse along the streets between the south edge of Laundry Field and Hall Brow, such as Ladies Walk and Row Street.

Furthermore, there have always been occasions when a break or a smuggle would carry the ball, almost inadvertently, into the town centre. Indeed to many locals, the game is not quite the same if it does not go into the streets

Particularly between the two World Wars there were determined efforts by the police and some residents and shop owners to blockade these routes, met at times by equally determined

attempts by the players to break through. In 1921 policemen even joined the scrum in order to try and steer play back into more open spaces.

In 1909, nearing the Hall, some Uppies diverted down Row Street right into a Salvation Army gathering. The *Cumberland Pacquet* noted that 'the big drum had a narrow escape'.

The ball got stuck for a while, causing the traffic to stop, until an Uppie called Nesbitt emerged from the scrum, bent double and complaining of cramp. He then crossed the road quietly to the Hall gates, took the ball out from under his coat and hailed it before anyone could stop him.

In 1933 the ball landed in some neighbouring allotments, from »

Key:

U Uppies goal (at entrance to Workington Hall)

D Downies goal (on promontory at site of former capstan)

1 Throwing off point (on the footbridge crossing the Beck)

2 Allerdale House (Council Offices)

3 **Derwent Park** (Rugby League and speedway)

4 **Tesco supermarket**

5 **Borough Park** (football)

6. **Lonsdale Park** (site of)

7 **Laundry Field**

8 **Workington Bowling Club**

9 **Workington Cricket Club**

10 **Magistrates Court**

▶ As at Kirkwall, one Workington goal is a water goal, the other is on land. Moreover, given that games often end after nightfall, photographs of goals being hailed are rare.

To hail at Workington the **Uppies** must enter the grounds of **Workington Hall** – home to the Curwen family from the early 13th century but now in a state of ruin – carry the ball up to the hall's central archway and throw it in the air three times.

In former years, when the Curwens were still in residence, goals were hailed at the main gate. But on Easter Tuesday 1889 Henry Curwen, then Mayor of the town, opened the gate and received the ball from the Uppies, earning three cheers for his gesture. This Mr Curwen was also known to give a sovereign and some ale as a prize to the hailing Uppie.

The relocation of the goal to the Hall courtyard dates from 1925.

So valued was this concession that in 1940 the players muscled aside four unwitting soldiers who had been detailed to guard the Hall (at that time requisitioned by the Border Regiment).

Getting as far as the park usually leads to a swift victory for the Uppies. But on Easter Tuesday 1858 the ball was thrown against the wall of the park only for the Downies to regain possession and fight their way back to the Derwent and to eventual victory.

The Hall itself is a poignant example of a great house allowed to fall into decay. The oldest surviving element is a 14th century pele tower – this was a defensible house typical of the Border region. But the main buildings we see today were developed by Henry Curwen in the mid 18th century, financed by his profits from the

coalmining industry and designed by the leading northern architect, John Carr. Thomas White laid out the parkland in a style influenced by Capability Brown.

The Hall survived in reasonable condition until the death of Alan Curwen in 1930. The house and park was then gifted in 1946 to Workington Borough Council, who chose not to maintain the buildings and allowed them to be stripped to the bones during the 1970s.

The former Uppies goal, the main gate, can still be seen, next to a modern magistrates court built on the site of the old stables.

The **Downies** also have to throw the ball up three times to score, their goal being the site of an old capstan (*below*), on a promontory where the beck (which flows from the left) meets the Derwent, opposite the Prince of Wales dock (on the right). In the distance lies the Irish Sea.

≫ where it was swiftly returned to the Cloffocks by the watchful gardeners. They stood guard every year, just in case, as members of the bowling club do now, protecting their green.

Tactics

Because Workington balls are thrown off at 6.30pm, the action can start in semi-darkness, depending on the date of Easter and whether the clocks have been put forward by then.

Thus failing light plays a part in how the game is played. But so too does subterfuge.

On Good Friday 1947 the game looked certain to end quickly at the harbour, until the outnumbered Uppies managed to send the ball over a wall and back into the town. After a convoluted journey via several pubs in Church Street, the scrum finally reached the bus station. From there the larger part of the crowd moved up Vulcans Lane, only for the Downies to begin shouting 'The ball's here! Milligan's got it'.

Milligan was a Downie so the Uppies, sensing danger, promptly dashed to the larger group. In fact, Milligan was hiding in a doorway with the ball up his shirt. As the dummy succeeded, he and his guard slipped away to score.

On Good Friday 1951 things were going well for the Downies, until an Uppie seized the ball and jumped onto a passing bus.

But such tactics do not always succeed. In 1931 an Uppie called Clegg picked up the ball in Lonsdale Park and headed for the Hall. Seeing Downies in pursuit, he veered left for the Derwent and swam across, intending to lie up in Siddick, a mile to the north. But this required him to travel through Downie territory, and being wet through from his immersion, he soon aroused the suspicions of two walkers, who managed to stop him long enough for his pursuers to catch up. The Downies then gained hold of the ball and followed a wide anti-clockwise arc to the harbour, where they were able to hail with ease.

As at other games, brute force is undeniably important at Workington. But the scrum rarely stays together all the way to goal. Far more likely is a break by one or a handful of players.

Certainly the Workington game is often highly unpredictable. A couple of games, in 1871 and 1939, have finished in under 10 minutes. Others have not been settled until well after midnight.

It is equally possible for the ball to be lost, usually temporarily, or to be hidden; a common tactic in a breakaway once darkness falls, if there is still a long way to the goal.

The player or players hiding the ball will sometimes wait hours, until the opposition have all given up and gone to bed, as happened on Good Friday 2006.

Even a draw is possible. On Easter Tuesday 1804 the ball was dropped and no-one could find it in the darkness, so a stalemate was declared. The following day, once recovered, the ball was cut in two and the honours shared.

The future

Undoubtedly the greatest threat to the character of *Uppies and Downies* in Workington is the potential loss of yet more space on the Cloffocks.

In 2001 a referendum resulted in a vote of 1,560 to 736 against Tesco's proposals to expand to a new site on Laundry Field. The turnout was only 12 per cent, but all wards outside Workington were excluded from the vote, even

though many of their residents participate in the Easter games.

Since then the Save Our Cloffocks campaign (*see Links*) has fought hard against the plans.

SOC's supporters have been elected onto Allerdale Council as independents in both 2003 and 2007. But their attempt to list the Cloffocks under the Commons Registration Act of 1965 failed.

Then aptly enough, on Good Friday 2007, a new piece of legislation came into force, The Commons Act of 2006.

This offered new hope, given that the criterion for land to be recognised as a common is that it must have been used for lawful sports and pastimes for at least 20 years 'as of right', without permission, force or secrecy.

Again though, SOC failed to get the County Council to agree to list the Cloffocks.

As for the supermarket plan, the final planning hearing is scheduled for January 2008.

But if passed, will this signal the end of *Uppies and Downies*?

Hopefully not, for although there is no actual committee, there are several well-rooted families working hard to keep the tradition going. Collections and a variety of social functions also now raise several thousand pounds annually for a chosen charity.

For these reasons, if the worst does happen and the Laundry Field does disappear under the aisles of a supermarket, the *Uppies and Downies* of Workington will surely find a way around, or through, whatever obstacle is placed in their path. They already have to deal with rivers and mud, roads and railways. A few trolleys and petrol pumps will surely not stop them now.

Workington is unusual in that two watercourses come into play, the River Derwent and (*above, in 2007*) the much narrower Beck. As the starting point straddles the Beck, action in the water is often immediate, and because from there it then meanders round the west and south sides of Laundry Field it can be crossed often during the course of a match. But at least, unlike the Derwent, its waters seldom run deep.

21. School Games

In every footballing code the type of ball used dictates the form of the game. This cheese-shaped, three panel ball is used for Harrow School's distinctive brand of 'footer'. But although similar in shape to the ball used at Ashbourne, where handling is more common, this one contains an inflatable bladder, and is therefore more suited to kicking (if not heading). Harrow's balls are made by Gilbert of Rugby, who also supply the Atherstone balls, which are of a similar design but larger in diameter.

Although they hardly qualify as games of *Uppies and Downies*, there are today four versions of football played at three English public schools – Winchester, Harrow and Eton – that meet the description of this book's subtitle. That is, they are indeed extraordinary, and show only few signs of having been influenced by the standardisation process that began in the mid 19th century.

This might seem odd, given the role that, history tells us, public schools played in the formulation of rules for both Association and rugby football. But in fact although alumni of public schools were involved in drawing up the first Association rules in 1863, the schools themselves remained largely aloof, showing little desire for 'outside' matches, other than against teams of Old Boys'.

As JC Thring, assistant master at Uppingham School declared at the time, 'it would be quite impossible, even if it were desirable, to induce the different schools to give up their time-honoured vanities, and to adopt a uniform game.'

Action from the Eton Wall game in 2006, surely one of the most extraordinary games of football ever to have evolved. Yet compared to play up against the churchyard wall at Hobkirk perhaps it is perhaps not so unique after all. At Eton they call the scrum a 'bully', at Winchester a 'hot'. Ashbourne's equivalent is the 'hug', Haxey's is the 'sway'.

Of course most public schools did then go on to adopt the standardised codes, so that by the end of the 19th century, few kept up their own idiosyncratic forms. One of the last of these, a rough and tumble game played between unlimited numbers at Shrewsbury, called 'dowling' (after the Greek for slave), succumbed to the march of soccer in 1903.

One headmaster, Samuel Butler, had described dowling as 'more fit for farm boys and labourers than young gentlemen'.

But at Winchester, Harrow and Eton the old forms did survive, and today they co-exist on the school timetables with soccer and rugby.

Each game is, in its own way, a complex affair. Where *Uppies and Downies* are largely free of rules, the public schools have developed almost a fetish of them, so that it is impossible to understand the minutiae without playing, or at least watching on a regular basis.

In these rule-bound codes, literacy and the capacity to absorb detailed instructions are as vital as physical prowess. Yet while it would be wrong to make too many comparisons between these games and those we describe as *Uppies and Downies*, their shared roots cannot be denied.

One of the common threads that links most early public schools is that they started life in town centres, where little space was available for pupils to play freely, other than on the streets, where they would inevitably have to mix and contend with other boys.

In 18th century Rugby, for example, football was played in the town on New Year's Eve, a nuisance which persuaded the constable in 1743 to pay a man called Baxter two pence 'for Crying no football play in ye street...'

Did Rugby pupils join in? It is entirely possible, for as Jennifer Macrory has pointed out (*see*

Links), boys at the school certainly engaged in mass snowball fights with the town boys until the late 19th century, with the latter trying to storm the school gates.

Schoolboys also tried to set the town bonfire alight in the Market Place in advance of November 5.

At any rate, in 1748 the school's trustees applied to Parliament for new premises because their existing site was 'in a place too much confined, and without any ground or inclosure adjoining, for the recreation of the youth...'

By 1750 a new site on the edge of town was able to boast a two acre field given over to sport.

It was on this field, of course, that a Rugby pupil, William Webb Ellis, is said to have changed the course of footballing history in 1823 by catching a ball and running with it, thereby giving rise to a new form of the game.

In truth this notion did not surface until 1876, four years after Webb Ellis's death. Nevertheless Rugby was one of the first schools to publish its own set of rules, in 1845, and it was largely these rules, with their emphasis on handling, that formed the basis of the Rugby Football Union, set up in 1871 after a split with those who preferred to adopt the Association code. (Interestingly the school itself only joined the RFU in 1890.)

But if Webb Ellis, or any other pupil, did indeed pick up the ball, what prompted him to do so?

We know from previous chapters that a number of street football games, for example in Jedburgh (see page 112), made the transition from a kicking game to a handling game around this time (so as to minimise breakages in built up areas). Stephen Glover's description of Shrovetide football in Derby in 1831 makes it clear

that the ball was 'carried in the arms of those who have possessed themselves of it.'

It is further known that there were three boys from Ashbourne at Rugby School at the same time as Webb Ellis; Barnard and Granville Dewes, and Edward Webster, all slightly older than Webb Ellis.

So had these boys told him about their own Shrovetide game, with its handling in the hug?

According to the source of the Webb Ellis story, a former pupil Matthew Bloxam, writing half a century later, football at Rugby around 1820 involved equal sides made up of older boys. The remaining pupils, the younger 'fags', were then split into two roughly equal groups, each to protect their own goal area.

As in mass football, the action had to take into account natural obstacles, such as several elm trees on the field. Matches could last beyond a single afternoon.

And it was common for the younger boys to be offered a chance to kick the ball, as happens in the early stages of another Warwickshire game, at Atherstone (where the balls have long been made by the same firm that provided Rugby's first balls).

A lack of open space also dictated the form of football played at London schools.

At Charterhouse's original site in the City there was a turfed area called The Green. However, on wet days, a covered passageway known as 'Cloisters' was the favoured venue for football. Seventy yards long, it measured only 9 feet wide.

In a passage that might seem familiar to any veteran of the Kirkwall Ba', E Eardley-Wilmot and E Streatfield (see Links) recalled in 1895, 'At the appointed time the Fags would assemble, and take

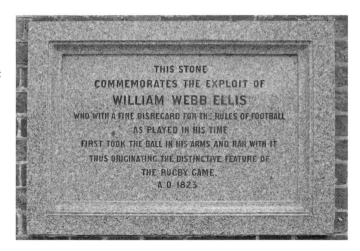

up their position twenty strong at each end of Cloisters... The boys of the higher forms would then range themselves down Cloisters... The ball very soon got into one of the buttresses, when a terrific squash would be the result, some 50 or so boys huddled together, vigorously "rouging", kicking and shoving to extricate the ball.'

Similarly constrained, until playing fields at Vincent Square were secured in c.1810, the boys at Westminster School had to be content with playing in the Abbey cloisters or in Great Dean's Yard. There, goals were scored by kicking the ball between two trees at either end, so that it either hit or passed over the railings (similar to the method of scoring at Ancrum).

Writing in 1903, a former pupil, Captain Markham (see Links) recalled that, 'The small boys, the duffers and the funk-sticks were the goalkeepers, 12 or 15 at each end, and were spaced out across this wide space; if any fellow who was playing out showed any sign of "funk", or failed to play up, he was packed off into goals at once, not only that day but as a lasting degradation...'

That these more arcane forms of football failed to outlive the advent of soccer and rugby is hardly surprising, given that they were devised to suit specific locations and seemed largely designed to provide older boys with a chance to bully the weak. A series of riots at schools from the 1790s onwards also confirmed that senior pupils enjoyed virtual autonomy.

This rising anarchy had inevitable consequences. Pupil numbers dropped – alarmingly at Harrow for example (see page 178) – forcing desperate schools to adopt widespread reforms.

So it was that during the 1830s and 1940s, organised sport assumed a new significance. Not only did it assist in a boy's moral and physical development, as encouraged under the burgeoning creed of Muscular Christianity, but it also ensured that pupils were forced to remain within school grounds during their free time.

Hence the playing fields became a natural extension of the classroom, and learning the rules of the game became as much a test of the intellect as any study of the Classics or mathematics.

▲ Caps off at **Stonyhurst College, Lancashire,** as portrayed by FP Barraud in 1890. Founded by Jesuits in France, the college had relocated to England in 1794, and each year at Shrovetide celebrated what former pupil Percy Fitzgerald called 'a high football festival'.

This entailed a Grand Match on three different days, 'fought with perfect desperation' by pupils, old boys and members of staff, divided into two teams: the English (seen in the foreground) and the French.

After breakfast the ball was placed on a small mound in front of the imposing south façade. Both teams then rushed towards it from marks 50 feet distant. Goals were scored 'by a fair kick or forced through in a squash' (although pushing was officially discouraged 'to save clothes'). After play ended at midday each scorer would be rewarded by extra pancakes at the subsequent 'Lemonade' celebration.

Barraud's painting probably depicts the last Shrovetide game played at the College in 1889. After this rugby and soccer became the winter staples. But the imposing façade is little changed and the building is now listed Grade 1.

▶ Known as 'Winkies', the form of football played at **Winchester College, Hampshire** is far too complex to explain in a single page. As Wykehamist Budge Firth wrote in 1936, 'it would take a Parliamentary Counsel to draft it intelligibly.'

But its myriad rules, arcane conventions and rakish vocabulary (players are termed 'hotmen', 'hotwatches' and 'kicks', and one is called an 'OP', meaning 'over the pillock'), plus the unique form of pitch on which it is played (known as the 'canvas'), are the accumulations of hundreds of years of history. The college itself was founded in 1387, and there is evidence of football being played there as early as the 1640s.

Originally it is thought the boys played on Kingsgate Street, just outside the college, until at some point they were shunted out (most likely for causing a nuisance) to the summit of St Catherine's Hill, a mile and a half away. There, on a turfed plateau, the site of an Iron Age hillfort, the boys devised a new game, called Hills football.

Hills was perfectly simple. A goal was scored when the ball crossed the opponents' line into an area called 'worms'. What made the game unusual, however, was that in order to prevent the ball from dropping down the hillside, younger boys were lined up around the edges and given the unenviable role of 'kickers-in'.

The pitch used today is in an area called **Meads**. This was first set aside for the recreation of Winchester's 70 scholars, known collectively as 'College', in 1790.

Measuring 73m x 24.5m – much the smallest playing area of any game featured in this book – its perimeter was first marked out by posts and ropes, it having

been decided that the kickers-in interfered too much with play. But the younger boys were still needed to contain the ball, until in 1844 they were superceded by the erection of a tall canvas fence on an iron frame. It is from this fence that the name 'canvas', for the whole playing area, derives.

Finally, in 1866 Meads took on the appearance we see today when the canvas fence was replaced by netting, which was not only less susceptible to the wind but also allowed other boys to spectate.

Two years later games on St Catherine's Hill were brought to a halt, while an increase in pupil numbers required the formation of a third team, called Old Tutor's Houses, to challenge the existing College and Commoners teams. At the same time the teams were reduced from 22 to 15-a-side.

Despite this the game was still notorious for its ferocity, and would remain so for many years.

The final refinement to the field of play took place in the 1880s, when a winch was introduced to tension the ropes between the posts so that they could withstand the weight of players during the course of play, as shown here in a match between the Commoners (in red and white) and the OTH (brown and white) in 2007.

Each of these elements – the posts, the ropes and the netting – their precise dimensions and placings, play a role in the rules of Winkies and in the complex method of scoring and accumulating points.

Otherwise, the ball used is a standard soccer ball, and matches last 30 minutes each way.

Because the canvas is relatively compact – one explanation is that the measurements echo those of a particular stretch of Kingsgate Street, but it may simply be due

to a lack of space – games today are played between sides fielding 15, 10 or even six players. Some now feel that the six-a-side game better reflects the modern craving for speed and quickness of thought. In this respect the complexity of the rules allows a real advantage to smart tacticians.

As to what those rules are, we recommend the school's website.

◀ Two more extraordinary forms of football are played on the famous playing fields of Eton. These are known as the **Field Game** (shown here in 2007), and the Wall Game (*see opposite*). There was a third form of Eton football, called Lower College, but this was superceded in the 1860s by soccer, which, together with rugby, is also still played by the pupils.

Eton College itself, near Windsor in Berkshire, was founded in 1440 with the help of masters and fellows from Winchester. From a Latin primer of 1519 there is mention of Eton boys playing 'with a ball full of wynde'. However, this was clearly for handball, whereas in the Field Game handling is forbidden. Even so, some form of football must have been played at the College before the 18th century, because records for the Wall Game go back to 1766 – the actual wall was built in 1717 – and that game was patently a variation of a pre-existing Field Game. (Indeed the terminology used is similar in both.)

Of the two codes, the Field Game is much the simpler, and is played by pupils from the whole school, starting in the first year (whereas the Wall Game is confined to a more select group of older boys).

There are certain similiarities with soccer. For example the teams are 11-a-side, and a size 4 soccer ball is used (one size down from the standard issue). The goalposts, which have no nets, are also smaller, measuring 12 feet wide x seven feet high. These dimensions, it may be noted, are exactly those used in hockey, a game also played at Eton from the 1830s onwards, the same period during which the rules of the Field Game evolved into their current form. A note in *Bell's Life*, in December 1841, for example, makes it clear that the game, 'which was not previously countenanced by the masters', was now well established. This was despite its rough edges and the fact that games were occasionally suspended when discipline broke down. Referees were introduced in 1845 and a first set of rules drawn up two years later.

(As to which came first, the football goals or the hockey goals, we cannot say, but clearly it was more practicable for the two games to share the same posts.)

As for the pitch, the modern Field Game pitch measures 120 x 80 yards (larger than now used in hockey and slightly larger than soccer). During the season several of these pitches can be seen laid out on three playing fields, known as Dutchman's, South Meadow and, the expanse illustrated here, Agar's Plough.

Since the 1850s, there have been a number of rule changes, but the game retains, as in the 1850s, elements that were also common in early soccer and rugby. Thus three points are awarded for scoring in the goal, and five points for a 'rouge', which is akin to a try. As in rugby a rouge can also be converted, for an extra two points.

The game is dominated by dribbling. No passing is allowed, and as seen here (*lower left*), the team is built around a nucleus of seven players forming the 'bully' (like the scrum in rugby), backed up by a 'fly' and three 'behinds'.

Since 1971 the Field Game has been played during the Lent Term (January to March), having been switched from the previous Michaelmas term to allow Eton to compete more effectively at soccer and rugby against other schools.

Needless to add, no other schools play the Field Game.

▲ Whereas the Field Game can in theory be played on almost any stretch of turf, there is only one location for the **Eton Wall Game**.

Erected in c.1717 and listed Grade II, the red brick wall rises some eleven feet above College Field and seals off the school from Slough Road. Seen here in 2006 the wall is obscured by boys, but is more clearly visible on page 172.

Close to where the wall kinks slightly in the centre there is a metal ladder, used by the College players to climb over from Slough Road, before jumping theatrically down to enter the field.

The pitch is 118 yards long but only 6 yards wide. However play is mostly concentrated up against the wall, where it can remain virtually static for much of the game's 60

minute duration. This makes the game as much a test of endurance for spectators as for players, not least since, bizarrely, no goals have been scored in the St Andrews Day match since 1909.

One of the elusive goals, a green door, can just be seen in the garden wall at the far end, with the College buildings and the roofline of the 15th century chapel beyond.

▲ To score in the **Eton Wall Game** at the Slough end, the ball must be thrown (for ten points) or kicked (for five) at the trunk of this plane tree, below the white ring, from a zone known as the 'Calx' (denoting the chalk marks that can be seen on the brickwork).

Being a harder target to hit, the tree is called 'Bad Calx', while the goal at the Eton end – the door in the wall – is deemed to be the 'Good Calx'. But as a goal attempt must not touch the ground or a defender, and as each goal is easily defended, one hardly seems better than the other, and it is small wonder almost a century has passed since the last recorded goal.

More commonly, however, single points are also awarded for a 'shy'; that is, when an attacker in either Calx, facing towards goal, manages to trap the ball against the wall but off the ground, with his lower leg, while either he or a team-mate touches the ball with a hand, calling out simultaneously 'Got it!'

If the umpire declares 'Given' an attempt on goal can then be made.

A host of other equally fiendish rules apply, but as the players hunker down into yet another 'bully' the scene is not so dissimilar from many of the rule-free street games we have visited elsewhere.

▲ Highlight of the Eton Wall Game season is the **Collegers v. Oppidans** match held on a Saturday close to November 30, an encounter first recorded in 1766 when the game was called 'Scrambling Walls'. In the 1820s teams numbered 18 or 20 players each. Since 1945 this has been reduced to ten a side.

Seen here before the 2006 match (*top*) are the Collegers, in their purple and white stripes (with optional war paint). Below, Oppidans players parade the ball, a smaller version of a soccer ball.

As is evident, at this time of year the turf soon churns up, so that every yard is hard fought in sapping mud. But then given the near impossibility of scoring, it is the taking part and not the winning that counts in the Wall Game.

▶ If a brick wall is the defining factor at Eton College, at **Harrow School** in Middlesex, it is mud.

And not just any mud but claggy, unrelenting mud, thick with clay; a mud which tests the fittest of limbs and only adds to the weight of the distinctive Harrow ball (*see page 172*) that even before a match weighs a hefty 820g, twice the weight of a soccer ball.

Founded in 1572, there were no playing fields at Harrow until 1750, and nearly no football at all by 1844, when only 69 boys were on the roll. Thereafter, under CJ Vaughan, a disciple of Thomas Arnold, numbers grew, and in 1853 a Philathletic Club was set up to organise and regulate sport.

The school's first football rules were then drawn up in 1865, at a time when Old Harrovians John and Charles Alcock were active in the formation of the Football Association. Charles in fact became Secretary of the FA and was largely responsible for establishing the FA Cup, supposedly based on a knock-out tournament played at Harrow (although the Youdan Cup in Sheffield provided another model).

Harrow 'footer' has changed little since that era. Each team fields eleven players. Goals, known as 'bases', are formed by two 12 foot posts, 18 feet apart, with no crossbar. The pitches are the same size as for rugby.

Once again the rules cannot be easily summarised, but remarkably, considering the conditions, the emphasis is on dribbling. The ball can also be caught, at which point the catcher can call 'Yards!' and take three strides before punting the ball upfield.

Another feature is that because the ball is too heavy to head it can be controlled on the shoulder, a skill known confusingly as 'fouling'.

 From **Football Lane** in Harrow School to football fame at Wembley Stadium is barely two miles.

But even at Harrow 'footer' has become increasingly overshadowed by soccer, particularly since the autumn term was given over to rugby in 1927, leaving footer and soccer to vie for attention during the shorter spring term.

To add to the old game's marginalisation, the expanse at the foot of Harrow Hill on which footer had long been played, known as Duckers, has recently been drained for other sports. That said, Sheepcote Fields, where matches now take place on former farmland (*left*), appears to offer equally ripe and testing conditions.

Indeed Harrovians say that if a flock of seagulls descends to feed after a match, then the mud levels must have been just right.

Note: Readers interested in viewing any of the games in this chapter should note that school playing fields are private and permission may be required.

22. Conclusions

Uppies and Doonies at Ancrum in the Scottish Borders get down to basics at their Shrovetide match in February 2007. After over 150 years of annual encounters the game appeared to have died out in the 1970s, only to be revived in 1997, thanks to the efforts of one villager. Throughout the history of *Uppies and Downies* there have been numerous peaks and troughs. But could a nationwide revival be possible in today's risk averse Britain?

Having completed our tour of the extraordinary football games of Britain, what conclusions can be drawn that might assist in securing a better future for the *Uppies and Downies* of the early 21st century?

In each chapter there appeared brief comments on the prospects of the 15 surviving games, and as seen, these are mixed; positive in some instances, not so in others.

We therefore hope that this book will form a source of encouragement – and hopefully useful information – for those many hard working individuals without whom the games could not take place. This includes not only the players and voluntary organisers, but also the many sponsors, publicans, council officials, property owners and representatives of the police and emergency services whose support for these age-old games is crucial.

The festival football tradition in this country is centuries old – 900 years or more if we take William Fitzstephen's account of 1174 as the first piece of evidence. So whatever the difficulties and challenges that are inherent within the staging of this type of public, potentially risk-laden event, they are surely well worth the effort in maintaining what is an important element of our national heritage.

At the same time it is recognised that within the world of *Uppies and Downies* there exists no single body that might represent festival games as a whole. Nor is it our intention to propose that such a body be formed. The very autonomy of each game, and the consequent lack of an organising framework is part and parcel, not only of the games' appeal but also of their heritage.

Nevertheless, knowledge and experience can be usefully shared, and so some form of informal networking between the leading supporters of the various games could reap benefits in the long term. Certainly they share much common ground between them.

Insurance and litigation

One of the principal reasons why those who oversee festival games are reluctant to set up formal organisations is that this avoids the likelihood of such bodies being held accountable for breakages or injuries.

Better, they argue, to raise funds beforehand to cover the cost of any damages, and donate the balance to charity, as is the usual practice, and simply to warn all players that they participate at their own risk, as for example at Alnwick (*see opposite*).

At Ashbourne, the role of the committee is deliberately confined to the raising of funds, the supply of the balls, the selection of a guest and the organisation of the pre-match luncheon. Now and then they might amend the rules, such as they are, but once a game starts they exercise no jurisdiction until the game ends and the post-match celebrations commence.

Other than at Alnwick and Duns, where there are umpires, it is the players who run and self-police games of *Uppies and Downies*.

This is also true of the Ba' Committee at Kirkwall, while at Workington, where there is no committee, the leading supporters of the game are mainly concerned with fundraising and social events.

In today's litigious climate, this is of course the ideal way to continue. But it does mean that the future depends almost entirely on the players themselves. They have to take responsibility by acting with due care and consideration for their fellow participants.

On the whole they do this with great success. As we have seen, instances of death and serious injury in games of *Uppies and Downies* are far lower than is commonly believed. Nonetheless it has to be recognised that a combination of unlimited playing numbers, uneven ground, darkness and, in some places, a lack of sobriety, does make fractures and sprains inevitable.

The world of *Uppies and Downies* can only survive if it remains free of the shackles of insurance, and does not invite the attention of health and safety inspectors. Otherwise, it could soon become swamped under a welter of regulations it can ill afford.

No one concerned with any of the surviving games will need reminding of this, and so it can only be hoped that they will be able to maintain this status quo.

The twin issues of insurance and health and safety do beg one further question, however.

Could long lost games of *Uppies and Downies* ever be revived, and if so, in what form?

Revivals

In fact there have been a number of revivals. In Scotland, Hawick's game went into abeyance between 1780 and 1842, then continued until its second demise in 1939. In Duns the game was revived in 1949, having ceased in 1886, while in Ancrum, as noted opposite, the game was revived in 1997 after a 22 year hiatus.

South of the border, Alnwick's game was revived after a twelve year break in 1952. St Ives restarted theirs in 1972.

So might there still be hope for those communities that have lost their games, the likes of Kingston, Dorking, Derby, Chester-le-Street and Hawick?

Clearly there would be major legal and organisational obstacles to overcome for this to happen, in the same way that it would be extremely hard for many of this country's other more outlandish customs to start from scratch in today's risk averse society. Imagine, for example, the difficulties that would arise in attempting to initiate the carrying of flaming tar barrels in Ottery St Mary, Devon – a custom which almost certainly evolved in the 1890s from a much older Shrovetide game of Uppards v. Downwards. Yet this potentially lethal custom was revived in 1956 and is still enjoyed today.

Similarly, who today would think of sanctioning from afresh a madcap event like the downhill pursuit of cheeses that takes place each May on Cooper's Hill in Gloucestershire?

Yet might there be other, more workable ways of reviving, or even initiating from scratch modern games of *Uppies and Downies*?

One way is to follow the example of Alnwick in 1828 and stage games on open fields. The result may not be an accurate rendition of mass participation *Uppies and Downies*, but in towns like Dorking, Kingston and Chester-le-Street it would at least encourage interest in local traditions.

An example of this approach is the children's game of Easties and Westies, played in the Border »

Alnwick's committee warns that all who attend Shrovetide matches do so at their own risk (*top*). But accidents do occur, as at Jedburgh in 2005 (*above*) and every game depends on the goodwill of the emergency services. Indeed most games of *Uppies and Downies* take place only because the police and other agencies adopt a tolerant attitude.

▶ Reaching for the sky during the **Callants' Ba'** game in **Jedburgh** on Shrove Tuesday 2007. The Scottish Borders town is one of four locations where youth games precede the open-age games, the others being at Ancrum, Kirkwall and Haxey. Some would argue that all games of *Uppies and Downies* should cater in a similar fashion for young players, as the best means of securing their future (as well as providing good exercise and helping to build community spirit).

But when enthusiasts in Wales tried to do exactly that by organising for young players a modernised form of **cnapan** *(see pages 24–25)*, the games eventually had to end owing to the difficulty of securing affordable insurance. Having started in 1985 and been staged in playing fields in **Newport, Pembrokeshire** *(right)*, the last series of cnapan games took place in 1995, so that Wales is now the only country in Britain to have no game of *Uppies and Downies* played in any form.

Apparently the main obstacle to obtaining insurance was that cnapan was not recognised by any sports authority, and therefore not by the underwriters either, as a *bona fide* activity. Therein lies the problem for all would-be revivalists. Having no system of its own, *Uppies and Downies* cannot fit easily within anyone else's.

》 village of Lilliesleaf, where the main game ceased during the 1920s *(see pages 104-105)*.

Similarly in Selkirk, also in the Scottish Borders, as noted on page 105, a children's game has been recently set up to commemorate the famous Carterhaugh match of 1815, as part of the town's Sir Walter Scott festival in December. Apparently there are plans to move this game to the summer to allow senior members of local rugby and soccer clubs to take part. There is even talk of relocating the game to the site of the 1815 game, where the Ettrick meets the Yarrow.

For handba' devotees from the surrounding area this would surely be most welcome, particularly as the 200th anniversary of Carterhaugh approaches.

Outside Scotland, two recent revivals have been in Yorkshire and Pembrokeshire.

In Maltby, near Rotherham, 'Beck Ball' was invented in April 1928, quite possibly inspired by the Prince of Wales's visit to Ashbourne a few weeks earlier (an event widely covered by cinema newsreels). Four teams, of miners, policemen, teachers and churchgoers played on land bisected by Maltby Dyke, which was dammed to deepen the water.

Each team defended a different goal in four quarters of play and had to score in the goal opposite. To add spice, two balls were used simultaneously, one from soccer and one from rugby. Money was collected for the school sports' fund and the experiment was repeated in 1929 and 1930.

Beck Ball then disappeared, but was revived in 1986 as part of the town's festival, in a bid to improve community relations after the Miners' Strike (in which Maltby was heavily involved).

This time groups of miners, emergency service workers, teachers and rugby players formed the teams. No doubt the tackling was fierce, particularly between miners and the police, but the game was a success and was repeated over the next two years.

But by this time the cost of maintaining public liability insurance cover had risen so high that the organisers felt they could no longer bear the expense, and so Beck Ball lapsed a second time.

The same fate befell attempts to revive cnapan during the 1980s (*see opposite*).

No-one is therefore under-estimating the practical difficulties that any revival might face. But that is not sufficient reason to dismiss the possibility out of hand.

Shrove Tuesday

There has for many years been a debate in Britain concerning the addition of an extra Bank Holiday.

Summer is assumed to be the preferred time. But if there is one day in the year which Britons once celebrated far more widely than now, it is surely Shrove Tuesday.

One reason for proposing it is that there are currently no Bank Holidays between New Years' Day (or January 2 in Scotland) and Good Friday, so Shrove Tuesday would slot comfortably between the two. But secondly, what better way to revive interest in festival football than to make the day a public holiday. Certainly in those towns where schools are given a day off on Shrove Tuesday, as in Ashbourne and Atherstone, festival football is highly popular.

But football is not the only Shrovetide custom that would benefit. Perhaps a revival of cock fighting would not be appreciated, but the sounding of pancake bells would. Indeed this custom has long been enjoyed in Scarborough, North Yorkshire, where an added and wonderful custom is a community skipping festival, held on the South Foreshore.

(Incidentally, although football is no longer played, Shrove Tuesday has been known in Scarborough as 'Ball Day' since at least 1853.)

In short, Shrove Tuesday could be reinvented as a day on which the British are actively encouraged to indulge in some form of communal outdoor exercise, whether it be football, skipping, jogging, aerobics, or whatever.

With pancakes as an added sweetener, naturally.

Commemorations

Because festival football was once an important part of popular British culture, there is a strong case for the provision of memorials – perhaps in the form of plaques or public art works – to be placed in key points where the game no longer survives.

Candidates would include the former throwing up points on Front Street in Chester-le-Street, the High Street in Dorking, and the Market Place in Kingston, and among the current games, the site of the Country goal in Sedgefield and the Clock Mill in Duns.

No doubt readers will have their own suggestions, which would be welcomed via the *Played in Britain* website.

Attention should also be directed towards the formal marking and acknowledgement of at least one or two camping closes in Eastern England. As the prototypical football grounds of Britain, these sites deserve to be commemorated, as do those which staged the once epic games of cnapan held in Pembrokeshire.

Heritage and research

Nowadays we can barely escape from stories in the media regaling us with the innermost thoughts of sportsmen and women. For historians of the future these stories will no doubt add considerably to their understanding of contemporary sport and society.

It is now time to record the testimonies of festival footballers.

Already this process has started in Kirkwall and Ashbourne, where John Robertson and Lindsey Porter have conducted in-depth research.

Folklorists such as Doc Rowe have also amassed considerable material, not only for festival football but a whole range of traditional games and pastimes.

This is to be applauded, but we should not forget to record details of exactly how each festival game is played; its tactics, its subtleties, its rivalries and its tensions.

There is also more scope for the active conservation of balls and games' ephemera, as has already been done, for example, at the museum in Hallaton.

An asset not a liability

Sport is often credited with promoting the so-called 'feelgood factor'. Festival football does this in a number of ways. It provides good honest exercise, brings communities together, attracts visitors and tourists, and gives back to the people, for a few precious hours at least, the right to roam freely, and play, in the public realm. A rare gift indeed.

Finally, therefore, as we hope this book has demonstrated, there lies the hope that games of *Uppies and Downies* will continue to be regarded for what they are, and that is as an asset to their host communities, and not a liability.

Hardly the archetypal football star, Joss Entwhistle hailed the ball for the Downies at Workington on Good Friday 1947 after a classic 'dummy' manoeuvre that saw two packs head in different directions from the bus station, while a fellow Downie called Milligan hid with the ball in a doorway. Every game in every town has stories such as this, yet only recently have historians started to record them in a considered fashion. Compared with the efforts of celebrity sportsmen and women today, Joss's feats were of minor import. But they are part of football history all the same.

Links

Where no publisher listed assume self-published by organisation or author

Where no publication date listed assume published on final date within title, ie. 1860–1960 means published 1960

Abbreviations:
UP University Press

General sporting history

Arlott J ed. *The Oxford Companion to Sports and Games* Oxford UP 1976

Birley D *Sport and the Making of Britain* Manchester UP (1993)

Brailsford, D *A Taste for Diversions: Sport in Georgian England* Lutterworth Press (1999)

Burnett J *Riot, Revelry and Rout: Sport in Lowland Scotland Before 1860* Tuckwell Press (2000)

Collins T, Martin J, Vamplew W (eds) *Encyclopedia of Traditional British Rural Sports* Routledge (2005)

Gomme AB *The Traditional Games of England, Scotland and Ireland* Reprinted Thames & Hudson (1984)

Griffin E *England's Revelry: A History of Popular Sports and Pastimes 1660-1830* Oxford UP (2005)

Jewell B *Heritage of the Past: Sports and Games* Midas Books (1977)

Malcolmson R *Popular Recreations in English Society 1700-1850* Cambridge UP (1973)

Strutt J *The Sports and Pastimes of the People of England* (1801)

Football History

Alexander M *Shrove Tuesday Football in Surrey* Surrey Archaeological Collections (1986)

Dymond D *A Lost Social Institution: The Camping Close* Rural History 1 (1990)

Goulstone J *Football's Secret History* 3-2 Books (2001)

Harvey A *Football: The First Hundred Years, The Untold Story* Routledge (2005)

John B *The Ancient Game of Cnapan* Greencroft (1985)

Magoun F *History Of Football From The Beginnings to 1871*
Kölner Anglistische Arbeiten (1938)

Magoun F *Shrove Tuesday Football* Harvard Studies and Notes in Philology and Literature (1931)

Marples M *A History Of Football* Secker & Warburg (1954)

Punchard F *Survivals Of Folk Football* (1928)

Walvin J *The People's Game* (1975)

Willughby F *Book of Games* (1606)

Young P *A History Of British Football* Stanley Paul (1967)

www.britishpathe.com (archive film of Ashbourne, Alnwick etc)

www.rugbyfootballhistory.com

British customs and folklore

Hole C *A Dictionary of British Folk Customs* Helicon (1976)

Hutton R *The Stations of the Sun* Oxford UP (1996)

Palmer G and Lloyd N *A Year of Festivals* Frederick Warne (1972)

Shuel B *The National Trust Guide To Traditional Customs Of Britain* Webb & Bower (1985)

Whitlock R *A Calendar of Country Customs* Batsford (1978)

Sykes H *Once a Year* Gordon Fraser (1977)

www.cheese-rolling.co.uk/

www.docrowe.org.uk

www.homersykes.com

www.tarbarrels.co.uk

www.wackynation.com

www.collectionspicturelibrary.com/folkcustoms

Ashbourne

Porter L *Shrovetide Football and the Ashbourne Game* Landmark Publishing (2002)

www.ashbournenewstelegraph.co.uk

www.ashbourne-town.com

Atherstone
Freeman C *Images of England: Atherstone* Tempus (2006)
www.atherstone.org.uk

Chester-le-Street
Simpson D *Chester-le-Street and Washington* Business
Education Publishers (2007)

Cnapan
Bradley AG *A Welsh Game of the Tudor Period* Badminton
Magazine (Jan-Jun 1898)
Owen G *The Description of Penbrokeshire* J Clark (1892)

Cornish Hurling
Greenaway R *Cornish Hurling* Oakmagic (2004)
Rabey I *The Silver Ball* (1984)
http://telematics.ex.ac.uk/realcornwall/sportsandgames/hurling.
asp

Denholm
Sellar M *A History of the Village* (1989)
www.denholmvillage.co.uk

Dorking
Alexander M *Tales of Old Surrey* Countryside Books (1985)

Hallaton
Morison J & Daisley P *Hallaton, Hare Pie Scrambling & Bottle
Kicking* Hallaton Museum Press (2000)

Haxey
Cooper J *A Fool's Game: The Ancient Tradition of Haxey Hood*
(1993)
Newall V *Throwing the Hood at Haxey: A Lincolnshire Twelfth
Night Custom* Folk Life 18 (1980)
Parratt CM *Of Place and Men: Gender and Topophilia in the
Haxey Hood* Univ of Iowa (Summer 2000)
Peck W *A Topographical Account of the Isle of Axholme*
Thomas & Hunsley (1915)
www.wheewall.com/hood

Hawick
Wilson R *A Sketch of the History of Hawick* (1824)

Kingston
Ayliffe GW *Old Kingston – recollections of an Octogenarian
from 1830 onwards* Knapp, Drewett & Sons (1972)

Kirkwall
Robertson J *The Kirkwall Ba'* Dunedin Academic Press (2005)
The Ba' 1945-59 The Kirkwall Press
www.kirkwallba.co.uk
www.bagame.com

Scottish Borders
Groome FH ed. *Ordnance Gazetteer of Scotland: A Survey of
Scottish Topography, Statistical, Biographical and Historical*,
Thomas C Jack, Grange Publishing Works (1882–85)
Watson G *Annual Border Ball-Games* Transactions of the
Hawick Archaeological Society (1922)

Sedgefield
www.sedgefieldweb.co.uk

Workington
Godwin J *Mass Football in Cumberland and Elsewhere*
unpublished typescript (1986)
Wallace K *The Barbarians of Workington: Uppies v Downies*
(1991)

Schools
Macrory J *Running With The Ball: The Birth Of Rugby Football*
Collins Willow (1991)
Money T *Manly & Muscular Diversions: Public Schools and
the Nineteenth-Century Sporting Revival* Duckworth (1997)
www.etoncollege.com
www.harrowschool.org.uk
www.winchestercollege.co.uk

Newspapers and journals
Alnwick & County Gazette, Alnwick Journal, Ashbourne News,
Atherstone Herald, Atherstone News & District Advertiser,
Berwickshire News, The Border Magazine, Cumberland
Pacquet, Derby Mercury, Dorking Advertiser, Epworth Bells,
Hawick Advertiser, Hawick Express, Hawick News, Ipswich
Journal, Jedburgh Gazette, Market Harborough Advertiser,
Newquay Guardian, Northern Echo, Northumberland Gazette,
The Oppidan (Eton College), The Orcadian, Orkney Herald,
Royal Cornwall Gazette, Scunthorpe Evening Telegraph,
Southern Reporter, St. Ives Times, St Ives Weekly, West Briton,
West Cumberland Times & Star, Whitehaven News

General Reference
www.oxforddnb.com *Oxford Dictionary of National Biography*
Oxford UP (2004-07)

Credits

Photographs and images

Please note that where more than one photograph appears on a page, each photograph is identified by a letter, starting with 'a' in the top left hand corner of the page, or at the top, and continuing thereafter in a *clockwise* direction.

All English Heritage and National Monument Record photographs listed are either © English Heritage or © Crown Copyright. NMR. Application for the reproduction of these images should be made to the National Monuments Record, at Kemble Drive, Swindon SN2 2GZ. Tel. 01793 414600.

Maps reproduced by permission of Ordnance Survey on behalf of HMSO. © Crown copyright 2007. All rights reserved. Ordnance Survey Licence number 100047737

English Heritage/National Monuments Record photographs

Nigel Corrie: 172b, 178c; Bob Skingle: 89b, 90abcd, 91; NMR: 94, 151

Peter Holme photographs

back cover abc, front flap, 1, 4, 6abcd, 7, 8, 10, 11, 13abcd, 14abc, 16ab, 17, 27, 48abd, 49ab, 50ab, 51, 52, 54, 56, 58, 61, 62ac, 63ac, 64ab, 66ab, 67a, 70, 72, 73ac, 75b, 77a, 78abc, 80b, 83ab, 84, 85abc, 93abc, 95abcd, 96b, 98ab, 100a, 101, 106, 107, 109ab, 110ab, 111, 112, 115ac, 117abcd, 118abc, 119ab, 120, 121, 122bcd, 123abcd, 124abc, 125abcd, 126b, 127, 129b, 130, 131, 132, 133, 136a, 137abcdef, 138, 141ab, 142a, 144ab, 146ab, 147b, 148ab, 150a, 152abc, 153b, 154ab, 156b, 157abc, 158a, 160ab, 161bc, 165, 166b, 168ab, 170ab, 171, 172a, 179ac, 180, 181ab, 182a, 188

Commissioned photographs

Ken Amer: 31b, 55; Richard Cann: 19; Simon Inglis: back flap, 33, 173, 176abc, 177, 178ab, 179b; Andrew Tulloch, Duns Museum Office: 134

Archive photographs

Linda Ainslie: 128b, 129a; Archive CD Books Project: 167; Atherstone Heritage Centre: 80a, 82a; Photographic Library, Beamish Museum: 35, 93d; Birmingham Central Library, Benjamin Stone Collection: 155; ©Chick Chalmers. Licensor www.scran.ac.uk: 2; ©photographer, L.H. Chappell, Duns. Licensor www.scran.ac.uk: 136b; Cornwall Centre, Redruth: 149a; Jane Currie: 126a; Dorking & District Museum: 34ab, 40; Hawick Library: 103b; Helena Thompson Museum: 164a; Alan Holgate: 59; Brian John: 182b; McManus Galleries & Museum: inside front cover; Stuart Morcom: 82c; John Morison: 162; National Football Museum: 104; ©National Museums Scotland. Licensor www.scran.ac.uk: 44b, 46, 105a, 112; National Museum of Wales: 25ab; NCJ Media: 92, 96a; George Nairn, Picture the Past: 15, 39; Newquay Old Cornwall Society: 142b; Northern Echo: 89a; ©collection JB Oliver. Licensor www.scran.ac.uk: 113; Orkney Library & Archive, Tom Kent collection: 42b, 45, 48c; Penlee House Gallery and Museum: 140; Lindsey Porter: 69, 73b, 79a; Robert D Clapperton Photographic Trust: 103a; John DM Robertson: 18, 31a, 43, 47; Doc Rowe: back cover d, 57, 60, 63b, 64c, 65, 67b, 68, 147a, 158b, 161ad, 163b ; ©School of Scottish Studies. Licensor www.scran.ac.uk: 36, 100bcd, 102ab, 135ab; School of Scottish Studies Archives: 128c; ©The Scotsman Publications Ltd. Licensor www.scran.ac.uk: 116; Ian Spring: 86, 87, 88b; ©St Albans Museums: 23; St Ives Trust Archive Study Centre: 150b; Stonyhurst College: 174; by permission Suffolk Record Office, Ipswich branch, ref IRO.HD480.14: 26; Andrew Sollars: 175ab; Homer Sykes: 37, 77b, 79b, 149b; E.Torricelli: 42a; Keith Wallace: 164b, 166a, 183; by permission Warwickshire Museum Service, Warwickshire County Record Office PH1035/A9713: 82b; by permission Warden & Fellows, Winchester College: 21; Dr Tim Wright: 53

Agency photographs

Borderpics: 115b; Rob Grey/digitalpics.net: 105b; Getty Images: 41, 71, 75a, 143; ©Hedgerow Picture Library: front cover; Mary Evans Picture Library: 29; Mirrorpix: 163a; PA Archive/PA Photos: inside back cover, 76; National Media Museum/Science & Society Picture Library: 97; South West Image Bank, WMN-2-1 (W767_1): 153a

Acknowledgements

Firstly, thanks are due to Simon Inglis and Jackie Spreckley for their tremendous input and patience while I have been researching this somewhat elusive subject. In the sometimes fast moving crowds of *Uppies and Downies*, many anonymous people have provided useful information on the hoof. The staff of libraries and museums and officers of local history societies have also been helpful. I would particularly like to thank the following, some of whom I am now happy to call friends: John Robertson, Bobby Leslie, Gary Gibson, Edgar Gibson, Leslie Tait, Marie Sutherland, Walter Haywood (Kirkwall); Phil Coggon, Dale Smith, Alan Holgate (Haxey); Lindsey Porter (Ashbourne); Lorna Dirveiks, Harold Taft (Atherstone); Jack Deeble, Marjorie Brown (Alnwick); John Fishwick, Billy Gillies, Ronnie Notman, Iain Heard, John Johnstone, Henry Douglas (Scottish Borders); Ivan Rabey, Colin Rescorla, John Bartlett (St Columb); Malcolm Veal, Janet Axton, Brian Stevens (St Ives); John Burt (Corfe Castle); Joe Sandwith, Paul Grima (Workington); John Morison, Joe Cann (Hallaton); Angus Graham Campbell, Andrew Wynn, Paul Williams (Eton College); Simon Berry (Harrow School); David Fellowes, Penny McPherson, Andy Sollars, Dr Geoffrey Day (Winchester College); David Knight (Stonyhurst College); David Dymond, Clive Hartfield, Rex Hartfield (camp-ball); Neill Martin (School of Scottish Studies, Edinburgh University); Richard McBrearty (Scottish Football Museum); fellow enthusiasts for cold, dark festivals: Doris Davison, Patrick Malham, James Bamber, Sally Raynes, Dave Brewis, Doc Rowe, Norihisa Yoshida; John Hutchinson; Dave Russell; Phil Martin; Albert Clayton; and last but most of all, for his companionship and generosity throughout, Peter Holme.

The publishers would also like to add their thanks to: Sheila Whitehead (Duns), Emma Rummins (Kingston Museum and Heritage Service), Margaret Morgan (Royal Cornwall Museum), Lisa Little (The Northumberland Estates), Clara Young (McManus Gallery, Dundee), Emma Lile (Museum of Welsh Life), John Higton and Mary Turner (Dorking & District Museum), John Beedle (Hawick Library), Chris Shinner and Peter Hicks (Newquay Old Cornwall Society), David Mackie (Orkney Library and Archive), Zilla Oddy (Scottish Borders Council Museums & Galleries), Aileen Wilson (Clapperton Photographic Trust), Ian Bruce & family (for permission to use Spike drawing), Christine Freeman (Atherstone), Richard Cann (Gloucester Cathedral), Friends of Winchester College

The Best of Charles Buchan's Football Monthly (2006)

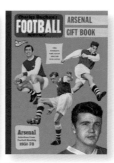

Charles Buchan's Arsenal Gift Book (2007)

Charles Buchan's Manchester Utd Gift Book (2007)

Engineering Archie Simon Inglis *(2005)*

Liquid Assets Janet Smith *(2005)*

A Load of Old Balls Simon Inglis *(2005)*

Played in Manchester Simon Inglis *(2004)*

Played in Birmingham Steve Beauchampé & Simon Inglis *(2006)*

Played in Liverpool Ray Physick *(2007)*

Future titles *Great Lengths – the indoor swimming pools of Britain* Dr Ian Gordon (2008), *Charles Buchan's Liverpool Gift Book* & *Tottenham Hotspur Gift Book (2008)*, *Played at the Pub* Arthur Taylor (2008), *Played in Glasgow* Ged O'Brien (2009), *Played on Tyne* & *Wear* Lynn Pearson (2009), *Bowled Over – the bowling greens of Britain* Hugh Hornby (2009), *The British Olympics* Martin Polley (2010), *Played in London* Simon Inglis (2011). For more information **www.playedinbritain.co.uk**

Calendar of games

Note, all times and dates subject to change. For an up-to-date list of the dates and times of all games see **www.playedinbritain.co.uk**

* if date falls on a Sunday, game played the day after

† if date falls on a Sunday, game played the day before

‡ usually a Saturday morning before November 30

January 1*	**Kirkwall, Orkney**	10.30am boys, 1.00pm men
January 6†	**Haxey Hood, Lincolnshire**	11.00am activities, 3.00pm game
January – March	**Winchester College Football** **Harrow School Football** **Eton College Field Game**	times vary
First Monday after February 3	**St Ives, Cornwall**	9.30am activities, 10.30am game
Monday before Shrove Tuesday or Monday following	**Hobkirk, Roxburghshire**	4.00pm approx
Shrove Tuesday	**Sedgefield, County Durham** **Alnwick, Northumberland** **Ashbourne, Derbyshire** **Atherstone, Warwickshire** **St Columb Major, Cornwall**	1.00pm 2.00pm 2.00pm 3.00pm 4.30pm
Ash Wednesday	**Ashbourne, Derbyshire**	2.00pm
Thursday after Shrove Tuesday or Thursday following	**Jedburgh, Roxburghshire**	12.00 noon boys, 2.00pm men
Saturday after Shrove Tuesday or Saturday following	**Ancrum, Roxburghshire**	11.00am boys, 1.00pm men
Monday after Shrove Tuesday or Monday following	**Denholm, Roxburghshire**	4.00pm approx
Second Saturday after Shrove Tuesday	**St Columb Major, Cornwall**	4.30pm
Good Friday	**Workington, Cumberland**	6.30pm
Easter Monday	**Hallaton, Leicestershire**	11.00am activities, 3.00pm game
Easter Tuesday	**Workington, Cumberland**	6.30pm
Saturday after Easter Tuesday	**Workington, Cumberland**	6.30pm
Friday of first full week in July	**Duns, Berwickshire**	6.00pm
St Andrew's Day ‡	**Eton College Wall Game**	11.00am
Christmas Day*	**Kirkwall, Orkney**	10.30am boys, 1.00pm men